STORM OVER MONO

STORM

OVER MONO

*The Mono Lake Battle
and the California Water Future*

JOHN HART

Cartography by Nancy Fouquet

UNIVERSITY OF CALIFORNIA PRESS

Berkeley   Los Angeles   London

University of California Press

Berkeley and Los Angeles, California

University of California Press, Ltd.

London, England

Library of Congress Cataloging-in-Publication Data

Hart, John, 1948–

 Storm over Mono : the Mono Lake battle and the

 California water future / John Hart.

  p. cm.

 Includes bibliographical references and index.

 ISBN 0-520-20121-3 (alk. paper) — ISBN 0-520-20368-2

 (pbk. : alk. paper)

 1. Water resources development—Government

 policy—California. 2. Water rights—California.

 3. Water withdrawals—California—Mono Lake.

 4. Water-supply—California—Los Angeles. I. Title.

HD1694.C2H27 1996

333.91′64—dc20   95-32190

Printed in the United States of America

9 8 7 6 5 4 3 2 1

Acknowledgment is made for permission to reprint material from the following sources:

Excerpt from "The Hamlet of A. MacLeish," *Collected Poems 1917–1985*, by Archibald MacLeish. Copyright © 1985 by The Estate of Archibald MacLeish. Reprinted by permission of Houghton Mifflin Co. All rights reserved.

Excerpt reprinted with permission of Scribner, an imprint of Simon & Schuster, from *The Sun Also Rises*, by Ernest Hemingway. Copyright 1926 by Charles Scribner's Sons. Copyright renewed 1954 by Ernest Hemingway.

Excerpt from "Bucolics: II Woods," from W. H. Auden, *Collected Shorter Poems 1927–1957*. Copyright © 1966 by W. H. Auden. Reprinted by permission of Random House, Inc., and by permission of Faber and Faber Ltd.

Excerpt from *Anabasis*, by Saint-John Perse, trans. T. S. Eliot. Copyright © 1938, 1949 by Harcourt, Brace. Reprinted by permission of the Fondation Saint-John Perse.

The publisher gratefully acknowledges the contribution provided by the General Endowment of the Associates of the University of California Press.

In memory of my mother and best colleague

JEANNE McGAHEY HART

1906–1995

PHILLIP ISENBERG Assemblyman, Democrat of Sacramento, 1983–. With Bill Baker, dangled money in front of Los Angeles to encourage a search for replacement water supplies.

JOSEPH R. JEHL, JR. Ornithologist. Documented the role of Mono Lake for grebes and phalaropes; clashed with David Winkler on the needs of California gulls.

HUEY JOHNSON Secretary of Resources to Governor Jerry Brown, 1978–82. Established the 1979 Interagency Task Force on Mono Lake.

STEPHEN JOHNSON Photographer. An early Mono Lake Committee activist, he launched the Bucket Walks and later curated the exhibit *At Mono Lake.*

LAWRENCE KARLTON Judge, Federal District Court, Sacramento. When *Audubon v. Los Angeles* strayed into his court, Audubon fought to keep it there.

RICHARD D. KATZ Assemblyman, Democrat of Los Angeles, 1981–. Pushed water law reform and efforts toward a solution to the battle over the lake.

KENNETH R. LAJOIE Geologist. Produced pioneering studies of the Mono Basin and led an early effort to preserve the lake.

PAUL H. LANE General manager and chief engineer, Los Angeles Department of Water and Power, 1983–89. His tenure at the top began with one legal setback, the 1983 public trust decision of the California Supreme Court, and ended with a second, CalTrout I.

ANDREA LAWRENCE Mono County supervisor; skier, conservationist. Founded Friends of Mammoth; serves on the board of the Great Basin Unified Air Pollution Control District.

RICHARD LEHMAN Representative, Democrat of Fresno, 1983–94. Led campaign for the Mono Lake National Forest Scenic Area; maintained federal interest in the alkali dust problem.

TIM LESLIE State senator, Republican of Lake Tahoe, 1984–. Represents Mono Basin; gave key support to the final settlement and water board decision.

JOSEPH B. LIPPINCOTT Engineer. As a federal irrigation bureaucrat, 1903–6, he worked against his own agency to capture the Owens River for Los Angeles.

WILLIAM MCCARLEY General manager and chief engineer, Los Angeles Department of Water and Power, 1994–. Formerly an aide to Mayor Riordan, McCarley sought a quick settlement in the Mono Basin.

BARRETT W. MCINERNEY Attorney and fly fisherman. Managed the *Dahlgren* case and later launched a full-scale attack on Los Angeles's Mono Basin licenses for California Trout.

PALMER BROWN MADDEN Attorney. With Tim Such and Bruce Dodge, an architect of *Audubon v. Los Angeles.*

DAVID T. MASON Limnologist. In the 1960s, did the first systematic modern research on Mono Lake and sought to stir up a campaign on its behalf.

JOHN M. MELACK Limnologist. Conducted research at Mono Lake from 1978 on.

GEORGE MILLER Representative, Democrat of Richmond, 1975–. Pushed water law reform; co-wrote the 1992 Miller-Bradley bill which, among much else, funded water reclamation in Los Angeles to replace Mono water.

NATE F. MILNOR President, California Fish and Game Commission, 1940. Executed an agreement with the Department of Water and Power allowing it to dry up streams, in violation of state law.

ADOLPH MOSKOVITZ Attorney, Kronik, Moskovitz, Tiedemann, & Girard of Sacramento. A noted exponent of traditional water law, he represented the Department of Water and Power in Mono matters from 1980.

WILLIAM MULHOLLAND Engineer. The brilliant first chief of the Los Angeles Department of Water and Power who built the Los aged to avoid becoming associated with a "side."

MARTHA DAVIS Mono Lake Committee executive director, 1984–95. Seeking compromise and negotiation, she had to settle for a stunning victory instead.

MARC DEL PIERO Member, State Water Resources Control Board. Presided at endless hearings in 1993 and 1994; largely drafted the 1994 lake-level decision.

BRUCE DODGE Attorney, Morrison & Foerster of San Francisco. From 1979, championed the cause of Mono Lake at his own firm and in a seemingly endless succession of courts.

WALTER DOMBROWSKI Hunter and naturalist. Ran a lodge at the mouth of Rush Creek and counted ducks on pre-diversion Mono Lake.

KENNETH W. DOWNEY Assistant city attorney, Los Angeles. Veteran warrior for the cause of the Department of Water and Power.

HARRISON C. DUNNING Law professor, University of California at Davis. In 1977–78, headed the staff of Jerry Brown's Governor's Commission to Review California Water Rights Law; saw how the public trust doctrine might be used to protect streams. A leading academic voice for water law reform.

FRED EATON Engineer; Los Angeles mayor; Long Valley rancher. Initiated the Los Angeles Aqueduct.

JIM EDMONDSON Fly fisherman and conservationist. From 1990, oversaw the Mono Basin efforts of California Trout.

STAN ELLER Assistant district attorney, later district attorney, Mono County. In 1984, ordered Los Angeles to continue releasing water down Rush Creek.

JOHN FERRARO Los Angeles city councilman. In 1984, conducted hearings on the Rush Creek matter.

TERRENCE FINNEY Superior Court judge, Eldorado County. When the combined Mono cases came into his hands in 1989, he

passed the major issues to the State Water Resources Control Board.

PATRICK FLINN Attorney, Morrison & Foerster, Palo Alto. Has spent his entire career to date working on Mono Lake.

EDWARD FORSTENZER Attorney, later Justice Court judge, Mono County. Launched *Dahlgren v. Los Angeles* in 1984.

MIKE GAGE President, Los Angeles Board of Water and Power Commissioners, 1990–92. Attempted to produce a Mono compromise but balked at the Mono Lake Committee's demands.

DAVID GAINES Activist. Co-founder and leading light of the Mono Lake Committee; died 1988.

SALLY (JUDY) GAINES Activist and publisher. Co-founder of the Mono Lake Committee and, after David's death, co-chair.

RUTH GALANTER Los Angeles city councilwoman, 1987–. Became a leading voice for a resolution at Mono.

JOHN R. GARAMENDI State senator, Democrat of Stockton, 1976–90. Advocated Mono preservation.

DUANE L. GEORGESON Assistant general manager for Water, Los Angeles Department of Water and Power, 1982–90. In this and earlier departmental posts, confronted opponents in the Mono Basin and the Owens Valley.

THOMAS J. GRAFF Attorney, Environmental Defense Fund. In 1988, sought replacements in the Central Valley for Los Angeles's Mono Basin water.

LEROY GRAYMER Head, Public Policy Program, University of California at Los Angeles. Worked to mediate a settlement between the Mono Lake Committee and the Department of Water and Power.

ED GROSSWILER Executive director, Mono Lake Committee, 1982–84. Professionalized committee affairs and remained a key adviser for years.

DAVID B. HERBST Biologist. Nicknamed "Bug," he studied the Mono Lake alkali fly intensively.

Contents

Maps

Acknowledgments

The lengthy preparation of this book was made possible by Watermark, a consortium of persons who wish to see this complex story told as fully as possible. Through Watermark, Gerda Mathan provided invaluable new portrait photography for the project and Joan Rosen took on the major task of pulling together the color images. My thanks.

When I began work, the Mono Lake controversy was approaching its climax. I found myself writing a mixture of history and news. Many people who figure in the tale took the time to inform and advise me even in the midst of battle; I am grateful to all of them.

At the top of the list must come three key and continual informants: Mono Lake Committee Executive Director Martha Davis, geomorphologist Scott Stine, and hydrologist Peter Vorster. These experts gave me material enough for a book apiece, and none of them can be quite satisfied with mine. Any outright mistakes that occurred in the compression go of course to the author's account.

At the Los Angeles Department of Water and Power, I've had the generous assistance of Mitchell Kodama, departmental point man on Mono affairs. Thanks also to James F. Wickser, Dennis C. Williams, Kenneth W. Downey, Gerald A. Gewe, Valerie Roberts Gray, Steve McBain, Brian White, and the capable staffs of the library and the photo archive. I had most helpful conversations with former department leaders Mike Gage, Duane Georgeson, and Mary Nichols, and with Los Angeles City Council members Ruth Galanter and Zev Yaroslavsky.

On legal matters I'm indebted especially to Virginia A. Cahill, Harrison C. Dunning, Patrick Flinn, Cynthia L. Koehler, Barrett McInerney, Richard Roos-Collins, Jan S. Stevens, and Tim Such; also to Bruce Dodge, Stan Eller, Judge Edward Forstenzer, Joe Krovoza, Palmer Brown Madden, Antonio Rossmann, Joseph L. Sax, Mary J. Scoonover, Laurens Silver, and Bryan J. Wilson.

In Lee Vining and the eastern Sierra, I've had many hosts and informants. I must mention first Sally Gaines, Ilene Mandelbaum, and John Cain; among many other favors, John jeeped me up the steep road to Mono Dome and around the lake's mysterious east side. Warm thanks also to Jerry and Terry Andrews, Don Banta, Carlisle Becker, Jim Edmondson, Scott English, Brian Flaig, Augie Hess, Rick Knepp, Andrea Lawrence, Wallis R. McPherson, Geoffrey McQuilkin, Sally Miller, Shannon Nelson, Arlene Reveal, E. Woody Trihey, and all the staff of the Mono Lake Committee offices in Lee Vining and Burbank.

On natural history, I've taken lessons from researchers Roy A. Bailey, Bob Curry, Gayle L. Dana, David B. Herbst, N. King Huber, Joseph R. Jehl, Jr., Kenneth Lajoie, David T. Mason, John M. Melack, David Shuford, and David W. Winkler.

My thanks to Barbara A. Bates of the U.S. Environmental Protection Agency; Thomas A. Cahill of the Air Quality Group, Crocker Nuclear Laboratory, University of California at Davis; Jim Canaday, environmental specialist with the State Water Resources Control Board; David Carle of the Mono Lake Tufa State Reserve; Marc Del Piero of the water board; Deana Dulen, Lucy McKee, Dennis Martin, and Nancy Upham of Inyo National Forest; LeRoy Graymer of the Public Policy Program at UCLA; Gary E. Smith of the California Department of Fish and Game; and Elden H. Vestal of that department (retired).

Pieces of the story were filled in by David Brower of the Earth Island Institute; Russ Brown and Tim Messick of Jones & Stokes; Hal Candee of the Natural Resources Defense Council; Thomas J. Graff of the Environmental Defense Fund; Assemblyman Phil Isenberg; Huey Johnson of the Resource Renewal Institute; George Peyton and Dan Taylor of the National Audubon Society; and Mono Lake Committee board members Ed Grosswiler, Dave Phillips, and Genny Smith.

More gaps were filled by Rick Battson, Michael Bowen of California Trout, Gray Brechin, Dick Dahlgren, Grace DeLaet, David de Sante, Cecilia Estolano, Joe Fontaine, Robert Golden, Brian Gray, Jeff Hansen, Jon S. Heim, Mike Jimenez, Stephen Johnson, Bob Jones of the *Los Angeles Times*, William L. Kahrl, Assemblyman Richard Katz, Louis Lee of the Los Angeles City Administrative Office, former Congressman Richard Lehman, Richard May, Jason Montiel of the *Mammoth Review-Herald*, Peter Moyle, Randy Pestor, Phil Pister, Betsy Reifsnider, Judge Ronald Robie, Mark Ross, Bob Schlichting, Jan Simis, Felix Smith, Jan Stevens, John Stodder, Dean Taylor, Michael Verzatt, and Dave Weiman.

In chasing sources and odd facts, I've relied on countless libraries and editorial staffs. It would be unpardonable not to mention at least Ann Crawford of the Geological Society of America, Joel Ellis of the Mono Basin National Forest Visitor Center, Barbara Gately of the Marin County Law Library, Vineca Hess of the Mono County Free Library, Shirley McDermott of Resources for the Future, Chris Renz of the National Geographic Society, and Laura Williams of the Point Reyes Bird Observatory.

Special thanks to the photographers for the use of their color and black-and-white images, and for letting them be held for many months as the story and the manuscript evolved.

The process of making a book out of it all was smoothed by John Evarts of Cachuma Press, Steve Fisher, Dane and Wendy Henas, Don Jackson, Dotty LeMieux, David Sanger, and Mary Anne Stewart. It has been a pleasure working with project editor Rose Vekony and copy editor Jane-Ellen Long at the University of California Press.

Some Characters of the Story

BILL BAKER Assemblyman, Republican of Danville, 1981–92, then representative. In 1989, joined with Democrat Phil Isenberg to help Los Angeles find replacements for Mono Basin water.

THOMAS W. BIRMINGHAM Attorney with Kronik, Moskovitz, Tiedemann, & Girard of Sacramento. In later years headed the Los Angeles legal team.

CECILY BOND Superior Court judge, Sacramento County. Her 1989 decision not to force early restoration of Mono Basin streams led to the momentous appellate court decision known as CalTrout II.

TOM BRADLEY Mayor of Los Angeles, 1973–93. This generally environment-minded Democrat was passive on the Mono Lake issue.

WILLIAM BREWER Member of the California State Geological Survey of 1860–64. Recorded his vivid impressions of the Mono Basin.

DAVID BROWER Veteran conservationist. Played a brief but important role in launching the Mono Lake public trust lawsuit in 1979.

EDMUND G. ''PAT'' BROWN State attorney general, 1951–58; governor, 1959–66. As attorney general, declined to enforce stream-protection laws; as governor, launched the State Water Project.

JERRY BROWN Governor, 1975–82. Promoted water law reform. See Harrison C. Dunning; Huey Johnson.

THOMAS A. CAHILL Researcher, University of California, Davis. From 1979, studied Mono Basin dust storms.

JIM CANADAY Biologist, State Water Resources Control Board. Coordinated the massive staff effort leading to Decision 1631 of 1994 restoring Mono Lake.

HILARY COOK Superior Court judge, Alpine County. The first judge in the Mono Basin cases and the one most attuned to the views of Los Angeles.

DICK DAHLGREN Fly fisherman. In 1984, caught brown trout in temporarily rewatered Rush Creek, triggering a second round of Mono Basin legal cases.

GAYLE L. DANA Biologist. She studied the unique Mono Lake brine shrimp and man-

Angeles Aqueduct, confronted rebellion in the Owens Valley, and laid plans for tapping the Mono Basin streams.

MARY NICHOLS Attorney. In 1979, at the California Air Resources Board, initiated Mono Basin air studies; in 1992, as a member of the Los Angeles Board of Water and Power Commissioners, sought compromise with the Mono Lake Committee.

DAVID OTIS Superior Court judge, Siskiyou County. In 1985, as a visiting judge, issued the first rulings in *Dahlgren v. Los Angeles*.

GEORGE PEYTON Attorney and National Audubon Society board member. Brought the organization into the center of the Mono Lake campaign and oversaw *Audubon v. Los Angeles* for many years.

RICHARD J. RIORDAN Mayor of Los Angeles, 1993–. Moved quickly to settle the Mono Basin controversy.

RICHARD ROOS-COLLINS Attorney, Natural Heritage Institute, San Francisco. In 1991, became lead attorney in the Mono efforts of California Trout.

ANTONIO ROSSMANN Attorney. From 1976, represented Inyo County in its dispute with Los Angeles; sought an Environmental Impact Report on Mono Basin diversions.

ISRAEL C. RUSSELL Geologist. In the 1880s, did the first major study of the Mono Basin.

DAVID SHUFORD Ornithologist. Succeeded David Winkler as a leading gull researcher at Mono Lake.

NORMAN SHUMWAY Representative, Democrat of Stockton, 1979–90. Introduced the first bill for a Mono Lake National Monument.

LAURENS SILVER Attorney. At the Sierra Club Legal Defense Fund, pursued his own strategy on behalf of Mono Lake.

SCOTT STINE Geomorphologist. His findings about landscape evolution in the Mono Basin did much to shape the outcome of the battle.

TIM SUCH Legal researcher. Originated the public trust approach to "saving Mono Lake" and served on the Mono Lake Committee board for many years.

E. WOODY TRIHEY Stream restoration consultant. In charge of repair work on the Mono Basin streams 1990–93, he found himself in a philosophical and political crossfire.

MARK TWAIN Writer. On a visit in the late 1860s, he reported Mono Lake repulsive—but found it very good copy.

ELDEN H. VESTAL Fisheries biologist. In 1941, protested the diversion of Rush Creek. Fifty years later, his testimony was key to its restoration.

PETER VORSTER Hydrologist. Passing up a chance to work for the Los Angeles Department of Water and Power, he instead became the hydrological guru of the opposition.

NORMAN S. WATERS Assemblyman, Democrat of Plymouth, 1977–90. Carried early Mono protection bills in Sacramento.

JAMES F. WICKSER Assistant general manager for water, Los Angeles Department of Water and Power, 1990–. Successor to Duane Georgeson, he sought to defend a crumbling position.

PETE WILSON U.S. Senator, Republican, 1985–90, then governor. In both roles he found occasions to support the preservation of Mono Lake.

DAVID W. WINKLER Ornithologist. Studied the California gull at Mono Lake and helped to launch the Mono Lake Committee.

ZEV YAROSLAVSKY Los Angeles city councilman, 1975–94. First councilmember to advocate preservation of Mono Lake.

Prologue: The Bucket Walk

What in the world are these people doing? Is it a demonstration, a publicity stunt, some sort of exercise in sympathetic magic?

It's September 9, 1979, on the pale shore of a great lake at the eastern foot of the Sierra Nevada. A crowd of 250 people—longhairs and shorthairs, locals and visitors, biologists, birders, a noted photographer or two—has gathered. Every third person or so totes a banner or a sign, and everyone's carrying a container of some sort: a plastic jug or a plumped-out waterbag, a soft-drink bottle or a pail.

The odd group stands on an odd bright littoral, a seacoast far from the sea. Gulls come at a slant and cry. From the rippling surface rise curious white towers, built of a limy stone called tufa. Beyond them, dusky waterbirds dive and reappear, stuffing themselves with invertebrate fodder against migrations to come. A streak of high ground makes a path. At the end is a homemade sign: "Rehydrate here."

People clump together for the cameras, steadying the placards they carry: "Save Mono Lake!" "California Gulls Need Love, Too!" "Only God Has Water Rights!" Containers tip. Into a brine almost three times as salty as the sea (and getting saltier), fresh water falls, glittering.

"There," somebody says to the lake. "Have a drink."

The inland sea called Mono Lake can use it. It's been nearly half a century now since engineers of the Los Angeles Department of Water and Power diverted most of the

Bucket Walk. (Photo by Larry Ford)

creeks that feed this lake, forty-eight years since an artificial river began flowing south out of the Mono Basin toward a booming city 338 miles away. Without the normal inflow from these streams, the level of Mono Lake has been dropping a foot or so each year. Shrinking, the lake has grown saltier. Result: the slow impoverishment of a bizarre but prolific ecosystem, accelerating, there is reason to fear, toward collapse.

Today, by unconventional means, a little mountain water has made it down to the lake. Several hours ago and five miles away, on an aspen-shaded creekbank, these people dipped their containers into a living stream. Sloshing a little, they hiked down a glaciated canyon, past the city's diversion dam, through the village of Lee Vining, and out to this sunstruck shore. Now, pouring their pitiful quarts for the cameras, they make their point. They demand that the streams be allowed to run again—for real. They ask the city of Los Angeles to take less water from its dams and permit more flow to reach the lake—enough to let the salty surface rise, or at least stop sinking.

Why is it that they care?

"This solemn, silent, sailless sea," Mark Twain called Mono. "This loneliest tenant of the loneliest spot on earth." For most of a million years—and possibly for two or three—Mono Lake has lain in this basin at the eastern foot of the mountains, gaining water from streams and springs and glaciers and losing it to the air, forming its own peculiar web of living things, becoming stranger and stranger. Twain caught the strangeness. He missed the richness, the colors, the beauty. Intrigued though he was, he could not forgive the lake for being salty, nor for being set in what all but botanists usually call a desert.

Others have made Twain's mistake. We are trained to expect big lakes to have green surroundings, a cool northern look. That beer-commercial freshness isn't here, and it takes a while to appreciate what is. A quick drive past Mono Lake in the hot, bright middle of the day may well leave you wondering what all the fuss is about.

But if you hang around, be careful. In earliest morning, when the first light comes slanting in from Nevada; in midafternoon, when the sky grows lively with thunderheads; in the evening, when sunset colors the spikes and ramparts of tufa; toward the end of summer, when the lake is alive with a million migratory birds; in winter, when snow lies to waterline, you cannot stop and look without risk of being caught, of becoming what they call a Monophile.

The Bucket Walkers of 1979 were Monophiles. Buoyed by the company of the likeminded, they almost persuaded themselves that they might get their way. They indulged in the fantasy that Los Angeles would consent, rather soon, to give up the water they demanded. But to people who knew the odds and the politics—people who knew power—their effort seemed quixotic, doomed.

Between the Mono Lake advocates and their goal lay the weight of one of the most powerful bureaucracies in California. Even then the annual budget of the Los Angeles Department of Water and Power was close to a billion dollars. Its rights to the Mono Basin water were seemingly absolute. It was not about to share that precious substance for the sake, as one writer put it, "of some tiny shrimp and a flock of birds."

Challenge the Department of Water and Power for even a small part of the aqueduct flow that keeps Los Angeles going? As well undertake to "rehydrate" Mono Lake with a canteen.

Yet this peculiar shore—wet where you'd look for dry, rich where you'd count on poor, wind-ripped, volcano-pocked, at the mile-high foot of a mile-high mountain wall, possessed of a beauty that is slow to penetrate but haunting once perceived—is a place where unusual things happen.

By the end of the 1980s, the battle over Mono Lake was to change the landscape of water law and policy in California. Called to umpire the controversy, one court would expand the ancient idea that major bodies of water are the people's property and that government has a special and inescapable duty to protect them. Another court would revive old, disregarded laws against the drying up of streams. Finally, in 1994, the state agency in charge of water rights would hand down a decision more favorable to the lake than any of the Bucket Walkers could have dreamed.

These events inevitably recall the legend of David and Goliath. But to leaders in the

Storm, south shore, 1979. (Photo by Stephen Johnson)

Department of Water and Power, they must bring to mind instead the tale of Gulliver immobilized, unbelievably, by the thousand threads of the Lilliputians.

The Mono Lake controversy brings us back to the first but often flouted principle of conservation: "You may use, but you may not ruin." It reminds us, too, that this is a country in which determined citizens can take on mighty established powers and, occasionally, bring about real changes in the world.

Here is the place, and here is the story.

1

THE PLACE

In the middle distance there rests upon the desert plain what appears to be a wide sheet of burnished metal, so even and brilliant is its surface. It is Lake Mono. At times the waters reflect the mountains beyond with strange distinctness and impress one as being in some way peculiar, but usually their ripples gleam and flash in the sunlight like the waves of ordinary lakes. No one would think from a distant view that the water which seems so bright and enticing is in reality so dense and alkaline that it would quickly cause the death of a traveler who could find no other with which to quench his thirst.

Israel C. Russell, *Quaternary History of the Mono Valley, California* (1889)

MOST PEOPLE ENTER THE MONO BASIN from the south, from the direction of Los Angeles; or they come from the west, across the Sierra Nevada. Neither approach gives them much of a view. Better to get one's first look down into the basin from its northern gateway, from the minor pass called Conway Summit.

At Conway, finishing a long, gentle ascent, you arrive all at once at the rim of a great void. Your foot touches the brake; your gaze leaps outward and down. It is irresistible to see the lowland ahead just as geologists see it: a broken place, a sunken block, a graben.

If the first impression is of space, the second is of the mountains that contain it. To the west, rising directly out of lakewater, is the 7,000-foot eastern scarp of the Sierra Nevada, uncompromising, raw; its farther peaks curve left and seem to spread in front of you. Off east, the basin is bounded by lower ridges, Cowtrack Mountain and the wonderfully named Anchorite Hills; the eye runs beyond them to the prow of the White Mountains, highest of a hundred arid ranges out that way. South of the lake, not so conspicuous from Conway's height, lies the newest and strangest highland: the Mono Craters, symmetrical purplish piles of lava rock and volcanic ash, formed mostly within the last ten thousand years.

It's a hard-edged country, and it is a restless one. The Sierra, the White Mountains block, and the lesser ranges are rising now. The floor of the basin is dropping now. Lava is simmering deep underground and could force its way to the surface again at any time. This is a place where the planet changes fast.

Mono Basin aerial photo, taken from the east, 1968. (Photo by U.S. Air Force)

If there were no lake in the Mono Basin, the very shape of the country and the lively drama of the shaping would make this place remarkable. But there is a lake, a center, a Cyclops' eye in the great stony visage. You somehow never get used to its presence in the basin: so much water, carrying so much color of reflected sky and hill or glitter of bounced-back light, at this dried-out edge of California. One traveler recalls his first reaction: "What *is* that thing?"

Mono Lake is a roundish sheet of water, twelve miles across and, at the deepest points, about 150 feet deep. Don't note those figures in ink, though, for the lake is constantly changing its outline and dimensions, rising and falling from season to season, year to year, century to century. It fluctuates thus because it has no outlet. Water enters it chiefly from the Sierra side, from three big creeks—Mill, Lee Vining, and Rush—and leaves only by evaporation. Loss to the air varies with weather but probably runs somewhere between three and four feet a year. Streamflow varies much more: when the creeks gush, the lake rises; when they trickle, it falls.

High or low, the lake has been here a very long time. Mono has mirrored a stubbier

Opposite: *The inner line is the outline of the lake, with a surface elevation near 6,376 feet above sea level, reached several times after 1977. The outer line is the lake as it stood in 1940, at surface elevation 6,417 feet. Between them is the lake at 6,390, a level last seen in 1970—and the level to which the lake will now be allowed to rise once more.*

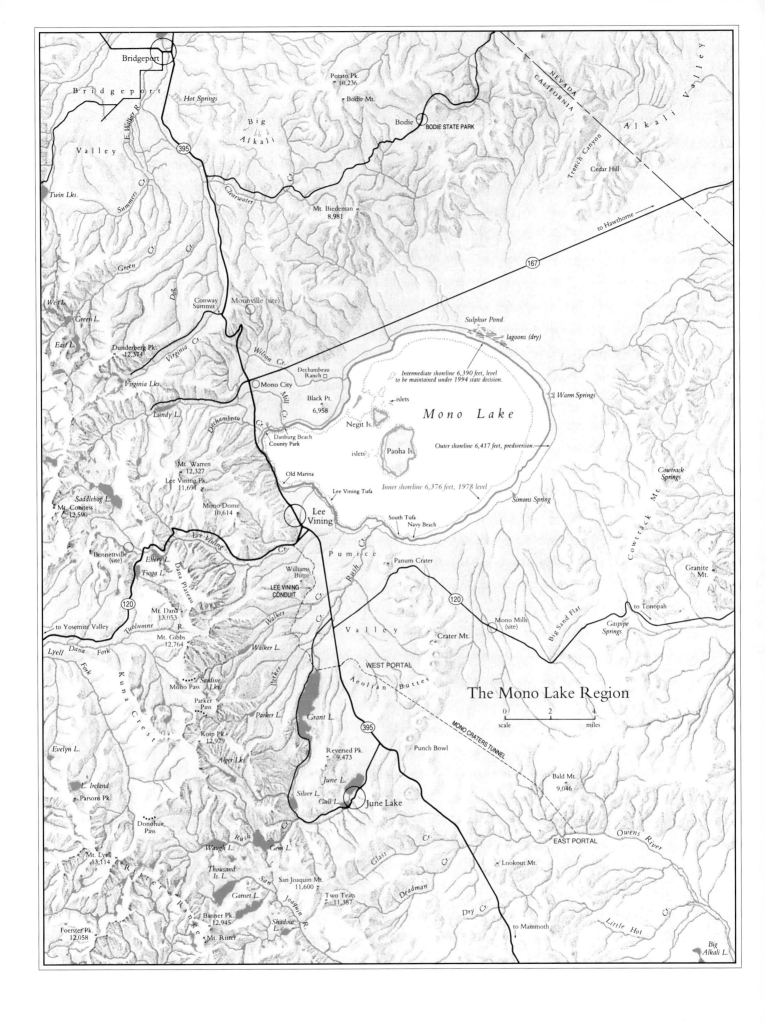

The Mono Lake Region

Sierra and seen the Mono Craters rise from the plain. Flows of lava have hardened in it; tongues of glacier ice have melted on its shores. Pumice boulders and icebergs have floated on it. Volcanic ash and cinders have rained into it and left datable layers, like tree rings, in its bed. This body of water is literally older than the hills—the newer hills, anyway. Somehow, it looks it.

THE MAKING OF MONO

To have so durable a saline lake you need a natural basin and just the right amount of incoming water. Too little precipitation and runoff, and your lake dries up; too much, and the water level rises to find an exit from even the deepest hole. The geology of the American intermountain West has produced hundreds of closed basins; it has also produced a climate too arid, by and large, to put permanent lakes in them.

The relevant part of the geologic story begins three or four million years ago. The Sierra Nevada was already fairly lofty then, but the land immediately east of it was utterly different from what we see today. Instead of dropping away to desert and steppe, the country continued high. The Sierra merged with a high plateau. Rivers drained west across this cool plain; one major stream flowed out of today's Nevada, across the present site of Mono Lake, and on westward to the sea.

But changes were approaching from the east. In a vast area of what is now Nevada, the crust of the earth was fracturing on parallel north-south lines. Between these faults, huge blocks lurched and tilted, forming new mountains and new valleys. As time passed, this splintered area expanded both east and west. We call it the Great Basin. When Great Basin faulting reached California, slices of terrain split off from the rising Sierra block, leaving today's precipitous eastern scarp.

What caused this revolution in the landscape? It signals nothing less, geologists now believe, than the secession of a continent. The western United States is in the process of rifting, calving off a new Pacific land mass, a California island. The faults found here are of the type that form when a region is stretching, pulling apart. Some one of these fractures, millions of years hence, may widen into a narrow sea connected with the ocean, like today's Red Sea. The fracture might occur along the Sierra's eastern foot— right here.

As the terrain grew more dramatic, the climate too became more extreme. For the shattered lands east of the Sierra Nevada, that mountain chain became a fence against rain. Storms off the Pacific dumped their moisture on the western slopes of the range; few peaks to the east rose high enough to wring much precipitation from the depleted clouds. Faulting and lava flows cut off the flows of old rivers too feeble to maintain their courses across the changing surface. Just over three million years ago, the river that had flowed across the Mono region became a casualty. The westward reach of the stream became a short river on the western slope, the Middle Fork of the San Joaquin.

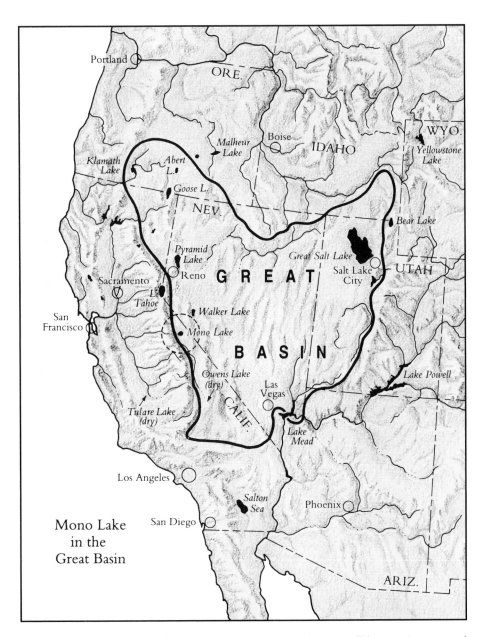

Mono Lake lies at the western edge of the Great Basin, a vast region of parallel mountain ranges and valleys, most of which drain to salt lakes or desiccated playas.

By three million years ago the Mono Basin seems to have become an isolated bowl, a likely place for standing water. Indeed, fish fossils suggest that a lake formed here very early; they show, moreover, that it was fresh and had an outlet to the north. It is possible, though not proven, that the original lake has persisted, changing but never entirely drying up, from that day to this.

If scientists can't document three million years' worth of lake in the Mono Basin, they are pretty sure, thanks to a datable volcanic spasm, about the last three-quarters of a million. Not far away, about 760,000 years ago a great boil of lava swelled and burst, leaving a pit, a caldera; that cavity forms the next basin south of Mono along the Sierra escarpment and is called Long Valley. The Long Valley eruption was 2,500 times the size of the 1980 blast that decapitated Mount St. Helens; it dropped ash as far east as Missouri and a thick layer of it, known as the Bishop Tuff, over 450 square miles of local terrain. If you drill a deep enough hole in the bed of Mono Lake, you encounter what appears to be the tuff, with younger lakebed sediments above it—and older ones below.

Most of the terminal lakes in the Great Basin have dried up now and again since the time of the Long Valley eruption. That Mono Lake has not is due to its favorable site: high and cool (reducing evaporation) and tucked in right under the snowy Sierra Nevada. Nearby, moreover, is a weather gap, a door for storms. West of Long Valley, the Sierra crest sags like an ill-pitched tent; several passes are as low as 9,000 feet. This low region is not accidental but marks the general path of the ancestral San Joaquin; one of several saddles here, Deadman Pass, nearly coincides with the notch last occupied by the vanished river. Storms off the Pacific funnel up the broad valley of what is now the Middle Fork, slip over the low crest, and have water left to dump on the east side. Heavy winter snowfall sustains one of the nation's largest downhill ski resorts, at the town of Mammoth Lakes. It also supports a surprising forest on the heights just south of Mono Lake: the world's most extensive stand of the handsome, plate-barked Jeffrey pine. And the same high precipitation swells Rush Creek, the lake's most voluminous inflowing stream.

ICE AND FIRE

As far as we know, Mono Lake has never sunk much lower than in recent times, but it has certainly risen very much higher. As recently as 120,000 years ago, it mounted far enough to find an outlet from its basin—to the east and south, that time, into the Owens Valley.

About 36,000 years ago, as ice began to gather in Sierra canyons, the lake again grew large, but it did not overspill. During the heart of the most recent glacial period, from 20,000 to 15,000 years ago, the present site of Lee Vining was a shoreline, and Lee Vining Creek was laying down the delta on which the town now sits. About 12,500 years ago, the lake mounted still higher; you can see its highest shoreline etched onto the slopes, hundreds of feet above the rooflines and satellite dishes.

Sometimes in winter a dense fog forms over Mono Lake. The Paiutes called it *po-conip*. In Lee Vining it obliterates the sun for days and gives every branch and twig a cold fur of rime. From the sunny surrounding heights, the fog layer mimics a higher lake: what the basin looked like in glacial times is not hard to imagine.

The approximate scope of the glacial lake can also be judged by Black Point, a

Fissures on Black Point, formed when lava cooled under the waters of ancient Mono Lake (Lake Russell). (Photo © Jim Stimson)

LAKE RUSSELL
7,060 feet above sea level – Maximum depth 800+ feet

MONO LAKE
Prediversion level 6,417 feet

W. D. Johnson, Topographer   UGES. LITH. & LIBERTY PRINTING CO N Y   I. C. Russell, Geologist.

THE MONO BASIN IN QUATERNARY TIME.

Scale 1: 250 000.

Contour interval 200 feet – datum mean sea level.

Mono Lake during the Tioga Glaciation, as mapped by pioneer geologist Israel Russell. During this last major glacial period, advancing ice and rising lakewater reached the same elevation line, but they reached it at different times: when the lake attained its high point, about 13,000 years ago, the glaciers had already shrunk well back. If "Lake Russell" had climbed another 120 feet, it would have found an outlet from the Mono Basin at a saddle to the east (arrow). The Mono Craters, which were differently configured at the time, are incorrectly shown.

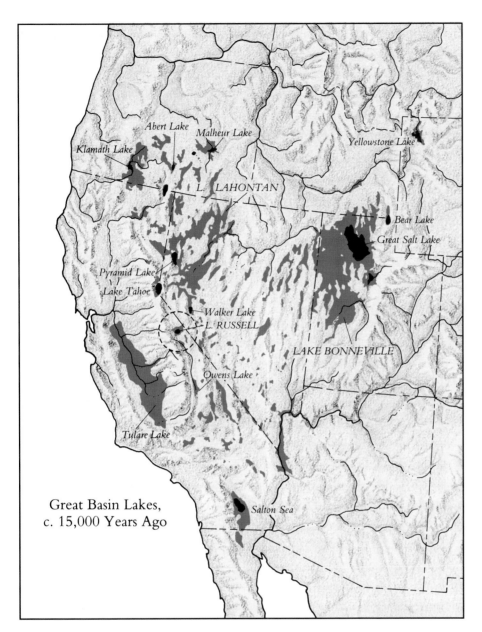

During the last glacial period, lakes covered much of the Great Basin: sprawling Lake Lahontan to the northwest, vast Lake Bonneville to the northeast, and lesser lakes and rivers by the score. But now water is scarce in the region, and the remaining lakes are precious.

broad-shouldered, gentle mass of basaltic cinders on Mono's north shore. This volcano erupted underwater about 13,300 years ago. Cooling quickly, the lava that formed the core of the cinder cone cracked, forming crevasse-like fissures. The very top of the mass seems to have reached the lake surface, where waves beveled it off, giving it an almost dead-flat summit. Black Point is said to be the only volcano in the world that formed underwater and is now completely exposed.

By 9,000 years ago, at the latest, Mono had shrunk to something like its present outlines. (Technically, only after this subsidence is it called Mono Lake: in all earlier incarnations it is known as Lake Russell, in honor of nineteenth-century geologist Israel Russell, the pioneering researcher there.) The shrunken Mono kept fluctuating, within a range of about 130 vertical feet. Its upward "transgressions" and downward "regressions" appear to correspond to century-scale sunspot cycles (which in turn reflect variations in the energy output of the sun).

Volcanic activity continued, adding numerous new summits to the Mono Craters. The pace of this mountain-building seems to have picked up in the last 3,000 years. Panum Crater on the south shore of the lake, a young and perfect example of a plug-dome volcano, built itself in the fourteenth century A.D. Its peak of rhyolite obsidian rises within a ring of light pumice gravel. To get a visual grasp of the Mono Basin, you can't do better than to walk the Forest Service trail around this crater.

The present lake islands are volcanoes, too. The smaller, darker island, Negit, is made up of many flows of blocky lava, mostly formed between 1,700 and 300 years ago. Java islet, one of the specks of land near Negit, was raised about A.D. 300, when the lake was very low; the Java eruption spat out tens of thousands of blocks of pumice that floated across the lake, grounded on its shores, and rest there, tufa-encrusted, today. Paoha, the large "white island," emerged sometime in the seventeenth century. Then the rising lava did not reach the surface but burrowed into the lake-bottom sediments, pushing them upward; the powdery surface found on most of Paoha is simply the lake bottom, high and dry. Sediment slid off the island's flanks to the west as it rose and produced shoals that sometimes break the surface of the water as the Paoha islets.

A GRAIN OF SALT   Terminal lakes always turn salty in time. Inlet streams bring in salts and other minerals dissolved from the rock of their watersheds; evaporation removes only pure water. The other compounds stay behind. It is estimated that 285 million tons of chemicals are now dissolved in Mono Lake. How concentrated the solution is, by the gallon, depends on how much water is diluting that load. Before Los Angeles began diverting its feeder streams, Mono Lake was about a third again as salty as the sea; in 1981, it was three times as salty as ocean water.

You can make Mono Lake brine, more or less. Take a gallon of pure water. Add ten tablespoons of table salt. Add eighteen tablespoons of baking soda. Add eight teaspoons of epsom salts. Add a pinch or so of laundry detergent and borax, and you've about got it. Taste it, and you'll feel no urge to swallow.

Chemically, Mono is known as a triple-water lake: it is saline; it is alkaline; and, due to its volcanic surroundings, it is sulfurous. Fluoride, boron, and arsenic levels are also extremely high, and there are surprising amounts of uranium, thorium, and plutonium. Salt lakes are known for peculiar chemistries, but even among them Mono is outstandingly bizarre. Some scientists speculate that the oceans of the pre-Cambrian era, half a billion years ago, may have contained a fluid similar to Mono Lake water.

"The waters are clear and very heavy," wrote William Brewer, an early visitor. "When still, it looks like oil, it is so thick, and it is not easily disturbed. The water feels slippery to the touch and will wash grease from the hands, even when cold, more readily than common hot water and soap. I washed some woolens in it, and it was easier and quicker than any 'suds' I ever saw. . . . I took a bath in the lake; one swims very easily in the heavy water, but it feels slippery on the skin and smarts in the eyes."

This "heavy water," very reflective, makes Mono an outstanding mirror of its surrounding mountains. When wind works the water up into waves, the lake foams more readily and more lastingly than the ocean.

All salt lakes get compared to the Dead Sea, that hypersaline sink of the Jordan River in Palestine. The Dead Sea, where the chemical mix is so strong as to preclude all life except bacteria and protozoans, deserves its name, but the typical salt lake does not. Certainly Mono doesn't. In the spring and summer it explodes with life, growing algae and other microscopic plants by the millions of tons. On the algae feed two simple, prolific organisms: a specially adapted, tiny crustacean, the brine shrimp, *Artemia monica*; and a specially adapted, tiny insect, the alkali fly, *Ephydra hians*. The shrimp can be found throughout the lake, in the oxygen-rich upper level of water; the flies, related to houseflies but without their annoying habits, make a band around its entire shoreline.

The Mono brine shrimp is unique to this lake. The creatures are about half an inch long, translucent, tinged many colors but most often red. Oarlike appendages, eleven on each side, scull the water and sweep algae particles to the mouth. The shrimp hatch out in the spring from cysts in the bottom muds and go through several stages of maturation. A second generation is born live during early summer. With cool weather the animals die off, having sent another shower of dormant, partially developed, encysted embryos to the lake floor. Shrimp in the lake, at their annual peak, typically number seven *trillion*.

Alkali flies hatch from eggs laid underwater in algae mats. The larvae live on submerged rocks (the pumice blocks from Java islet are ideal for them) or on drowned vegetation, pulling themselves along with clinging "prolegs" and grazing. After two or three months of growth and three molts, they clamp themselves down and pupate, emerging in one to three weeks as adults. Several generations hatch each year, and flies are present even in winter. These vegetarian insects aren't pests or scavengers; indeed, it is hard to touch one. Whenever feet approach the shoreline, the flies retreat, a humming cloud. You can herd them into swirls with your hands.

LIFE CYCLE of the BRINE SHRIMP

In the spring, miniature shrimp called *nauplii* hatch from egg-like cysts and mature in about two months. In early summer, the cyst-hatched shrimp produce a second, live-born generation. Before dying in the fall, the shrimp release the next year's cysts, which sink to the bottom muds. *Artemia monica* is the only brine shrimp species whose cysts sink rather than float.

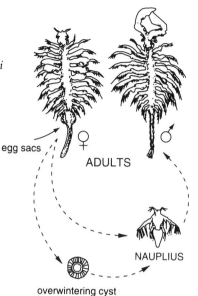

egg sacs

♀ ADULTS ♂

NAUPLIUS

overwintering cyst

LIFE CYCLE of the ALKALI FLY

Females crawl under water to lay eggs, which hatch into aquatic larvae. After feeding on algae for a month or more, the larvae secure themselves to tufa or drowned vegetation, pupate, and emerge one to three weeks later as winged adults.

ADULT

EGG

TUFA
lake bottom

PUPARIUM
(pupa inside)

LARVA

Brine shrimp and alkali fly life cycles. (Adapted from drawings made by Joyce Jonté for the Mono Lake Guidebook.)

THE BIRDS   Millions of flies, trillions of shrimp: food by the ton for something or someone. But who'll play top-of-the-food-chain? The lake is not just too salty for fish; it is also too salty for the liking of most water birds. So the harvest is left to a few bird species adapted to fill this peculiar habitat niche.

The bird you can't miss in the summer, anywhere in the basin, is *Larus californicus*, the raucous California gull. Unlike most of the twenty-five North American species known as "seagulls," this species leaves the coast in summer for breeding sites far inland. The largest breeding population is at Great Salt Lake, the second largest at Mono.

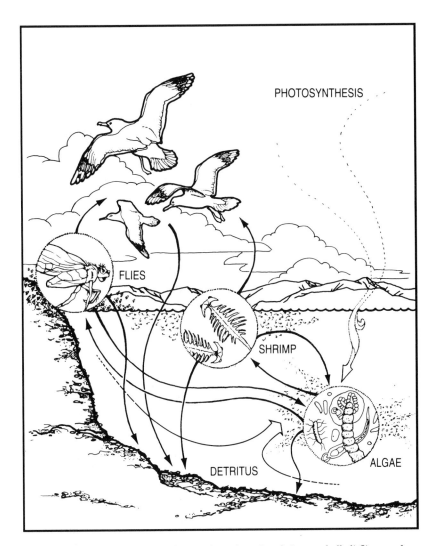

PHOTOSYNTHESIS

FLIES

SHRIMP

DETRITUS

ALGAE

The food chain at Mono Lake is short and simple. Brine shrimp and alkali flies eat algae. Birds eat shrimp and flies (the latter are scarcer but nutritionally superior). Nitrogen and other nutrients return to the algae by way of excretions and decay. Available nitrogen appears to be the main limit on productivity. High salinity makes algae less efficient at "fixing" nitrogen from the air and slows the whole system down. (Adapted from a drawing made by Rebecca Shearin for the Mono Lake Guidebook.)

The Mono gulls nest on various islets, almost invisible from the shore, and on the prominent "black island," Negit, when it is available. But when the lake is low enough, first Negit and then the larger of the islets fuse to the shore, and coyotes prey on eggs and young, soon driving away the birds.

The gulls range far from the lake. One of them once scooped a trout out of a tarn near Koip Peak Pass, far up among the Sierra summits, and lost it onto the grass at my unlicensed feet. I had fish for dinner anyway. Gulls also haunt garbage dumps and

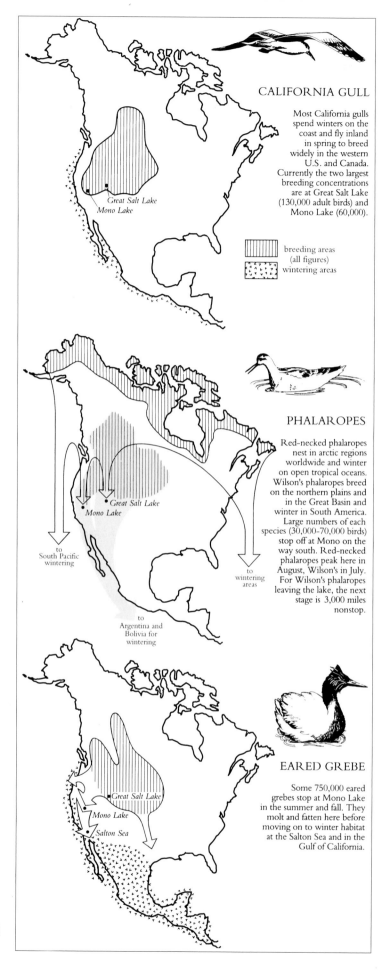

CALIFORNIA GULL

Most California gulls spend winters on the coast and fly inland in spring to breed widely in the western U.S. and Canada. Currently the two largest breeding concentrations are at Great Salt Lake (130,000 adult birds) and Mono Lake (60,000).

| | breeding areas (all figures) |
| | wintering areas |

Great Salt Lake
Mono Lake

PHALAROPES

Red-necked phalaropes nest in arctic regions worldwide and winter on open tropical oceans. Wilson's phalaropes breed on the northern plains and in the Great Basin and winter in South America. Large numbers of each species (30,000–70,000 birds) stop off at Mono on the way south. Red-necked phalaropes peak here in August, Wilson's in July. For Wilson's phalaropes leaving the lake, the next stage is 3,000 miles nonstop.

Great Salt Lake
Mono Lake

to South Pacific wintering

to wintering areas

to Argentina and Bolivia for wintering

EARED GREBE

Some 750,000 eared grebes stop at Mono Lake in the summer and fall. They molt and fatten here before moving on to winter habitat at the Salton Sea and in the Gulf of California.

Great Salt Lake
Mono Lake
Salton Sea

Bird Migrations. (Birds drawn by Joyce Jonté.)

scavenge on the streets of Lee Vining. "Rats of the air," somebody called them. But the landmark *Ecological Study* of 1977 has it right: "In winter, when the gulls have returned to the oceans where most of their congeners breed, the inland sea at Mono seems barren without them."

The eared grebe, *Podiceps nigricollis*, might be the totem creature of Mono. It is a small, dark bird with patches of gold on each side of the head (the "ears"). Grebes are specialists. They dive superbly, fly unremarkably, and barely walk at all. They feed, sleep, court, and mate on water. Though grebes don't breed at Mono Lake, up to a million birds stop off here in summer and fall. They arrive scrawny, with worn and damaged feathers; here, floating safely well out on the lake, they molt and feed, and feed, and feed. At its peak, the throng consumes brine shrimp at the rate of sixty tons a day. When cool weather comes and the shrimp supply crashes, the grebes move on to the Salton Sea and the Gulf of California, 350 miles to the south. The overfattened birds must work off some of their weight in futile takeoff attempts before they can actually get into the air.

Phalaropes are delicate, diminutive sandpipers. They have sharp, straight beaks and black-and-white markings touched with brownish red. The females are larger, more brightly colored, and dominant. There are just three species of phalaropes in the world; Mono Lake is important to two of them.

The northern or red-necked phalarope, *Phalaropus lobatus*, breeds in the far north and winters at sea, on the open subtropical oceans. Mono and Great Salt Lake are major stopover points in between. Red-necked phalaropes at Mono eat, almost exclusively, alkali fly larvae, pupae, and adults. They feed on the open water.

Then there is the Wilson's phalarope, *Phalaropus tricolor*. Of all these birds it is the Tuesday's child, the one with far to go. After breeding in a widespread North American range, up to 60,000 birds—perhaps 10 percent of the adult world population—converge on Mono Lake. Like grebes, they arrive worn and depleted, molt and regrow their pelages, and rebuild their fat reserves with flies and shrimp. You sometimes see the birds charging through the lakeside cloud of flies, beaks wide open, swallowing as fast as they can. (Gulls feed in the same manner.) The phalaropes double their weight during an average five-week stay and waddle back into the air.

They need every calorie for the second, longer, nonstop leg of their journey: 3,000 miles, largely over the open Pacific, to winter quarters at saline lakes in Bolivia, Chile, and Argentina. Returning to North America in the spring, they fly in more moderate stages, east of the Andes and the Rockies.

Another very noticeable migrant is the American avocet, *Recurvirostra americana*. This large, long-legged, long-billed wader has been called "the most graceful of all shorebirds." It has black-and-white markings and, in summer, a cinnamon-colored head and neck. Several thousand avocets stop off at Mono in the spring (northbound) and summer (southbound); a few nest on Paoha Island.

Because Mono Lake lies in a region of scanty aquatic habitat, the arid Great Basin, its importance to these migratory birds is magnified. The lake is one of the three or four most significant shorebird habitats in the western United States; it is internationally recognized as a unit in the Western Hemisphere Shorebird Reserve Network.

Another notable bird at Mono Lake is one you need luck, and probably a birder's telescope, to see. The snowy plover, *Charadrius alexandrinus*, is a bulbous sort of shorebird, white-bellied and brown-backed, that nests on dunes and alkali flats on the lake's east side. Mono Lake's population of several hundred birds is one of the largest in the state. Plovers primarily eat alkali fly larvae and adults and a couple of kinds of beetles.

Still other species, rare today at the lake, used to be as numerous as grebes and as ubiquitous in their season as gulls: the various types of ducks. Before Los Angeles took the creeks, a long-time local resident remembers, "There were so many ducks along the shore sometimes that when they'd move out all together [it was] like the shore itself was moving out." As late as the 1940s, the lake was a fine place for migrating northern shovelers, mallards, green-winged teals, redheads, and numerous other duck species— and a correspondingly popular place with hunters. At times in the fall a million birds would use the region, feeding on the flies and shrimp as well as on land insects and vegetation. Mono water was too salty for them even then, and the lake too choppy when the wind blew, so they gathered in sheltered spots where the surface layer of water was fresher: near creek mouths, in coves, and on the brackish lagoons that bordered the northeast shore of the lake. When those habitats disappeared, so did the great flocks, though there are still a few thousand ducks at Mono Lake today.

THE TUFA TOWERS   After years of calendars and magazine photographs, to say "Mono Lake" is to call up an image of pale stone monuments: the fabulous tufa towers.

The same chemical composition that makes Mono Lake a fishless filling station for birds produces these features. Tufa consists of several forms of calcium carbonate, or lime. The lakewater is full of carbonate ions; fresh water draining into it contains lots of free calcium to combine with them. Wherever the waters mix, the constituents precipitate out as stone. When runoff is vigorous, the mixing can occur almost anywhere; at times a sheet of fresh water spreads across the entire lake, and wave action is enough to cause tufa to form. Every stationary object on the shores of Mono Lake eventually gets coated with the stuff.

But tufa takes the dramatic tower shape only where freshwater springs issue under the lake. Lime precipitates on contact. The fresh water, lighter than the salt, keeps rising, producing a growing sponge of stone. Other processes give this porous trunk a solid rind. Algae that grow on its outer surface alter the chemistry of the nearby water, causing a harder form of tufa to precipitate around them. Even alkali flies get into the act: as larvae, they have special "lime glands" that filter calcium carbonate from their blood; when the adults emerge, little globules of lime are left behind. Generations of larvae, grazing on existing tufa, thicken it as they pass.

You can walk dryshod among tufa towers, whole groves of them left high and dry by the receding lake, but the towers you see so readily are dead. They no longer grow; with few exceptions, they no longer contain their springs. They are like sapless snags that will eventually crumble in the air.

To see tufa towers alive, you must take to the water. Skimming along in a canoe, you'll see pale shapes growing toward the surface, some of them sending up fresh water in greater or lesser plumes. Above these spots brine shrimp swarm most densely. Where a tower just reaches the surface, it may bubble like a drinking fountain.

Divers get the best view of tufa. Biologist David Herbst reports "columns of tufa that on land could not support their [own] weight . . . often covered with veils of bluish-green algae and sparkling crystals of the mineral gaylussite" (an evanescent tufa form). Canoe guide Gary Nelson says, "Beneath the lake, tufa are as close as rocks can get to being living organisms. The rocks are covered by a light green patina of algae, speckled with dark clumps of alkali fly pupae, and are literally crawling with adult flies encased in tiny bubbles of air."

Tufa occurs at saline lakes around the world, but nowhere, apparently, in this abundance or in this range of shapes—all these pinnacles, ramparts, mushrooms, knobs, and domes. Mono Lake tufas rise from the water, strange archipelagos doubled by reflection. They lean on upland slopes like menhirs, casting the only shade for miles. In this tree-poor landscape they serve the same functions as snags. Falcons and owls and small mammals nest in them. They also draw photographers, who may seem, at dawn and dusk, the most numerous creatures of all.

2

BEFORE LOS ANGELES

But men have known
The secret a long time. Men, forgotten,
Few . . .
Knew in the old time the standing before us of
Strangeness under the clear air.

Archibald MacLeish, *The Hamlet of A. MacLeish*

ONE MAY STILL READ THAT *MONO* is an Indian word for "beautiful." This is
pure European sentimentality. *Mono* is a Yokuts Indian word for "fly." The Yokuts did
not live here, but they traded with the tribe that did, a subgroup of Paiutes known to
themselves as the Kuzedika, the Fly Larvae Eaters. What the Kuzedika called Mono Lake
itself their descendants do not remember.

The Kuzedika, like all their Paiute kin, were expert hunters and gatherers. Like other
groups, they harvested nuts from pinyons and edible moth larvae from Jeffrey pines.
Like their relations, they hunted rabbits, pronghorn antelope, and other game. They
caught gulls and grebes when they could, and harvested gull eggs. They ate roots and
seeds and berries. But they named themselves for their distinctive food source and stock
in trade: the pupae of the alkali fly, the *kutsavi*.

When an alkali fly larva is ready to pupate, it clamps itself onto a hard surface by its
prolegs and grows still. Its soft outer layer becomes a hard husk, a puparium, within
which the creature transforms itself into an adult. Some pupae get dislodged by wave
action, float to the surface, and drift to shore. This drift used to be much heavier than
now. The Kuzedika sieved it from the water in finely woven baskets and spread it to
dry. Early observer Israel Russell described the next step: "The partially dried larvae
[*sic*], the kernels, are separated from the inclosing cases, the chaff, by winnowing in the
wind with the aid of a scoop-shaped basket; they are then tossed into large conical
baskets, which the women carry on their backs." Traveler William Brewer recorded:
"The worms [*sic*] are dried in the sun, the shell rubbed off, when a yellowish kernel

*John Muir with Kuzedika Paiutes.
(Photo courtesy the Bancroft
Library)*

remains, like a small grain of rice. This is oily, very nutritious, and not unpleasant to the taste." Kuzedika families had harvest rights to certain strips of shore, larger or smaller depending on their status, and were known to do battle over them.

The Kuzedika had no fixed settlements but followed the food sources. In the spring and early summer they lived on the west side of the lake, along Rush Creek, Lee Vining Creek, and Mill Creek. In late summer they moved to the lakeshore for the *kutsavi* harvest. In the fall they shifted to the pine woods. In the winter they moved away from the gigantic shadow of the Sierra to sunnier, less snowy lands east or north of the lake, living largely on pinyon nuts from the adjacent wooded hills. In a bad year, when the pine nut crop was low, they might trek east or south to Paiute relatives, or even west to the Miwoks of Yosemite.

For in fact the Kuzedika lived at one end of a highway of the day, a major trade route between the east-side Indian groups and the rest of California. This transalpine path went up Walker Creek, a tributary of Rush Creek, to Mono Pass and on down the western slope to Yosemite Valley and beyond. West along it trade parties carried *kutsavi*, dried caterpillars, pine nuts, salt, paints (red and white), pumice, rabbit-skin blankets, sinew-backed bows, and arrows tipped with obsidian. East came acorns, manzanita berries, paints (black and yellow), shell beads, and bear skins. Differing styles of baskets went both ways.

The Kuzedika were artists of basketry, bending local willow bark, fern fronds, grass roots, and rose stems into elaborate patterns. (Travelers in the eastern Sierra should not miss the Kuzedika baskets in the Bridgeport Museum, each different, each made without model or pattern. Most striking is the late beaded work, combining traditional skills and manufactured beads in a product that was made only for a short while.)

The Kuzedika life was competent and hard. It seems not to have changed, in the

Mono Basin, for a very long time. Not far to the south, in the Owens Valley, another group of Paiutes had apparently instituted regular irrigation. But the Mono Basin, a higher and harsher landscape, was perhaps an unlikely site for such an innovation.

INVASION In 1833 the explorer Joseph Reddeford Walker trekked east to west across the Great Basin. On its way to "discovering" Yosemite Valley (probably) and the giant sequoias (certainly), the party visited an alkali lake. It is tempting to identify that lake as Mono; historians doubt it, however. The indisputable American entry into the region came remarkably late, in 1852. In June, Lieutenant Tredwell Moore of the U.S. Army went into the Sierra after Miwok Indians who had reportedly attacked prospectors on the Merced River. Following the Indian trade trail through the high country, he learned that Chief Teneiya, the object of his pursuit, had moved on ahead of him, into the Mono Basin. Sometime that summer—the exact date is not known—Moore crossed Mono Pass and descended the abrupt east flank of the Sierra to the Mono Basin floor. The party found no Chief Teneiya; they had some friendly contact with the Kuzedika, gave the lake its modern name, and sampled some gravels that seemed to promise gold.

In August the *Stockton Journal* told the story. By fall, one Leroy Vining, after whom the town of Lee Vining was later named, was prospecting in the basin. He had no luck and switched to logging, but other miners struck it rich. A series of gold and silver rushes brought to the basin populations much larger than today's.

Most of the action was north of the lake, in the gaunt Bodie Hills that spread east from Conway Summit. The first boom was in 1857 at Dogtown, on the north slope of those hills, just outside the Mono Lake drainage. The second, in 1859, was nearer the lake at a place called Monoville or Mono Diggings, the first proper town east of the Sierra crest and south of Lake Tahoe. Local streams had too little water to wash the gravels, so ditches were dug to tap Virginia Creek on the north side of the hills—a diversion *into* the Mono Basin that continues to this day. Then the miners' attention shifted to Bodie, near the crest of the little range in a chilly and windswept bowl. The fourth boom was in silver and produced Aurora, farther east along the range. After a few quiet years, the excitement returned to Bodie and outdid itself. During the early 1880s Bodie was the hub of the region. It was also infamous for gunfights, murders, and prostitution. An apocryphal story has a little girl in Truckee saying in her prayers, "Goodbye, God, I'm going to Bodie."

With Bodie booming, any number of satellite mining districts opened up, especially on the Sierra side of the lake. There were little towns, ambitious while they lasted, up Mill Creek (Lundy Canyon) and near the headwaters of Lee Vining Creek.

At its height, Bodie had a population of well over 5,000. A local agriculture grew up to sustain it. So did a local lumber industry. In 1879 a five-ton steamer was hauled from

The ghost town of Bodie, onetime economic capital of the Mono Basin. (Photo by Gerda S. Mathan)

San Francisco to the lake to tow lumber barges across from Lee Vining Canyon. The next year Bodie interests constructed a narrow-gauge railroad around the east side to reach the vast Jeffrey pine forest on the south shore. Extensions were planned to link this local line with other western railroads, but they never materialized.

The birds, too, helped sustain the mining towns. The red-necked phalaropes, known as "Mono Lake pigeons," were hunted for the pot. Egging expeditions went out to Negit and in a few years greatly reduced what had been a large gull population, if contemporary impressions can be trusted. In 1860, gull eggs sold for seventy-five cents a dozen.

As for the lack of fish, the settlers quickly rectified that. Freight wagons with water barrels carried Lahontan cutthroat trout up and down the region, stocking streams. After 1900, hatchery-raised trout of several species were planted; the German brown trout naturalized best and came to dominate in most local waters.

The boom at Bodie was a brief one, but the town flickered on. In 1917 the logging camp at Mono Mills was abandoned, and with it the railroad. In 1932 a fire put a final stop to operations in Bodie itself.

Today, the sites of Dogtown, Aurora, Mono Mills, and Lundy are identified only by historical markers. Monoville is a scatter of scars and foundations; you need a local guide to find it. At Bodie, about one-twentieth of the buildings survive, preserved in Bodie State Historic Park, perhaps the most visited ghost town in the world. In a mod-

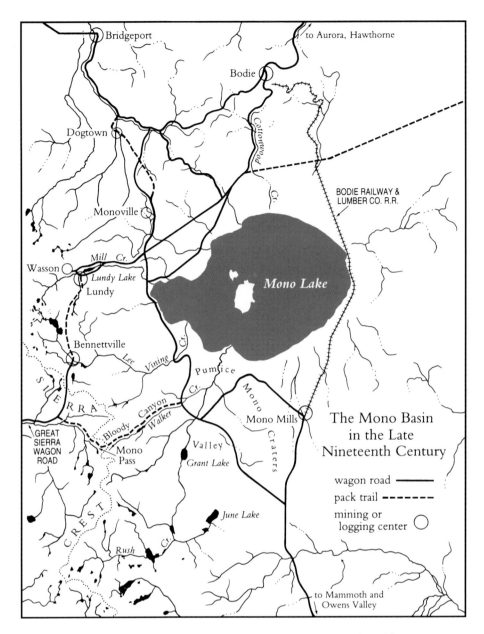

For fifty years after 1859, mining was the key activity in the Mono Basin. (Adapted from a map created by Thomas C. Fletcher for Paiute, Prospector, Pioneer.*)*

ern twist, preservationists have recently worked to prevent further and presumably less picturesque mining in the region around Bodie.

EARLY REACTIONS   From the beginning, everybody who saw Mono Lake had an opinion about it. Some marveled, some recoiled.

Alexis Waldemar Von Schmidt, who came to the basin in 1855 to do the first land survey, called the scene "the most beautiful I ever saw." Mark Twain was here in 1861–62 and said it was "little graced with the picturesque." Judging by his descriptions in *Roughing It*, Twain found the region fascinating nonetheless. Like others, he noticed that the water was a good detergent, but he had a sharper eye than some for the life it supported: "millions of wild ducks and sea-gulls," and in the lake itself "a white feathery sort of worm, one half an inch long, which looks like a bit of white thread frayed out at the sides. If you dip up a gallon of water, you will get about fifteen thousand of these." He noticed the alkali flies, too, and the way they could walk under water, holding bubbles of air beneath their wings. He ate his fill of gull eggs and went out to Paoha Island to look for a hot spring that people said would cook an egg in four minutes. On the way back, a sudden afternoon windstorm swamped his boat. The same thing has happened to many on this lake, and not a few have drowned.

William Brewer, whose journal *Up and Down California* is a priceless source on the primitive state of the state, came over Mono Pass in 1863. "It is a bold man who first took a horse up there," he wrote of the steep eastern path. "The horses were so cut by sharp rocks that they named it 'Bloody Canyon,' and it has held the name—and it is appropriate—part of the way the rocks in the trail are literally sprinkled with the blood from the animals." As for Mono Lake itself, Brewer was of Twain's persuasion: he found it not quite pleasant but entirely intriguing.

In 1865, journalist J. Ross Browne came for *Harper's*. He admired most of what he saw: the mountain shapes reflected on the water; the tufa towers, especially when they resembled classical architecture; the clear air; the flocks of ducks. But he thought the rim of *kutsavi* rather disgusting.

John Muir tramped over the old Indian trail not long after. He loved the country in general for its mix of glacial and volcanic landscapes, "frost and fire." In his account of the trek he says much about this setting, rather little of the lake itself. Perhaps, like many first-time visitors, he didn't know what to make of this uncommon piece of water. On a second visit, he went to Paoha Island in "an old waterlogged boat," got into wind-storm trouble, and seems to have warmed to the place.

Then came Israel Russell. The young geologist arrived in the region in 1881, when the Bodie railroad was under construction, and he stayed for several years. He seems to have been the first to set aside alpine standards of scenery to admire Mono Lake as the desert phenomenon it is. He clearly saw it as strange—"a sea whose flowerless shores seem scarcely to belong to the habitable earth"—but he was captured by the beauty in the strangeness. His 1884 monograph, *Quaternary History of Mono Valley, California*, is well worth reading today.

Russell described journeys throughout the basin and up and down the ranges, made shrewd guesses about the geology, and puzzled out much of the natural history of tufa. He gave their modern names to the Mono Craters and Negit and Paoha islands, using

Paiute words though not the original Kuzedika names (now lost). *Paoha* refers to water spirits—dangerous ones, though Russell seems not to have known that. Russell thought *Negit* meant "blue-winged goose." This is uncertain, but, logical though it might seem, *Negit* does not mean "gull."

In 1890, when Congress was debating the bill to establish Yosemite National Park in the mountains to the west, Robert Underwood Johnson of *Century* magazine called for a preserve extending "to the Nevada line." (Johnson was a friend of John Muir's, and the plan may really have been Muir's as well.) The indicated boundary would have taken in about the southern third of Mono Lake. As first enacted, the park did at least include the upper reaches of all the important Mono Lake feeder streams. The presence of parkland in the Mono watershed might, perhaps, have drawn earlier attention to the fate of the lake below. But in 1905 the park was shrunk back to the Sierra crest. Yosemite and Mono, two of California's most debatable landscapes, would henceforth be fought over quite separately.

LIFE AFTER BODIE

As mining petered out, the Mono region needed a new basic industry. Three possibilities offered: oil, tourism, and irrigated agriculture on a new and grander scale.

It's hard to believe it now, but there was a brief, roaring oil boom in the Mono Basin. Sediments have been accumulating on the lakebed so long that old plant matter has indeed been transformed into small amounts of primitive petrochemicals. Wells were drilled on Paoha Island and on the north shore. There was talk of a city of 20,000 on the western shore. But the wells yielded mostly hot water (and geological information).

As roads improved, a trip to the Mono Basin became something less than an expedition, and a tourist trade evolved. In 1915, the transmountain road over the Tioga Pass began to carry traffic from the crest down the canyon of Lee Vining Creek to the basin floor. The rancher who owned the land where the new road met what is now U.S. 395, the highway along the eastern base of the Sierra, saw his chance. Laying out a town at the junction, he named it after pioneer logger Leroy Vining. The speculation took, and Lee Vining became the commercial crossroads of the little region.

The largest town, however, took shape in a curious nook in the Sierra front, invisible from U.S. 395. Just southwest of Mono Lake, an isolated mountain stands out from the main mass of the range. When the glaciers advanced, they split around it, an inverted Y of ice. Rush Creek flows down the stem and north branch of the Y. In the south branch, dammed by the old moraine, is June Lake. Today its outlet stream runs backward, *into* the mountains, to join Rush Creek. The town of June Lake, which grew up in the 1920s, was to become the local base for Sierra recreation, with skiing in nearby resorts, fishing in nearby lakes and streams, and hiking in nearby wilderness areas.

It would be said, later on, that local people made little of their other potential tourist draw, Mono Lake itself. This is false. The lake at the time was only half again as salty as

Lee Vining. (Photo by Jim Stroup)

the sea and fairly swimmable; it also had plenty of beaches. And it was the only sizable recreational lake in a vast region. One local family, the McPhersons, made a project of putting these attractions on the map. After their plans for a lavish health resort on Paoha Island fell through, at the northwest corner of the lake the McPhersons opened the Mono Inn, a landmark ever since. You could stay at the Mono Inn for $2.50 a night, go hiking, fishing, swimming, or skiing, buy evaporated lake salts to cure whatever ailed you, and visit the islands daily, or on a moonlit night, on board the forty-two-passenger cabin cruiser *Venita*.

In 1928, Venita McPherson organized the first Mark Twain Day. The name was something of a joke, for the purpose of the event was to prove that the writer who had called the region "a hideous desert" was wrong. Twain Day was held, of course, at the inn. There were speeches, skits featuring Twain characters, races on land and lake (including one for motorboats and one for swimming horses), a bathing beauty parade, and dance tunes by the Bridgeport Orchestra. Twain Day (later Days) became an August tradition and lasted until World War II. After a hiatus, they were started up again in 1968.

By 1910, hydroelectric dams and powerhouses began to go up on the major Mono Basin streams. Various interlocking power companies arose and were absorbed, in time, by Southern Sierras Power, which in turn gave place to Southern California Edison. Mono Basin energy, like its water, was to flow south.

Hoping for a railroad connection to markets in the outside world, local promoters

DAMS AND DITCHES

were meanwhile planning to apply the creeks to large-scale Mono Basin agriculture. The loudest talk came from the Rush Creek Mutual Ditch Company: it proposed to send water from Rush Creek clear around Mono Lake to irrigate the fertile but arid lands on the southern, eastern, and northern sides. The ditch was begun—the steam shovel that built it stands today in front of the Mono Basin Museum in Lee Vining—and made it as far as the Mono Craters. But when the unlined channel was tested, the water sank into its porous bed and vanished.

The Mutual Ditch Company's more successful competitor, the Cain Irrigation District, was part of the hydropower combine. In 1915, the Cain District built a small dam at an inviting site on Rush Creek where the stream breached one of the recessional moraines of the last glacier. The resulting reservoir, called Grant Lake, submerged a natural pond of the same name. In 1925, the Grant Lake dam was raised. Large areas on either side of Rush Creek, in what is called Pumice Valley, were brought under irrigation. Much of the water sank into the ground and fed springs along lower Rush Creek and in the bed of Mono Lake itself. Researcher Scott Stine believes that the tufa towers at the southern arc of the lake, at the spot called simply South Tufa, date from this period.

As time went on, all this activity began to seem rather pointless. Even in the 1910s it was rumored that the waters of the Mono Basin would be called on for export south. In the 1920s the rumor became a certainty. As they lavished water on the leaky fields of Pumice Valley, the local irrigators were not so much raising a crop as making a point about their water rights. They were boosting the value of a commodity they knew they would soon be forced to sell.

3

THE COMING OF THE CITY

---

*The attempted taking of said waters by the said
plaintiffs means the destruction of a part of the
body politic of the State of California, to wit: the
County of Mono.*

From the pleadings, *Los Angeles v. Aitken, 1930*

ALMOST FROM THE MOMENT CALIFORNIA became part of the United States,
the Anglo residents of the old Spanish pueblo of Los Angeles had big ideas. For no
special reason other than local patriotism, they intended to make theirs the premier city
of the West Coast. What we forget, in reading the story of Los Angeles, is that numerous
small frontier communities had like ambitions. What set Los Angeles apart was not its
bumptiousness but its astonishing success.

Outsiders didn't predict it. At the turn of the century, William E. Smythe, first executive secretary of the National Irrigation Congress, thought California growth would occur where water was naturally plentiful, especially along the Sierra and Cascade chains.
Of southern California he wrote, "It is perfectly true that this charming district is not
within the field of the largest future developments." Among the future growth centers,
he predicted, would be the Owens Valley, that great trough behind the highest part of
the Sierra, south of the Mono Basin and Long Valley.

Los Angeles wasn't listening. Its first imperial step had already been taken: to claim
all the water available from the Los Angeles River, the stream on whose banks had been
founded the original Spanish pueblo of Nuestra Señora la Reina de Los Ángeles de
Porciúncula. In 1895 the California Supreme Court agreed with the city that it had an
overriding pueblo water right, going back to Spanish rule, to the river's entire flow. Later
students have concluded that this decision was in error—that the Spanish never dealt
in absolute water rights but, rather, balanced competing claims. Nevertheless, the
pueblo water right passed into legal doctrine.

By 1900 it was clear that even the entire flow of the Los Angeles River would not support the growth that civic leaders had in mind. Where next?

An engineer named Fred Eaton saw the answer, but he stood alone for a dozen years. As head of the privately owned Los Angeles City Water Company, he had encountered a radical notion. Just maybe, some unidentified genius suggested, an aqueduct could be built to the Owens River, 235 miles away and 4,000 feet uphill, through which Sierra Nevada water would run to the city by gravity alone. The very region Smythe had seen as a growth center would instead support the growth of Los Angeles.

Eaton saw an opportunity for public service—and great personal profit, for he had hopes of becoming the proprietor of the Owens River source. He made the wild idea his own. During ensuing years, in various leadership roles in and out of government, he pushed the plan. But not even during a term as mayor could he get many people to listen. William Mulholland, an Eaton protégé who succeeded him as chief engineer of the water company, wasn't convinced. Neither were the federal water bureaucrats. "On the face of it," one said, "such a project is as likely as the City of Washington tapping the Ohio River."

That assessment, however, overlooked the difference between the water-rich East and the generally arid West. And it made no allowance for the zest of engineers.

By 1904 the landscape of opinion in Los Angeles had changed. The city had bought out the old private water company, retaining the indispensable William Mulholland as chief engineer. Mulholland had already spent several fruitless years looking into water sources closer to home. Meanwhile, the new U.S. Reclamation Service, the dam-building and irrigation agency established in 1902, had begun planning an Owens River project of its own, strictly to benefit Owens Valley agriculture. Eaton's madcap dream looked plausible now; it was also about to be foreclosed.

THE REACH   In the fall of 1904, Eaton and Mulholland made a secret trip to the Owens Valley of Inyo County.

It seems a long way now; it seemed much longer then. Traveling north and east from Los Angeles by buckboard, they first had to cross the mountains that ring the Los Angeles Basin. Next came the Mojave Desert, flat, heat-blistered. Presently a shadow began growing on the left, the southern reach of the Sierra Nevada. Converging on the escarpment, the road crossed the line into Inyo County. To the right appeared a vast saline sea, larger though far shallower than Mono: Owens Lake, the terminus of the Owens River. North from it stretched a grand valley, about 100 miles long, 4,000 feet above sea level, between the highest Sierra peaks on the west and the somber masses of the Inyo and White mountains on the east. Mountain creeks came down from the Sierra, one after another, to join and swell the river.

North of the town of Bishop, the fertile valley ended and the land tilted upward into Mono County. The road's course grew rough but the river's was rougher: it vanished from view in a narrow slot, the Owens Gorge, eroded into the volcanic Bishop Tuff. At the top of the 2,500-foot ascent perched Long Valley, the misnamed basin, more round than long, from which the tuff was long ago ejected. A few miles further upstream, at the northern edge of Long Valley, the Owens had its beginning in a group of gushing springs.

To Fred Eaton, the layout of the land was providential. It mounted in steps from Los Angeles to the Mojave, from the Mojave to the Owens Valley, and even from the Owens Valley to Long Valley. From Long Valley to Los Angeles, water could run by gravity all the way. Water pressure would drive it over a few low hills, and tunnels would take care of larger barriers. No pumping would be required. Quite the contrary, the mountain water could spin turbines and generate electricity at several points along the way.

The Owens River watershed yielded 300,000 acre-feet, on average, of water per year; its acquisition would quadruple the city's supply. (An acre-foot is about 326,000 gallons, enough, by traditional guidelines, to support three families for a year.) Los Angeles moved.

Many thousands of pages have been written about the stages by which the city fulfilled its plan. Some of them glorify the truly remarkable engineering; others concentrate on the skullduggery involved. The project needed both to succeed. In 1905, Fred Eaton, now working secretly as agent for Los Angeles, went up and down the Owens Valley, acquiring land and water rights for the city and—in one key case—for himself. (He purchased the obvious dam site in Long Valley, essential for full exploitation of the river, and kept a stranglehold on it for a quarter of a century.)

Then there was the role of prominent water engineer Joseph B. Lippincott, an Angeleno and a close friend of Eaton's. In 1902 he landed a job with the new federal Reclamation Service. For the service, he was studying the feasibility of the project Los Angeles feared, the one that would tap the Owens for local farms. But when Eaton's plan came along Lippincott switched his allegiance. He helped convince Mulholland of the virtues of the idea, and thereafter he worked from within the federal agency to smooth the city's, and Eaton's, way.

Even by the not very stringent ethical standards of the time, Lippincott's double role was a scandal; when it came out, he almost but not quite lost his federal job. A few months later, after doing the city several more favors, he moved on to a lucrative post at the Los Angeles Department of Water and Power.

There was scandal at the Los Angeles end of the aqueduct as well. Before the Owens River plan was officially announced, leading local citizens got wind of it and hurried to buy up property on the outskirts of the city, in the San Fernando Valley, that would benefit from the coming water supply. Critics charged that the water wasn't really

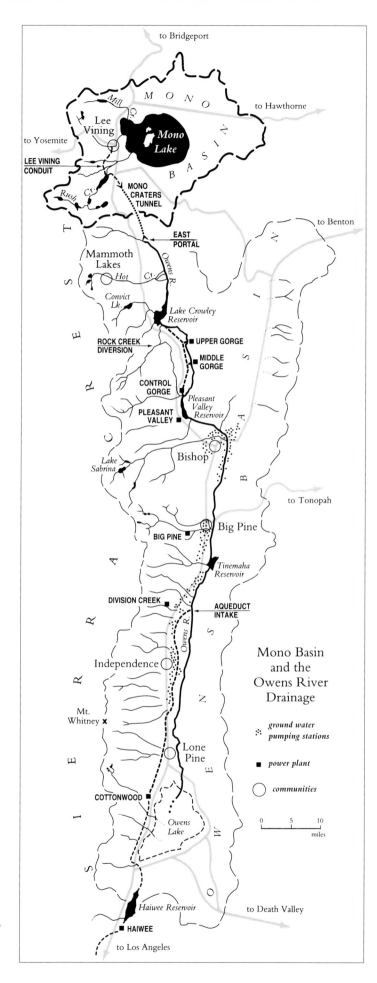

Los Angeles's waterworks, shown, bind these regions to each other and to the distant metropolis.

Map labels:

to Bridgeport

to Hawthorne

M O N O

Mill Cr.

Lee Vining

Mono Lake

to Yosemite

B A S I N

LEE VINING CONDUIT

Rush Cr.

MONO CRATERS TUNNEL

to Benton

EAST PORTAL

Mammoth Lakes

Hot Cr.

Owens R.

Convict Lk.

Lake Crowley Reservoir

ROCK CREEK DIVERSION

UPPER GORGE

MIDDLE GORGE

C R E S T

CONTROL GORGE

Pleasant Valley Reservoir

PLEASANT VALLEY

B A S I N

Lake Sabrina

Bishop

to Tonopah

Big Pine

BIG PINE

S I E R R A

Tinemaha Reservoir

DIVISION CREEK

AQUEDUCT INTAKE

Owens R.

Independence

Mt. Whitney ✕

O W E N S

Lone Pine

COTTONWOOD

Owens Lake

Haiwee Reservoir

HAIWEE

to Death Valley

to Los Angeles

Mono Basin
and the
Owens River
Drainage

∴ ground water
pumping stations

■ power plant

◯ communities

0   5   10
miles

Los Angeles water pioneers Joseph B. Lippincott (left), Fred Eaton (center), and William Mulholland. (Photo courtesy Los Angeles Dept. of Water and Power)

needed at all, that the whole project was a profiteering scheme arranged by the San Fernando speculators. The fact that the new water went at first to San Fernando farms, not city neighborhoods, gave credence to the claim. But the water was never intended for current needs; it was wanted for future growth. As Mulholland remarked, "If we don't get the water, we won't need it."

So the aqueduct was built. There had been nothing like it till then in the West. On November 5, 1913, William Mulholland pulled a lever that spilled the first Owens River water down a specially constructed ceremonial cascade into the San Fernando Valley. "There it is!" he told the crowd. "Take it!"

In the first few years, Los Angeles took only a portion of the flow of the Owens, and the only casualty was one nobody much cared about: Owens Lake, the inland sea the river had sustained. We know very little about Owens Lake as it was. It had brine shrimp and alkali flies, like Mono; like Mono, it had multitudes of waterfowl. It could float steamers. That's about it; even photos are hard to come by. Within a few years, the lakebed was becoming a vast salt pan where monster dust storms swirled.

Upstream along the Owens, though, agriculture prospered, and the initial bitterness in Inyo County gave way to an era of good feeling. Even Fred Eaton, in local eyes the villain of 1905, became popular. In the 1910s negotiations were undertaken to formalize the peace. Los Angeles proposed to guarantee water for 30,000 acres or so, enough to irrigate the valley's very best soils. Early construction of the dam at Long Valley, also under discussion, would have stretched the supply in drought years. Through such a settlement the city would have foregone some export water, but it would have avoided the famous Owens Valley "war" and kept off its record a black mark that refuses to fade. A binding commitment, however, was never made.

By 1921 the opportunity was gone. The city was growing even faster than expected. Dry conditions in the eastern Sierra were reducing flows in the aqueduct, while Owens Valley irrigation was actually expanding. Something, it seemed, had to give. In 1923, the department resumed its creeping purchases of land and water rights, closing in on the fertile farms around Bishop.

In 1924 a kind of guerrilla war broke out. Valley farmers dynamited the aqueduct several times, and, in November, briefly occupied the Alabama Gates, a control structure near Lone Pine, from which they shunted water back into the Owens River bed. The rebels attracted enormous sympathy and made some political headway in the next several years. But the revolt depended on two leading businessmen, the brothers Watterson, whose enterprises dominated the Inyo economy. As the L.A. land purchases throttled that economy, the Wattersons fell into financial trouble and started tapping the funds in the banks they ran. Los Angeles heard about this through some of its local allies, and in 1927 the Department of Water and Power tipped off the regulators. The Wattersons' banks shut down; they went to jail; their depositors lost their savings; the resistance campaign collapsed. Fred Eaton, till then a prosperous rancher, was among the casualties.

Los Angeles seems to have learned a lesson from this struggle: if you are going to take something, don't temporize. Take it swiftly, and take it all.

The city applied that lesson first by sewing up the Owens Valley. During the late 1920s and into the 1930s, it purchased 95 percent of the remaining private land in the valley, including most of the lots in Bishop and the other towns. (Ironically, this clean buy-out was all the rebels had been seeking, at the bitter end.) There could be no question now. Los Angeles owned the water, the waterworks, and the land. It was the biggest local taxpayer. In many ways, it was the local government. Though resistance continued in quieter forms, the Owens Valley had become a resource colony.

Outrage over what happened in that valley changed California law. In 1931 lawmakers passed the County of Origin statute, providing that areas from which water is exported must have their own economic needs served first. Inyo and Mono counties, however, were excluded. And nothing yet protected noneconomic uses of water; it would take a further change of attitude, forged not least at a place called Mono Lake, to accomplish that.

THE MONO
EXTENSION

Fred Eaton's water staircase had one step left. If you kept on going north from Long Valley, you would make one final ascent, over pine-forested ridges, before descending slightly into the Mono Basin. Eaton visited the basin in 1904, and he and his companions were already talking then about what would be called the Mono Extension. But that farther reach never became part of the original aqueduct plan. Rather, L.A. water leaders promised that the Owens River alone would satisfy the city's needs forever. Then came drier weather, combined with a gusher of new population. "Forever" had arrived.

The short-range solution, as we have seen, was to increase the take from the Owens. At the same time, Los Angeles considered two long-range projects, and it wound up building them both. The first was an aqueduct to the Colorado River. The second was the tapping of the Mono Basin.

The streams of the Mono Basin weren't anywhere near as water-rich as the Owens—Rush and Lee Vining creeks, the two largest, yield on average about 125,000 acre-feet a year—and they lay on the far side of the volcanic Mono Craters. For all that, they were temptingly near at hand and, best of all, they were uphill. Given a tunnel under the craters, Mono Basin water could flow south by gravity alone. Los Angeles would gain not only the water but also a very considerable amount of electrical power. With Mono flows added to the local supplies in the upper Owens, there would be all the more profit in building a dam in Long Valley at the head of the Owens Gorge, along with a series of power plants in the gorge itself.

The Department of Water and Power began acquiring land and water rights in the Mono Basin as early as 1912. But William Mulholland was slow to move ahead with an actual project. For one thing, he was still in a standoff with Fred Eaton about land around the Long Valley reservoir site; the reservoir, optional until now, would be essential to manage the new Mono water. Mulholland, unwilling to pay Eaton's price, was hoping to outwait him. To protect its interests in the meantime, the city once again found a back door to knock on. And once again the U.S. Reclamation Service let the city in.

In 1919, Mulholland turned to Reclamation Service head Arthur Powell Davis. The following year, the two agencies signed an extraordinary contract. The bureau would prepare plans, surveys, and cost estimates for an aqueduct out of the Mono Basin; the city would pay the $19,500 cost; and the results would be kept secret.

The Reclamation Service, of course, had no business designing a project for Los Angeles. It didn't even have any business designing a project whose purpose was largely to generate electricity, for Congress had entrusted hydropower matters to another agency. So the study had to claim that its subject was possible land irrigation in the Owens Valley. The Mono County Grand Jury got wind of the work and demanded an investigation by the state engineer; a state investigator, though denied key information, saw enough to cry foul. Shortly thereafter, Mulholland's friend Davis lost his job in a spasm of government reform.

But Davis had meanwhile done something very tangible and had made it stick: in the spring of 1920, he had withdrawn the public land in the Mono Basin from private settlement or claims.

Most of the land in the Mono Lake watershed was and is federal, controlled by the national government. At the time, federal policy made it easy for individuals to acquire government land by homesteading and by filing mining claims. "Withdrawal" blocked such transfers, sometimes permanently (to keep the land federal), sometimes temporarily (to prevent land speculation in advance of an irrigation project). In this case the latter reason, or pretext, applied.

In 1923, without informing its friends in the Reclamation Service, Los Angeles applied to the State Water Commission to appropriate the entire flow of the Mono Basin streams for *domestic* use and power generation, removing the irrigation pretext.

The Mono Board of Supervisors demanded that the deceptive withdrawals now be terminated. Davis's successor at the Reclamation Service, one Elwood Mead, saw the board's point very well, but he held urban use to be the highest: "There seems no question that the water of this region will soon be needed for domestic and industrial purposes in the City of Los Angeles, and its value for these purposes is far greater than for agriculture." Once more, the flouting of normal procedure seemed regrettable but unimportant. The greater good lay south.

To end the embarrassment, Mead pushed the city to act. Action was now possible. By 1929, Mulholland had retired; Fred Eaton was financially wrecked and in a poor position to bargain. It was clear that the Long Valley dam site would soon be in the city's hands.

There was some problem selling the new enterprise at home. The city and its neighbors, joined in the Metropolitan Water District, had in the meantime launched the Colorado River aqueduct project. In the process of selling that idea, Mulholland had dismissed the cheaper Mono option as "not promising." Now the department turned around and declared it vital. The Los Angeles public had doubts and an initial bond issue failed.

In 1930 the department went to the voters again, insisting that Mono water was essential to bridge the gap until the Colorado water arrived. The Department of Water and Power and its supporters cried "water famine"; city employees went out on campaign. This time the $38.8 million bond issue passed, by a margin of eight to one.

SEWING UP
THE BASIN

If the Mono project was actually to come on line ahead of the Colorado one, the city had to get cracking. The first task was to finish acquiring the private lands and rights needed for the project. The city already owned about 3,000 acres in the Mono Basin; it wanted ten times that much. Its targets included land along the aqueduct route; the farms that drew water from the creeks; the entire lake shoreline; and the islands. While the city did not require outright ownership of all this territory, it needed at least to extinguish certain rights the owners automatically possessed. Under California law, streamside properties had "riparian" rights to the use of the flows; lakeside properties had "littoral" rights to shoreline access. Since the streams were going to dry up and the lakeshore to recede, these rights now had to be bought and paid for.

This time there was no convenient Fred Eaton to do the city's work. In 1930, Los Angeles went to law, as governments can, to condemn lands and rights. It called to court irrigation companies, power companies, banks, and sixty-two individuals—seventy-eight defendants in all. *Los Angeles v. Aitken* (after Mono resident Nina B. Aitken, whose name happened to fall first on the list) was filed in Los Angeles County Superior Court in the spring of 1930, moved to Mono County Superior Court in the spring of 1932, and finally tried on neutral ground, in Tuolumne County Superior Court in Sonora, during 1934 and 1935.

By that time it was very nearly moot. Most of the owners had made their own deals with the city, usually selling their land outright. The largest block of land came from the Southern Sierras Power Company. Here we have one of the few instances in which the city faced a negotiating partner of equal strength. Southern Sierras, itself a utility, was not subject to condemnation. Moreover, it owned some properties that the city had to have: the power-plant sites along the Owens Gorge. Knowing its advantage, the company approached many of the private owners in the Mono Basin, assembling a high-priced land package that Los Angeles had either to take or to leave. The city grumbled, and took.

By the time the case went to trial, only four owners were seriously fighting. The most notable holdout was a prominent local family, the Clovers, who held some re-markable land.

If the old Mono Basin had an ecological crossroads, it was the lower reach of Rush Creek, owned largely by James B. Clover and his wife Anna.

Rush Creek, largest of the lake's feeder streams, comes down from the peaks, between the long embankments left by the last glacier, across the blankness called Pumice Valley, and on toward the salty shore. About three miles from the lake it crosses a granitic sill, making a rugged little notch. Below this narrows, in the old days, the creek broke into numerous deep channels, flowing in a wide band of cottonwoods, willows, and Jeffrey pines. Just before reaching the lake, the stream spread out even more widely, forming marshes and lagoons. In the lake itself, a cone of fresh creekwater spread out over the salt. Birds gathered here to drink and wash, and brown trout, swimming out to the deadly border, would dart across it and snap up shrimp from the brine. On either side of the creek mouth, sandy, shelving beaches curved away.

The Clovers' two parcels bracketed this lushest stretch of Rush Creek. Upstream was a piece containing the rocky narrows and a vital set of springs. These poured in from both canyon walls and ran to the stream in multiple rills packed with watercress. They never got warm, never froze, never failed. Even when summer irrigation above the narrows reduced the flow down the main Rush Creek channel, the Clover springs kept the stream healthy and full of trout from this point down. A sort of compensation was apparently taking place: the very irrigation waters removed from the creek higher up augmented some of the natural springs below.

The Clovers' lower and larger parcel included the Rush Creek mouth. It was developed, barely, as a resort ("finest of stream fishing, duck shooting unsurpassed, rates reasonable"). Caretaker Walter Dombrowski built some additional ponds for ducks and blinds for hunters. He also counted waterfowl, on a semiprofessional basis, for the federal government. Dombrowski estimated that as many as 400,000 birds, mostly ruddy ducks and shovelers, settled on the Rush Creek delta at times and flew up the stream corridor to feed in its drainage basin.

For Los Angeles, the Clover property was perhaps the most important prize of all. The *Aitken* jury awarded the family $42,800, or $89 an acre, for the riparian and littoral rights that constituted nearly the whole value of their land. Landowners who had thrown in with Southern Sierras Power had gotten up to $319 an acre.

The Clovers, and some other owners, found the jury awards too low. Los Angeles found them too high. In an attempt to have them reduced, the city went to the Third District Court of Appeal in Sacramento. The city did not challenge the sums allotted for loss of creekwater. But it argued that lakeshore owners—the Clovers included—should get merely nominal damages for the loss of lake access. Reasoning: the California constitution forbids water waste; discharge to Mono Lake of water that could otherwise be used domestically constituted waste; by diverting the streams and lowering the lake, Los Angeles was only practicing conservation. If a lakeside owner had in the past enjoyed or profited from the existence of a wastewater lake, that was just too bad.

The Third District Court didn't buy this argument. It ruled that, insofar as the shoreline owners could make commercial use of their special location, they were entitled to compensation for their loss. Lost enjoyment, to be sure, need not be paid for; lost opportunity for profit must be. The jury awards stood.

By the time the process was over, Los Angeles owned outright some 30,000 acres of land in the basin and had water rights and easements on thousands more. The city had spent some five million dollars. Private land in the region had become a scarce commodity. It was at this time that the Paiutes, who had owned fertile properties along Rush Creek and elsewhere, were rendered all but landless.

Opposite: *The federal government owns most of the land in the Mono Basin. In the 1930s, the Los Angeles Department of Water and Power became the second largest owner. The Mono Basin National Forest Scenic Area was created in 1984.*

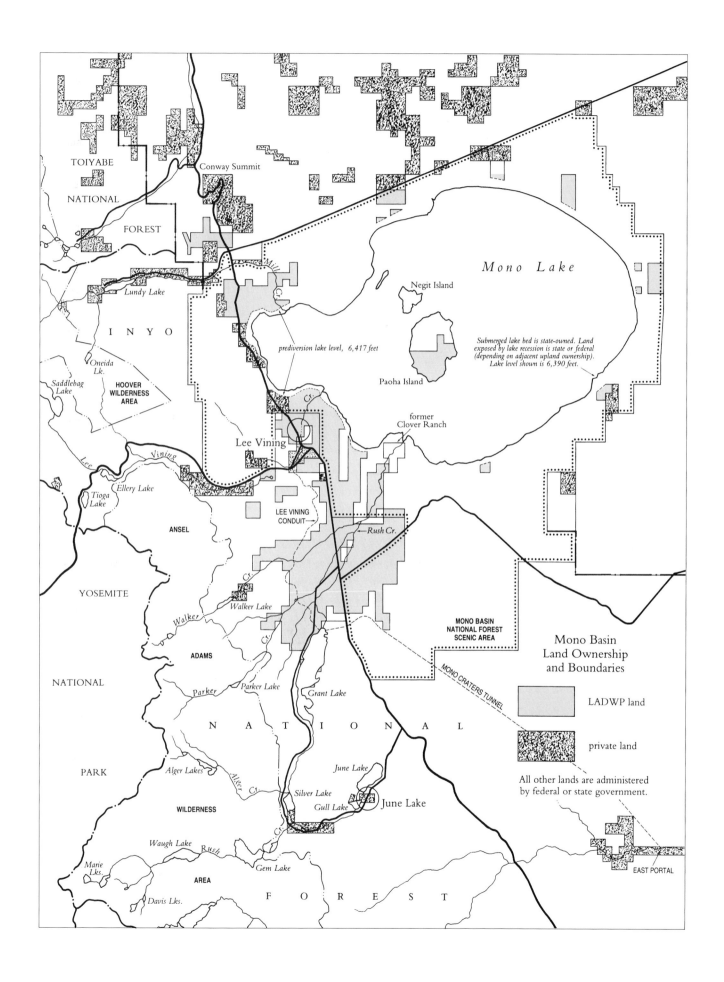

TOIYABE

NATIONAL

FOREST

Conway Summit

Lundy Lake

Mono Lake

Negit Island

I N Y O

predivision lake level, 6,417 feet

Oneida Lk.

Saddlebag Lake

HOOVER WILDERNESS AREA

Paoha Island

Submerged lake bed is state-owned. Land exposed by lake recession is state or federal (depending on adjacent upland ownership). Lake level shown is 6,390 feet.

Lee Vining

former Clover Ranch

Lee Vining

Ellery Lake

Tioga Lake

ANSEL

LEE VINING CONDUIT

Rush Cr.

YOSEMITE

Walker Lake

ADAMS

NATIONAL

Parker Lake

Grant Lake

MONO BASIN NATIONAL FOREST SCENIC AREA

Mono Basin Land Ownership and Boundaries

N A T I O N A L

PARK

Alger Lakes

June Lake

MONO CRATERS TUNNEL

LADWP land

WILDERNESS

Silver Lake

Gull Lake

June Lake

private land

Waugh Lake

Rush

All other lands are administered by federal or state government.

Marie Lks.

Gem Lake

AREA

Davis Lks.

F O R E S T

EAST PORTAL

What's interesting now about the *Aitken* case is the way it spelled out both the fate of Mono Lake and many of the values to be lost. Los Angeles's expert witnesses predicted that the lake would ultimately drop almost 100 feet in surface elevation, to a level of 6,322.4 feet above sea level, and would shrink in area by more than 50 percent. These estimates were far more credible than those of the defendants' experts, who claimed the lake would dry up entirely. For their part, the landowners offered lots of testimony about fish and wildlife, though only as assets to be considered in setting the purchase price. The possibility of alkali dust storms from the lakebed was also mentioned. No one seriously denied these consequences. Allowing for the many lessons that have since been learned, *Aitken* was a pretty good guide to what was to occur.

THE SYSTEM   Even before *Aitken* was resolved, the city's Mono Basin waterworks were under construction. They consisted of:

> A diversion dam on Lee Vining Creek, four miles up from the lakeshore and 338 miles from Los Angeles. This is the northernmost point on the Los Angeles aqueduct system; a further reach to Mill Creek, six miles farther north, had been rejected because of cost.
>
> A buried pipeline curving along the Sierra slope, scooping up Rush Creek tributary creeks Parker and Walker along the way and continuing south to the Grant Lake reservoir.
>
> Grant Lake reservoir on Rush Creek, eight stream miles above the lake. This impoundment would store the waters brought in from the northern creeks, as well as the flows of Rush Creek itself.
>
> Another stretch of buried pipeline running from Grant Lake to the base of the Mono Craters, at a spot called West Portal, where the major tunneling began.
>
> The Mono Craters Tunnel, leading at a constant descending angle 11.5 miles under the craters and the wooded heights beyond and down to East Portal, the discharge point on the upper Owens River.

Once through the mountain, the export water would flow down the upper Owens into Long Valley reservoir at the head of the Owens Gorge. Instead of running down the gorge, it would be sent on a parallel course through penstocks and power plants. (This gorge bypass was not completed until 1953.) Rejoining the Owens bed at the bottom of the defile, the flow would pass on down the river 50 miles to the aqueduct takeout point near Lone Pine.

One more element essential to the plan was not formally included in it: a second,

Inspecting the Mono Craters Tunnel. H. A. Van Norman (left) succeeded Mulholland as Water and Power general manager and chief engineer. (Photo courtesy Los Angeles Dept. of Water and Power)

parallel Los Angeles aqueduct from the Owens River south. Without this "second barrel," the city could take only part of the Mono water to which it was entitled. Construction, however, would be delayed for decades.

Of all the engineering achievements that make up the Los Angeles aqueduct system, the Mono Craters Tunnel may be the most remarkable. Burrowing from both portals and from two vertical access shafts, the crews encountered long sections of rotten rock that had to be supported with steel casings. Groundwater poured into the bore, and so did suffocating carbon dioxide; an additional vertical shaft had to be drilled to vent it. When the tunnel passed through the warm core of these volcanic domes, it collapsed; a mess of water and shattered rock backed up for nearly two miles, killing two men. The job took almost four years in all, and half a dozen lives.

For Lee Vining, the immediate effect of the project was to lift the community out of the Depression several years before World War II ended the slump for the rest of the country. Both East Portal and West Portal had encampments that were really towns, with schools, churches, bars, outlying brothels, and baseball teams playing in a local league. Among the buildings erected in Lee Vining then was a sort of Quonset hut that served as a dance hall for construction men; in a rather nice twist, it would wind up forty years later as the headquarters of the Mono Lake Committee.

Another twist was in the making. During this same period, hundreds of miles away, work was proceeding on the city's second and much larger new aqueduct, the one to the Colorado. The Mono Extension had been sold to the voters as an interim source, a

Wallis the Witness

Wallis McPherson lived most of his life in the Mono Basin—until distress at the condition of the lake drove him north over the hills to Bridgeport. (Photo by Gerda S. Mathan)

Wallis R. McPherson of Bridgeport hands you his card. It bears the blue outline of Mono Lake, his address, and the single word "Expert." An equally appropriate legend would be "Witness." From 1914 to 1977, McPherson seems to have been in on every phase of the Mono Basin story.

His father, Wallis D. McPherson, came to the basin in 1909 as an engineer for the Rush Creek Mutual Ditch Company. In 1917, when Wallis R. was three, the family moved out to a homestead on Paoha Island, where they hoped to build a sanitarium featuring goat's milk. Wallis loved the island: "There were dogs and horses and people and goats and chickens and ducks, and I was king of the whole works." The volcanic soil and artesian water (from an old exploratory oil well) produced amazing vegetables and corn.

After four years the family moved to the mainland and operated the Mono Inn. In 1934, young Wallis attended the Aitken trial in Sonora and spent several days on the stand. After Aitken, he worked as a surveyor on the Mono Craters Tunnel; among other tasks, he made sure that each new segment was properly aligned before blasting. "If you haven't heard a round of shots fired in a tunnel, you've missed a thrill." With the storyteller's trick of delaying the punchline, he recalls one dangerous moment underground: "I ran out of Shaft 2 one day as fast as I could and climbed the ladder, six hundred feet, which left me short of breath, and got to the top of the shaft. Just ahead of

the water." In August of 1938, when the crews met beneath the mountain, the tunnels joined precisely.

In that same year McPherson bought his tour boat, named the Venita after his mother, and started taking parties to the islands. He also tried, as a sideline, packaging brine shrimp for customers including Steinhart Aquarium in San Francisco. "They wanted them live or they wanted them dry. Live, the transportation was a little difficult. And a dead whale doesn't stink at all; just try drying several hundred pounds of shrimp!" McPherson helped to build the shrimp plant that still operates on the western shore. When a Hollywood crew used the lake as a set for Fair Winds to Java, *a forgotten movie of 1953, he was in charge of their boats.*

After World War II, the receding lake robbed the Mono Inn of its water access. In 1950, a freak windstorm picked up and wrecked the dry-docked Venita. The next year, McPherson went to work for the California Division of Highways, delegating management of the inn to a succession of hired managers. "Each manager bought himself a new car and went down the road, and I was still driving the old Buick." In 1977 he retired from his state job, sold the inn, and moved to Bridgeport, in the next valley north from Mono. "I don't particularly care to even look at Mono Lake any more," he says. "I realize that it's still a pretty lake. But it's not the Mono Lake I know. Not by a long shot."

stopgap pending the tapping of the great southwestern river. But it was the Colorado project that moved faster. The two new supplies would arrive at almost the same moment. The Colorado River, not the eastern Sierra, would serve Los Angeles as secondary source—an insurance policy, expensive but in the long run worth the price.

Considerable paperwork accompanied the construction. Water acquisition in the 1930s was no longer quite the free-for-all process it had been in 1905. Los Angeles had to get a dam-building permit from the State Department of Public Works. It had to get a diversion permit from the state water rights authority—the Division of Water Resources, as it was then called—before actually taking water. Finally, it had to ask a favor—two favors, in fact—from the California Fish and Game Commission.

The Department of Public Works was no obstacle. There was controversy, however, before the Division of Water Resources. At hearings in the fall of 1938, much of the Mono community turned out to oppose the granting of permits. The diversions, people complained, would "lay waste and desert" a large area, cut property values and property tax revenue, and choke off tourism. The water board seemed to sympathize but declared itself powerless. Domestic water supply was the highest use, and that was that. "It is indeed unfortunate that the City's proposed development will result in decreasing the aesthetic advantages of the Mono Basin," the staff observed, "but there is apparently nothing that this office can do to prevent it." On June 1, 1940, the division granted the permits Los Angeles sought.

The Fish and Game Commission was, or should have been, a higher hurdle. According to California fish and game laws, new dams were supposed to be built with fish passage facilities or "fishways" around them. In 1937, when Grant Lake dam was well underway, the legislature added a new requirement: all dams, old or new, equipped with fishways or not, must let enough water pass to maintain "in good condition" the fish in the streams below. Los Angeles proposed neither to add fishways nor to let water escape its new reservoirs.

The fishways rule was fairly easy to get around. The law allowed the city to offer as a substitute a hatchery, not necessarily on the stream being dammed. The Fish and Game Commission agreed to this substitution, and such a facility was built, on city land and partly at city expense, on Hot Creek in Long Valley. Today, the Hot Creek Hatchery supplies the fish planted in some 400 lakes and 900 miles of stream up and down the eastern Sierra.

The second provision, that water be released through dams, could not, in theory, be evaded. But in a breathtaking maneuver, the chairman of the Fish and Game Commission, acting all by himself, signed an agreement that purported to let the city off this additional hook as part of the Hot Creek Hatchery deal.

The west shore of Mono Lake in 1938, before diversions began. (Photo Burton Frasher, © Frashers Fotos, Pomona, California)

Could Chairman Nate Milnor do that? He couldn't. For one thing, he was going far beyond what the full commission had agreed to; for another, the bargain itself was patently illegal. Yet the Hot Creek Agreement of November 25, 1940, became an unchallenged landmark of California water law. Every student in the field learned about it; every citizen or biologist who thought to complain about the fate of streams in the Mono Basin and Long Valley stubbed a toe on it.

When the Hot Creek Agreement was signed, Los Angeles had already begun to impound the Mono Basin waters behind Grant Lake dam. Five months later, in April 1941, water began to flow southward under the Mono Craters.

4

THE STREAMS GO SOUTH

"How did you go bankrupt?" Bill asked.
"Two ways," Mike said. "Gradually and
then suddenly."

Ernest Hemingway, *The Sun Also Rises*

EARLY IN 1941 a young fisheries biologist sat down in his cabin near June Lake and wrote a letter to the Los Angeles Department of Water and Power. "On March 10," Elden Vestal reported, "I examined Rush Creek below the new Grant Lake dam and was dismayed to find that no flow, whatsoever, was occurring in the stream." The streambed had been dry most of the time since the previous October. Vestal made a modest request: "I would greatly appreciate the Department turning in and maintaining a flow at all times of not less than five cubic feet per second." This tiny flow, Vestal thought, would serve to keep the fine trout stream minimally healthy while he sought advice from his superiors.

The answer came quickly, and it came from the top. "Dear Sir," wrote H. A. Van Norman, Mulholland's successor in Los Angeles. "The Division of Fish and Game of the State of California and the Department of Water and Power of the City of Los Angeles have entered into an agreement relative to the operation of the Grant Lake and Long Valley Reservoirs, and it is suggested that you contact your central office to make yourself familiar with the terms of the agreement."

Vestal did check with his boss, chief of the Bureau of Fish Conservation. "The reply was a thinly veiled warning to stop my investigations into what was apparently a very sensitive political question," says Vestal. And so he learned that Rush Creek had been sold, so to speak, down the river. He also learned, as he put it later, that "the City of Los Angeles was God Almighty."

Elden Vestal of the Department of Fish and Game. His protest against the drying-up of Rush Creek earned him a sharp reprimand. (Photo by Gerda S. Mathan)

Vestal, one of the first professional biologists ever to work for California Fish and Game, had been in the region off and on since 1938. He had walked and fished the local waters—"One of the tools of the trade is a fly rod"—and knew lower Rush Creek as an extraordinary trout water, a place to catch fourteen-inch German browns. He was, of course, aware of the Los Angeles project—the region was swarming with construction workers, and the higher Grant Lake dam was taking shape upstream. But he had had no idea of how much water would be taken.

The initial alarm came to seem overblown. Once Grant Lake was filled, Los Angeles extracted less water than it was physically capable of taking. The early 1940s were wet years; there was flow to spare. Though Rush Creek below the dam suffered, the stretch farthest downstream, the three miles between the narrows and the lake, did not. Irrigation continued on the porous flats above the creek, and the springs near the narrows continued to flow, adding cold, clear water to the diminished main stream. The watercress beds continued to provide food and shelter. The spawning gravels, the multiple channels, the undercut banks, remained. It was still a good place for fish.

In 1946, rather daringly in view of the prospects, Fish and Game chose lower Rush Creek for an experiment in the planting of rainbow trout. Elden Vestal, back in the region after a stint in the army, supervised the Rush Creek test stream. He arrived in time to see the respite end.

The years from 1947 to 1951 were dry. Los Angeles exported all available water, shutting down local irrigation. Little or no water came down the channel from Grant Lake, and the springs, too, began to dwindle. During 1951, the mean summer flow was down to 2.5 cubic feet per second. Fishermen were complaining. The stream and the fish were barely surviving. The "vital thread," as Vestal calls it, was not yet snapped but was stretched to the limit. At the same time, down on the Rush Creek delta, the marshes and Walter Dombrowski's duck ponds were going dry.

Elden Vestal was not there to see the thread snap. In 1950 he left the region for another Fish and Game post, taking with him his copious notes.

The second major stream that Los Angeles tapped, Lee Vining Creek, was in many respects a scaled-down version of Rush. It had the same narrow, brimming channels, the same streamside gallery forest. But lower Lee Vining Creek had no significant springs. Except for a stretch immediately below the diversion dam, and occasional wet-year spills over it, the more northerly creek saw no water after the spring of 1947. Pines, cottonwoods, and willows died. In the early 1950s a fire completed the destruction of the riparian woodland. The creek became a desert gulch, littered with old tires sent bouncing down the embankment from Lee Vining above.

The effects on Mono Lake itself were delayed rather longer. In 1941, Mono's surface stood at 6,417 feet above sea level, well down from a historic high of 6,428 in 1919. Without diversion, the lake would now have begun rising; even with diversion, for several years it almost held its own. Even after it began to drop, in 1947, the recession seemed without practical consequence. Until the middle 1950s, in fact, Mono Lake was still within the range of recent natural fluctuations, no lower than it had been in 1861.

Then, in 1955, the water surface dropped below the 6,405-foot elevation mark, and in rapid succession several types of degradation set in.

At higher levels, the lake had lapped at hillsides; now increasingly its margins lay on gentle plains. At higher levels, the shore was sandy; now the adjacent sediments were finer, and mudflats formed. In the higher lake, currents had carried sand along the shore, building beaches and bars with brackish lagoons behind them; these wetlands, found especially on the northeast shore, were important duck habitats. As the lake sank below 6,402 feet, the sand sources were left behind. Moreover, shallows north of Negit Island began to block the "longshore" currents. The old lakeside lagoons drained, becoming dry bowls, and no new ones formed. On Paoha Island, several interior salt ponds (two of them named Heart Lake and Dollar Lake) dried up also.

At the mouths of the major creeks, additional lagoons and wetlands were lost. Here the retreating lake had steadily been exposing the underwater deltas, big fan-like deposits where the streams had dropped their sediments. In this same period of the late 1950s, the lake margin reached the abrupt outward edges of these fans. As it continued to drop, groundwater drained from the abandoned flats above, and large areas went dry.

In other areas around the shore, marshland and wet meadow actually expanded as the lake retreated. In some of these stretches—along the west shore, for instance—the green mat widened as the water's edge shifted; but in other and far vaster reaches, an alkali flat came to occupy the immediate shoreline. Separated from the shore, the wetlands lost much of their habitat value. Though springs tended to migrate downslope as well, they moved less far than the lake; there were fewer spots where fresh water pooled on top of the brine.

These shoreline changes affected the ducks most of all. There would still be waterfowl at Mono Lake, but at a fraction of the old numbers.

For people, too, the Mono shorelands became less pleasant, less useful. Miles of sandy beaches gave way to miles of sticky mud. In the early 1960s, a marina opened just north of Lee Vining. Water-skiing competitions were held there. By the end of the decade, though, the adjacent waters were too shallow and hazardous for boating. The place became known as "the Old Marina" or "Sneaker Flat" (for the guck that would suck off your tennis shoes). It was at this time that the Department of Water and Power opened its Grant Lake reservoir to recreation.

Not every change was a scenic loss. As the lake fell, the tufa displays were transformed. Tufa "groves" that had stood at water's edge were left high and dry and became less interesting. But new and more spectacular stands were exposed. Today's most extensive tufa displays, South Tufa and Lee Vining Tufa, were uncovered at this time.

Also revealed were the bizarre natural sculptures known as sand tufas. These form beneath the shifting lake margin, where sand is permeated alternately by salt water and fresh. When the waters mix, tufa precipitates, cementing the sand in intricate tubes and layers. By nature these structures are buried and hidden, but the prolonged modern regression of the lake exposed them. Some were displayed in cross-section in eroded banks; the most spectacular stood free. Here wind and gravity, removing the sand particles not bound by tufa, left fantastic chambered monuments up to six feet high. Sand tufas came to be sentimentalized as fairy castles, but that does not do justice to their weirdness: they seem, rather, the hives of some unearthly insect with an exquisite sense of form.

And what about the living things of the lake itself? Just what was happening to them during the years of recession is harder to estimate. We really don't know what, besides brine shrimp and alkali flies, lived in the pre-diversion lake, so we don't know what may have ceased to live there. There were apparently several water plants that vanished as the lake grew saltier. Old-timers recall drifts of an ivory-colored alga: "That's what your ducks really went to town on." There were certainly several types of microscopic animals now gone.

High salinities seem to reduce the crop of the lake's basic foodstuff, algae. Flies and shrimp had to spend more of their energy keeping their tissues free of excessive salt. Brine shrimp apparently became smaller, though not less numerous. Alkali flies grew

Portrait of decline: tufa towers at the northwest corner of the lake as seen in 1962 (top), 1968 (center), and 1982. (Photos courtesy Mono Lake Committee)

both smaller and somewhat fewer; the shoreline windrows of dislodged pupae, favored food of birds and Paiutes, grew less lavish. In the late 1950s, the Kuzedika stopped visiting the shores to gather *kutsavi*. Red-necked phalaropes, which subsist entirely on flies, later began to feel the effects of lessened food supply.

There was no collapse of the web of life at Mono Lake, no sudden die-off. In Hemingway's terms, it had not yet reached the sudden phase of bankruptcy. But there was a clear impoverishment, a definite loss of vigor.

David Mason

In 1961, U.C. Davis student David Mason arrived at Mono Lake to begin the first major limnological study since Israel Russell's. He knew and loved the region already. Mixing scientific research with a passionate personal concern, he set a pattern that many were to follow. But that is to put it just wrong, for Mason's task was not to mix two attitudes but to keep them strictly apart—to prevent the advocate from spoiling the researcher's scientific discipline. His successors have been facing that task ever since.

Before descending to the proper neutral tone, Mason's thesis gleams with his love of the place. "Water drains off the mountains and into this basin, nourishing a shrinking film of lake, an expanse of brine lying heavy in its bed," he writes on the first page. "The lake moves and breathes as the sun passes its yearly course; while a few small creatures in its waters bend the sun's energy to their purpose for a time, and then sink and die."

Like a general practitioner meeting a new patient, Mason gave the lake a thorough physical. He offered a theory to account for the lake's nearly perfect oval (except for the big stream deltas on the west). He performed what was then the most detailed chemical analysis ever made of the lakewater and described, for the first time, some of its behaviors. He noted how incoming creekwater mingled with the brine—a delayed mixing, completed only in the fall—and how the lake changed color through the year, greening with algae in the winter, clearing by summer as trillions of shrimp developed to graze the crop away.

In print, Mason called the continued decline of the lake "presumably inevitable." Privately he tried to arouse concern about it. He put together a slide show for local audiences. One day, working near Danburg Beach at the northwest corner of the lake, he bumped into roving photographer Ansel Adams and begged him to use his influence somehow on behalf of the lake. (Adams was indeed to help the cause, but mainly through his art.) Mason also approached several conservation organizations, receiving sympathy but not much practical interest: the cause seemed too thoroughly lost.

ALKALI AND DUST STORMS

As its surface fell further below 6,400 feet, Mono Lake began, for the first time, to appear distinctly shrunken, too small for its bed. On the north and east, the rim of exposed alkali, narrow at first, grew ever more broad. This strip is a chemical wasteland that plants are very slow to colonize. Sparse local rainfall might leach the surface in time, but the poison is constantly renewed from below. A few feet down lies groundwater even saltier than the lake; as capillary action draws it toward the surface it evaporates, leaving a salt crust that replaces itself as fast as it is blown or washed away.

As early as 1965, the expanding alkali band gave rise to something new in Mono Basin weather: the dust storm. This is windy country, especially in the spring and fall, and now the winds had long expanses of alkali to work on. They picked up the microscopic

Blowing dust on the east shore, seen from the old Clover Ranch. (Photo © Jim Stimson)

salt particles by the ton and built great clouds of them. The first storms were small, but within a few years they became immense. At times the eastern two-thirds of the lake, including the islands, would disappear in the gray-brown cloud. An airline pilot once mistook dust swirling off Paoha Island for a volcanic eruption.

Very fine dust, we now know, is particularly nasty stuff to breathe. Human nasal passages have defenses, mucus and traps of hair, to screen out larger motes and grains before they reach the lungs, but Mono-type dust particles are so minute that they slip right through. Being in the middle of an eastern Sierra dust storm subjects the lungs to more ultra-fine particles than being in the middle of a forest fire. You could think of alkali dust as albino soot.

In the short term, breathing the stuff is highly irritating and can cause real distress for the very young, the very old, and anyone with a lung disorder. Repeated exposure may injure lung tissue and possibly give rise to cancers, due mainly to physical irritation but potentially also to chemical effects. Mono dust contains the carcinogen arsenic in amounts that may warrant concern.

Such dust storms were nothing new down in the Owens Valley, where the desiccated playa of Owens Lake had been feeding them for years. The Owens storms often blow right up the trough of the valley, over the towns. Mono Basin residents are luckier. Most of them live on the western edge of the lake, upwind from the dust sources. The great storms here move north and east, into country that is sparsely inhabited and little visited (though this is changing).

"You just have to see it, to experience it, to understand how bad it is," says a man who does live northeast of Mono Lake. "If you go outside, your teeth are instantly gritty, and it stinks. It smells like brackish seawater. It hurts to breathe." In a really bad storm you don't have to go outside: "It was so dusty inside the house you could shine the flashlight through the house and see the same amount of dust inside as out."

THE CREEKS ARE RUINED

For the lake, the occasional wet year stalled or even reversed the changes that were occurring. But for the streams, those wet years only accelerated the damage. The first great season of destruction came in 1967.

By this time lower Lee Vining Creek was a desert landscape. Rush Creek had fared somewhat better. Intermittent irrigation on both sides of the creek, above the narrows, had maintained some flow in the springs. Streamside vegetation dwindled but did not vanish, and a few trout probably remained. Elden Vestal's "vital thread," though perilously stretched, was not yet actually broken.

In the winter of 1966–67 the snowpack was heavy, especially in the Rush Creek watershed. Spring was wet and cold. At the end of June, the weather suddenly turned hot and meltwater came with a rush—more water than the aqueduct could handle, more water than Grant Lake could store. The Water and Power managers guessed wrong and continued diverting from Lee Vining Creek far longer than they should have; this only increased the amount they had to release down Rush. In early July that stream may have carried more water than at any time since the last glaciation. The torrent, moreover, ran down the newly exposed steep front of the delta and into a lowered lake. By the laws of physics, flowing water works to adjust its course into a smooth elevational arc from source to mouth. That's what happened on Rush Creek in 1967. Cutting upward from the mouth, the temporary new river carved a twelve-foot gash into the old delta.

Lee Vining Creek was spared in 1967. Its turn came two years later. The 1969 flood sliced a ten-foot incision into the bed of the creek near the lakeshore. Farther upstream,

Flowing to a lowered lake, Rush Creek cut a new inner canyon into its old floodplain. (Photo by Geoffrey McQuilkin, courtesy Mono Lake Committee)

the rushing water tore itself a new, simplified channel and stripped the rather shallow soil off most of the floodplain. Left behind was a landscape of sunbeaten, cobble-sized stones.

Nobody much noticed what was happening to the creeks in the late 1960s. Officially, these creeks were not seen as streams at all. They were drains, escape valves for use when the system got out of control. The channel by which water was released, at need, into Rush Creek was called Mono Gate Number One; but the common expression was the Mono Wastegate.

THE SECOND BARREL

Such wastage was about to become rarer. Though the tunnel through the Mono Craters had been built large enough to take almost all the available water from the Mono Basin, there was a bottleneck far down the line, where the original Los Angeles Aqueduct had still not been expanded to match.

Left to itself, Los Angeles might never have gotten around to expansion. By this time the growing city had covered most of the land available to it; its water needs were no longer rising so steeply. Moreover, the city had signed on, through the Metropolitan Water District, to the State Water Project, a scheme to tap the Sacramento River for southern cities and agriculture. When this California Aqueduct came on line, in 1973, Los Angeles would be tied into rivers from Arizona almost to Oregon—would have, in truth, a world of water on call. The city also had a superb underground reservoir, in the gravels of the San Fernando Valley, for the long-term storage of its supply. By any reasonable measure, the city had reached its goal of water security.

It's a terrific irony, in view of all that would follow, that the nudge to speed up the destruction of Mono Lake came directly from the state.

In releasing to Mono Lake some of the water that might be taken south, the city was not living up to the terms of its 1940 diversion permit; it was, technically, "wasting" that water. Similarly, it was taking less than it might from the Owens Valley. In 1959, after issuing many extensions, the State Water Rights Board (successor to the old Division of Water Resources) issued a warning. If action was not forthcoming, the city could lose its claim on the water it wasn't yet using.

Now, losing water rights—whether you especially want to use them or not—is something no traditional water-man can abide. The whole California water law system is based on the principle of seizing, holding, and never, *ever*, letting go. No agency held that creed more righteously than the Los Angeles Department of Water and Power.

So a second Los Angeles aqueduct was built, parallel to the first one and about half its size, at a cost of about $89 million. This "second barrel" came on line in 1970. Given this new plumbing, the city had every reason to use it, to draw on the eastern Sierra rather than on its entitlements from the Colorado or the Sacramento. For one thing,

Major Aqueducts
Serving the Greater
Los Angeles Area

Three of California's largest aqueducts converge on Los Angeles and the southern California metropolitan region.

while the other sources were shared, the Los Angeles Aqueduct was under the city's sole control. For another, the water, coming straight from snowmelt, was simply of higher quality than that from the other sources. And for a very important third thing, eastern Sierra water spun turbines, producing very low-cost energy at the rate of 3,560 kilowatt-hours per acre-foot.

So the department proceeded to carry out the perfectly logical policy of draining the eastern Sierra first. In the Owens Valley, the city pumped more groundwater; falling water tables threatened to complete the desiccation process begun in the 1930s. In the Mono Basin, average diversions nearly doubled, to 100,000 acre-feet a year. The lake

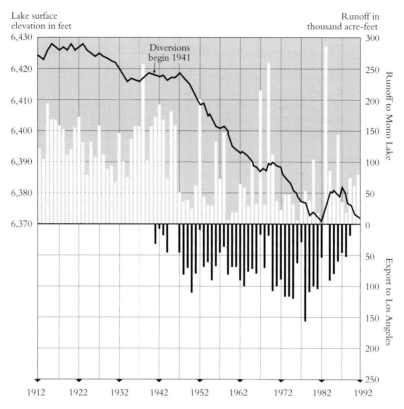

Lake surface
elevation in feet

Runoff in
thousand acre-feet

Diversions
begin 1941

Runoff to Mono Lake

Export to Los Angeles

1912 1922 1932 1942 1952 1962 1972 1982 1992

As water was diverted to Los Angeles (black bars), total streamflow into Mono Lake decreased (white bars) and the lake level dropped. Read left scale for lake level, right scale for streamflow and export volumes. Streamflow includes not only the four diverted streams but also Mill Creek and lesser streams that were never diverted from the Mono Basin. An acre-foot is about 326,000 gallons. (Adapted from California State Water Resources Control Board, Draft Environmental Impact Report, *1993, vol. 1, figs. 1-6 and 1-7.)*

sank faster, over two feet per year. Its volume shrank more rapidly. Salt concentrations grew. In both regions, these effects began to produce new citizen protest and to attract renewed sympathetic attention from the outside world.

THE SECOND OWENS
VALLEY WAR

In the decades after the turbulent 1920s, Los Angeles and the population of the Owens Valley had evolved a curious peace. There were conciliatory voices, conciliatory policies. Tourism became more and more important in the valley, replacing agriculture as the region's major industry. And many observers found themselves thinking the same thought: that if Los Angeles had not bought up water and land, the splendid high-desert landscape, mountain-rimmed, magnificent for its very emptiness, would be much more cluttered and, indeed, less to be treasured.

Then came the second barrel of the Los Angeles aqueduct, and a reminder that such benefits, however real, were purely accidental.

The city had permitted irrigated agriculture to continue, under lease, on approximately 30,000 acres of its lands. It now proposed to reduce this green area by half (though the remainder would have a more reliable water supply). Water and Power also proposed to increase the extraction of groundwater from its numerous wells. Pumping had been minimal for decades; water came to the surface in extensive wetlands and was "lost" (from an engineer's point of view) to evaporation. Now some of this groundwater would go to the remaining farms (freeing up river water for export); and in some years pumping would add directly to the aqueduct flow. Water tables would fall.

As soon as the new aqueduct was complete, the pumping began. By 1972, unadvertised effects were becoming obvious. Springs that had been familiar landmarks were drying up. Deep-rooted desert plants began to die off; dust storms seemed to increase.

In 1972, Inyo County went to court, demanding that Los Angeles prepare an Environmental Impact Report (EIR) on the effects of its actions. After some early maneuvers, the case wound up in Sacramento, bouncing back and forth between the Sacramento County Superior Court and the Third District Court of Appeal. The lower court generally saw things the city's way; the appellate court tended to side with Inyo County. The higher court required the EIR and was later to reject as inadequate two successive drafts. The courts also took control of the pumping, setting the permitted rates, amid much wrangling, from year to year.

This second Owens Valley controversy continued for more than a decade. In its early stages it prepared the way for action at Mono Lake. It showed that the Department of Water and Power was not, after all, legally untouchable and that citizen pressure could accomplish a great deal.

In Mono County, too, an opposition struggled to form. Inspired in part by limnologist David Mason, some shoreline property owners banded together as "Friends of Mono Lake," wrote letters, and tried to rally the community. They found it hard going. People resented Los Angeles, which operated somewhat like a feudal overlord, but few now saw the lake itself as worth much effort to defend. Unlike the citizens of Inyo, the Mono protesters did not try to persuade their Board of Supervisors to take any particular action.

Organizations based outside the region were also starting to take an interest. The National Audubon Society took an inconclusive look at the issue. The Toiyabe chapter of the Sierra Club addressed a protest to the Department of Water and Power. There was talk of adding the Mono Basin to Yosemite National Park. But the mobilization process was like starting a balky power mower: it took quite a few pulls on the rope before the engine finally caught.

What drew the attention of outsiders, at this point, was not the lake or the landscape as a whole but one dramatic feature within it: Negit Island. Bulging on the water like a big black hat, with rocky crown and level surrounding brim, Negit was romantic, photogenic, and doomed. In 1940 two miles of water had lain between island and mainland; now just two narrow straits interrupted a land bridge. When these closed, coyotes and other predators would reach the California gull nests. *American Birds* magazine predicted "total destruction of the population."

In 1972 the Bureau of Land Management, proprietor of the federal land on the lakeshore, took the ineffectual but symbolic step of declaring Negit an Outstanding Natural Area. In January of 1973, state Assemblyman Gene Chappie led a field trip to the island and called on "DWP and the people of Los Angeles to recognize their responsibility for the problems they are creating." He promised "to do a little disturbing in the Southland in the near future." Chappie seems to have found the colossus to the south rather hard to disturb, however.

That same year, the former McPherson place on the big neighbor island, Paoha, was for sale. The Department of Water and Power eventually picked up the property, "to assure a possible sanctuary for the gulls," aqueduct manager Duane Georgeson said. Though gulls had nested on Paoha in the distant past, they were to show no interest in it, this time around.

By 1974, then, Los Angeles was beginning to feel some renewed heat regarding its operations in the eastern Sierra. For Mono Lake, however, it appeared to be too late.

FROM PERMIT
TO LICENSE

With water flowing southward at a new and higher rate, the city's water rights could at last be "perfected." Ever since 1940, Water and Power had been diverting water under interim "permits." At the beginning of 1974, the state water rights agency—it had changed its name yet again and was now the State Water Resources Control Board—quietly converted these permits into permanent "licenses." Curiously, in view of the mounting concern about Negit Island, no one filed a protest. For its part, the water board did no fresh analysis. It felt that conversion from permit to license was an automatic process: the authorities were there only to do the paperwork.

In 1974, luck was still running with the Department of Water and Power. Had the licensing been delayed even three more years, the city would have faced a real battle. But the opposition had not taken form in time. Now the licenses were in hand. Effectively, Los Angeles owned Mono Lake. Whatever destruction ensued, the department leaders could well feel, they had now nothing to fear but a little more bad press.

5

THE REVOLT OF THE BIRD-WATCHERS

It is a place where the grand processions make you acutely aware of being alive on the planet. You watch the passage of moon, sun and stars over the knife-edged horizons, and the jagged shadows of evening reaching beyond the lake into Nevada and the sky beyond. You watch the birds in their arrivals, departures, and intricate ceremonies and stalking grace, and you take comfort from such order and cyclical permanence. It is hard to watch this spectacle crumble to dust.

Gray Brechin, 1976

NEAR THE END OF THE 1970S, a force arose that could actually challenge the Los Angeles Department of Water and Power at Mono Lake. The defining moment was May 12, 1979, when lawyers for Friends of the Earth, the National Audubon Society, and a new group called the Mono Lake Committee entered the tall, red-trimmed doors of the old Mono County Courthouse in Bridgeport to bring suit against the department. The parties who converged that day had gotten there by several different roads.

In 1974, even as Los Angeles was tightening its legal grip on Mono Basin waters, a junior at the University of California at Berkeley was seeking the means to loosen it again. His name was Tim Such.

Most Mono Lake campaigners have fallen in love with the landscape before they come to grips with its problems. For Tim Such, the process happened the other way around. In an environmental studies course he was asked to locate and analyze "an environmental disruption that had escaped review and accounting." Having seen the declining lake on his way to hikes in the eastern Sierra, he wondered now if the case might fill the bill. In fact Mono proved the perfect example: a scene of continuing environmental destruction, begun long ago, which no current law or policy appeared able to touch or even to acknowledge.

As Such continued his research he found his interest mounting toward obsession.

TIM SUCH

Kenneth Lajoie

Geologists love unnatural erosion. It lets them see what is otherwise hidden.

On the northwest shore of Mono Lake, a large stream, Mill Creek, is diverted into the bed of a small one, Wilson Creek. (This diversion, part of a hydropower operation, is not the doing of the Los Angeles Department of Water and Power.) Wilson Creek has responded by cutting a new, slotlike canyon.

Into that slot in 1964 walked Kenneth Lajoie, a graduate student in geology at the University of California at Berkeley. He saw recorded there, in fifty feet of layered silts and gravels, the history of the last high stand of Mono Lake, and he knew what his doctoral thesis would be.

In the lower layers were stream gravels and beach sands some 36,000 years old; these told Lajoie that the lake edge had been below the site at that time. Above these oldest deposits lay multiple layers of silts, which Lajoie named the Wilson Creek beds; this material had settled through lakewater. At the top of the column, beach gravels recorded the rapid drop of the lake, about 12,000 years ago. Interspersed were twenty or so thin layers of volcanic ash, white, pink, and silver: eruptions from the Mono Craters. A thick bed of chocolate-brown volcanic ash near the top of the silt beds recorded the underwater eruption of Black Point.

Some of the things Lajoie read in this record were puzzling, for they contradicted the results of more established researchers. For instance, the Wilson Creek strata suggested to Lajoie that Mono Lake had reached its highest level well after the glaciers had begun pulling back, yet the conventional wisdom held that lakes were high and glaciers large at the same time. In his thesis Lajoie ended by pulling his punches, avoiding confrontation over some of his ideas. "I've regretted doing that ever since," he says. "Most of those conclusions have withstood the test of time."

Since Lajoie worked at the lake, Mono has become a kind of master key to recent geologic events over a wide region. Other much-studied lakes, such as Searles in the Mojave Desert and even the Great Salt Lake of Utah, were dry for much of their history; the sedimentary records there have gaps. Mono endured. Mono Lake rises or falls very promptly in response to climatic changes, clearly recording these fluctuations in its bed. And Mono lies in a land of volcanoes. Layers of volcanic ash make distinctive "marker beds," which geologists use to correlate and date events within and even outside the Great Basin.

Something predictable, meanwhile, was happening to Lajoie: he was falling in love with the object of his study. A landscape this strange and marvelous, he felt, should be preserved outright. In 1974 he organized a Sierra Club Mono Lake Task Force to demand an end to stream diversions. (It was at this point that he met Tim Such and helped to fan the younger man's excitement over Mono.)

Among other things, Lajoie sought a way of hitching the Mono issue to Inyo County's suit against Los Angeles, which now was going full steam ahead. In August of 1976, Lajoie visited Antonio Rossmann, special counsel to Inyo County. An honest EIR on Los Angeles's Inyo pumping, Lajoie and Rossmann agreed, must include discussion of the effects water diver-

sions had on the Mono Basin. Lajoie prepared a declaration stating this view for use in the Inyo v. Los Angeles *court.*

In 1977, when it rejected the city's first EIR on its Inyo groundwater pumping, the Third District Court of Appeal signaled approval of Lajoie's idea. The court remarked in a footnote that all the city's water-gathering activities, including the Mono Basin diversions, should be analyzed as a whole. Had the Mono County supervisors been ready to take that hint and join in the case on their own behalf, the story might have unfolded very differently. As it was, the court's suggestion died.

Geologist Kenneth Lajoie (seated) led an early Sierra Club effort on behalf of Mono Lake; Tim Such researched the famous public trust doctrine that helped to save it. (Photo by Gerda S. Mathan)

Singlemindedly, without specific training, without funding, and with very little encouragement, he set out to discover what others had despaired of: a legal lever hefty enough to use against Los Angeles's water diversions. His modest paper had turned into a consuming avocation.

Early in his search, Such made the round of environmental groups and government agencies. For the most part, he heard discouraging words. "They thought the Mono issue was too complex," Such recalls. "They thought you couldn't fight Los Angeles. They said, 'If you find a good legal theory, come back.'"

During 1975 and 1976, interrupting his formal education, Tim Such pursued the elusive theory. Working as a private criminal investigator by day and a Mono Lake legal sleuth by night, he became a regular at the Berkeley and Stanford law libraries. Besides studying the history of the Mono Extension itself, he explored the laws and decisions of most of the fifty states, Mexico, England, and the Roman Empire.

Such looked at the California state constitution, which requires that the use of water be "reasonable and beneficial." In the past, these terms had meant chiefly that water had to be *used*; could they be interpreted to forbid uses that harm the environment? Well, probably not: the idea was too far ahead of its time.

He considered the theory that the federal government, owner of much land in the Mono Basin, had an automatic right to the water necessary to protect its assets, such as Negit Island. This approach had possibilities—in fact, the Sierra Club would shortly be pursuing it—but Such did not see it as key.

He looked at international treaties protecting migratory birds, which might impose a duty to protect Mono Lake. He looked, too, at the possibility of an alliance with the Kuzedika Paiutes to promote aboriginal claims.

Of all the many theories Tim Such examined, one grew on him: the theory of what is called the public trust. He read of it first in a 1967 article in the *Michigan Law Review* by eminent environmental lawyer Joseph Sax, but the doctrine is so ancient that, in further researching it, Such made some use of his prep-school Latin.

THE PUBLIC TRUST   Broadly speaking, the "public trust" is the concept that certain lands and resources belong to the whole people and that the government, which serves as guardian, has an inescapable duty to manage these properties well. This idea has been developed farthest in regard to one particular case: land covered by water.

Under doctrines going back to the Roman emperor Justinian and long since built into Anglo-American law, submerged lands—riverbeds, lakebeds, marshes, tidelands—have a peculiar status. The government—in our system, the several states—administers this territory for the public. But it does not do so with a free hand. Public trust lands are to be kept in condition to support certain appropriate uses. Usually, this means that shallow waters may not be filled.

The protected uses, in California, were originally navigation, fishing, and commerce. But in 1971, in a case called *Marks v. Whitney*, the California Supreme Court expanded the list. Thereafter, public trust values in California included wildlife habitat, nature study, and simple beauty of scene.

The trust expanded geographically as well. Some California courts wished to limit it to coastal tidelands, but the trend was to apply it also to navigable inland waters.

What about Mono Lake? Its water and its bed plainly belonged to the state. They were almost certainly covered by the public trust. And there was no doubt they were being damaged. But at Mono Lake the damage was indirect. The lake was not being filled; it was not even exactly being drained. It was dwindling due to the diversion of feeder streams, a victim of starvation, not mayhem. Moreover, those feeder streams (with the possible exception of Rush Creek) were too small to be navigable and thus not themselves subject to the public trust in the classic sense.

Could the public trust doctrine stretch to fit this case? Tim Such had a strong hunch it could. The state, he reasoned, could and should take steps to protect the people's property. That could only mean demanding more water. If the state would not seek greater inflows to Mono Lake, then citizens, acting as "private attorneys-general," could make the demand instead.

Even after all these years? Even after all these years. For the beauty of the public trust is that, with rare exceptions, *it cannot be given away*. Failure to enforce it does not automatically destroy it. It escapes the legal pruning saws known as "laches" and "estoppel," which serve to block delayed and untimely claims. Under the public trust, no claim is untimely.

This nutshell account of the submerged-lands public trust doctrine benefits from hindsight. When Such was researching the idea, it was regarded almost as an antiquarian oddity. The notion that it might be applied to curtail water rights was truly novel. There appears to have been just one other person in California in the mid-1970s who was aware of this possibility: Harrison C. Dunning, a law professor at the University of California at Davis, who will appear again in this story.

With his theory in hand, Tim Such made a second tour of environmental groups and government agencies. At this point he met Tony Rossmann, special counsel to Inyo County in its own dispute with Los Angeles. Rossmann was impressed by his argument. Elsewhere, though, Such found the reception little warmer than before. By this time environmentalists were gearing up for a fight concerning a new water project in the Sacramento/San Joaquin Delta, the Peripheral Canal. They feared the canal would open the way to the draining of northern California on a scale not yet seen. In general, the groups were unwilling to tackle another water issue at this time—especially this one, for saving Mono Lake could only mean less water for Los Angeles and thus more apparent need for the ominous new canal.

The major exception was Friends of the Earth. But at this point our story must backtrack to the early 1970s and trace another of the roads that led to the courthouse in Bridgeport in 1979.

Early in 1972, on the Davis campus of the University of California, a student named Sally Judy saw an ad in the student newspaper: "Bird Freaks Unite!" The author, drumming up membership for a student-run birding course, was one David Gaines. Sally Judy wasn't a bird freak—yet—but she turned out for the course. That casual decision changed her life.

Two years later, Gaines and Judy were a couple and staying at his parents' condominium in Mammoth Lakes. Gaines, who had just earned his Master's degree in ecology, was doing a quick inventory of Mono County for the California Natural Areas Coordinating Council. He was instantly captivated by Mono Lake and alarmed by the changes he saw taking place there. Sally, for her part, was not an enthusiast at first sight: "I didn't see enough of the lake to be impressed."

In 1975 Gaines was commuting between posts at Davis and at Stanford and talking up Mono Lake to students and friends on both campuses. One of these contacts, Jefferson Burch at Stanford, got word of something amazing: a federal program of research grants for *undergraduate* science students, called Student Originated Studies. Why not a study of Mono Lake? With Gaines's encouragement, Burch and two friends, Christine Weigen and David Winkler, worked up a proposal. To their astonishment, the $20,000 grant came through.

In 1976, the dozen members of the Mono Basin Research Group assembled in Lee Vining. David Gaines was on hand but not on the official, all-undergraduate roster. Most of the group camped out on a ranch on Dechambeau Creek near the northwest corner of the lake. (Landowner Jan Simis, a member of the local Friends of Mono Lake organization, had the welcome sign out for researchers.)

Looking at the group, you might have pegged them just as local folk certainly did: belated hippies, sixties kids in the wrong decade. In the Dechambeau encampment they sang, recited verse, lived largely on granola, beans, and rice, and were known to take in other nonstandard substances. But if you'd expected no results from such an outfit, you couldn't have been more wrong.

The study group made an orderly survey of the Mono Lake environment, building from the physical basics to the subject they knew would prove central: the birds.

FLOCKING TO MONO   Though people had long been remarking on the numbers of birds at Mono in summer, no one, as far as the students knew, had made a systematic count. (They were unaware of Walter Dombrowski's waterfowl estimates in the 1940s.) It's not hard to see why so little had been done. The lake was large. The flocks were vast. Some species spread over the whole lake surface. Others were secretive. All moved around. And why try to count birds at a doomed lake, anyway?

By car, by boat, and on foot, the group carried out five "all-lake censuses." Heading out at dawn with "mist nets," they trapped shorebirds. Perching on tufa towers (a practice later frowned upon), they panned binoculars and telescopes over miles of water. Boating to the islands, they inspected the gull colonies on Negit minutely, doing their

Ornithologist David Winkler holding a lizard, 1976. (Photo courtesy Sally Gaines)

best not to disturb the birds (spooked gulls will abandon eggs and young, and the neighbors tend to turn cannibal). They skimmed around the lower-lying islets by canoe and gave them names like Twain, Muir, Java, Pancake, and Little Norway.

When the figures were added up, they showed maximum populations, on any given day, of several thousand American avocets; 22,000 red-necked phalaropes; 93,000 Wilson's phalaropes; and three-quarters of a million grebes. All these totals were more or less surprising. The gull counts—46,000 birds, with 38,000 on Negit and 8,000 on the islets—were ten times higher than most earlier visitors had guessed. The impressive phalarope counts were completely unexpected. The group also made an important addition to the breeding-bird list: they spotted, for the first time, snowy plovers nesting on the remote east shore.

The most numerous species, the eared grebe, was an obvious target for close study. But the grebes, who favor open water, floated maddeningly out of reach. "We never caught a grebe," David Winkler recalls, "and we weren't willing to shoot one." The group did make a useful compilation of old grebe knowledge and confirmed Mono Lake as their major habitat in the western Great Basin, as Great Salt Lake is in the eastern.

The Wilson's phalaropes were almost as frustrating. By the time the group had mastered its shorebird-netting skills, *Phalaropus tricolor* had headed south from the Mono Basin. That left available for study the red-necked phalaropes and the gulls.

By sticking straws down the gullets of captured birds and extracting samples of the stomach contents, the students learned that red-necked phalaropes chiefly eat alkali flies—adults, pupae, and larvae. The students tried to estimate how far these migratory birds could fly from Mono by gauging their fat supply. This can be done by simply killing and boiling up the bird, or more humanely, as they did, through an elaborate computation based on weight and length of wing. The students concluded that the red-necked phalaropes left Mono fat enough to make it at least to the Salton Sea and perhaps to the Gulf of California. But they also concluded that Mono Lake was a mere stopover point for this species, not, as it is for the Wilson's phalarope, a vital last staging area before a heroic flight.

Because gulls regurgitate food for their chicks, it was no trick to check what they had in their crops: brine shrimp. Later research would suggest that gulls, like phalaropes and grebes, do in fact prefer alkali flies when they can get them; the more abundant brine shrimp appear to be the fallback, the staple.

The gull census had shown Mono Lake to have the world's second largest breeding population of the species; only Great Salt Lake harbored more. The group speculated that Mono gulls might be different from other groups of *Larus californicus*, a separate flock returning to this lake only, as salmon strains return to their natal streams. "If the gull colony at Mono Lake collapses," David Winkler suggested, "it will mean the demise of a population which . . . is, in all probability, unlike any other in the world." This idea seemed plausible, but Winkler's own later work would prove it flat wrong: *Larus californicus* is *Larus californicus*, wherever found.

Before the ecological study, Mono was vaguely acknowledged as a lake with a lot of birds. After the study, incomplete as it was, Mono had to be recognized as a habitat of the first importance. Over the years this recognition would only grow.

What would continued lake decline mean to these species? Possible problems were loss of nesting sites for the gulls, diminished food supply for all species, and physical stress from intake of salt water.

The Negit Island nesting ground would plainly go fast. In September of 1976, with the lake surface at 6,378 feet, the single remaining strait across the land bridge was less than a yard deep. In two years, maybe one, coyotes and other predators would cross. Could displaced gulls find room on the islets east of Negit, or might they move over to Paoha? The researchers couldn't say. In the long run, though, all existing islands, even Paoha, would be bridged; and though new ones would undoubtedly poke out of the water, the total available habitat would shrink dramatically.

HOW LOW CAN YOU GET?   To assess what would happen to avian food supply, the researchers had to figure out just how low, and thus how salty, the lake would get. Those answers come out of a formula called a water balance. In essence, it is like a personal budget. The lake has a certain natural income, mostly from creeks and from rain that falls on its surface. It has an unavoidable expenditure, in the form of evaporation. It has a bank account, the water in the lake itself. When the evaporation expenditure is greater than the liquid income—as it has been in most years since 1941—the bank account shrinks and the lake falls.

But getting from the simple theory to a practical formula is no easy task. For one thing, most of the numbers, including evaporation rates, are estimates. Only the larger streams are gauged, and the gauges are not near the shore. Every Mono Lake water-balance model makes its own simplifying assumptions; every model must be tested against the historical record; every model must be tricked out, in the end, with an extra, arbitrary factor to bring it into line with the facts observed.

Compared to previous efforts, the Ecological Study water balance, prepared by team member Robert Loeffler of Stanford, was quite sophisticated. Its results, though, lined up with predictions made as far back as 1934 by the Department of Water and Power. It suggested that if diversion continued at the recent clip of 100,000 acre-feet a year, the lake would wind up fluctuating around a level of 6,323 feet, it would have about half of its 1976 surface area, and it would contain less than a third of its 1976 volume. The model foresaw a lake almost four times as salty as it was in 1976 and seven times as salty as the sea.

How would alkali flies and brine shrimp do in this shallow, shrunken lake? Gayle Dana and David Herbst went to the lab at Lee Vining High School, boiled down lake-water to produce brews up to three times as salty as Mono Lake vintage '76, and put shrimp and fly larvae into them. The shrimp began dying massively as salinities approached double the then-current level of about 88 grams to the liter. Fly larvae did not die but went into a kind of dormancy; at concentrations above double, they seemed unable to move into their next life stage, pupation.

The sensitivity of Mono shrimp was a surprise. Brine shrimp from some other lakes can live in waters so full of salt that any additional chemical precipitates out as a solid. However, these "foreign" shrimp can't live in Mono water, which is charged not only with table salt but with sulfates and carbonates as well, nor can Mono shrimp live in the "foreign" waters. These and other differences would eventually lead the Mono Lake shrimp to be declared a separate species, *Artemia monica.*

Might Mono shrimp acclimatize to a saltier lake? Dana and Herbst doubted it, and later researchers have concurred. Saltwater creatures, it appears, have just a few methods for getting rid of salt and carbonate; with little natural variation, there's not much for natural selection to build on.

At what lake surface elevation would concentrations become lethal? The ecological study didn't try to pin this down, but later researchers would put the last-gasp surface elevation somewhere between 6,350 and 6,360 feet above sea level. As it sank toward that range, Mono Lake would be impoverished and probably subject to unpredicted disruptions; below it, the lake would indeed approach the state of a Dead Sea.

Gayle Dana, brine shrimp researcher, may know more about Artemia monica *than anyone else in the world. (Photo by Gerda S. Mathan)*

Without shrimp, no gulls and grebes. Without flies, no phalaropes. Though these bird species would hardly go extinct without Mono, the loss of the lake would be a serious blow. Just how serious remained for later research to show.

The 1976 workers flagged a third threat to the birds: stress on their systems from too much salty water, ingested with their food or *in* their food, as the body fluids of prey species grew more salty. This idea was to prove controversial; certainly such an effect would set in only when the lake became very salty indeed.

On quite another subject, the 1976 study asked what would happen, over time, to the alkali flats exposed by a falling lake. Would vegetation close over them? Or would they remain barren indefinitely, giving rise to plumes and clouds of dust? Preliminary studies suggested that vegetation was slow indeed to colonize this flat and poisonous environment, and that dust storms could only get more severe as the alkali rim expanded.

"Three months of field work," the report concluded, "could uncover only the beginning of an answer to the question of how water diversions are going to affect the lake and its basin." The authors made no outright recommendation but observed, "To maintain Negit with a five-foot buffer zone, no more than 25,000 acre-feet could be taken" per year. That would be only a quarter of what Los Angeles had recently been diverting.

THE MONO LAKE
COMMITTEE

One night, staring into a campfire at the Simis Ranch, the Ecological Study group realized they were on the hook. Their study done, they decided, they could not walk away. They would have to do something to prevent the losses they saw coming. They would have to make an attempt to save Mono Lake.

David Herbst, perhaps the world expert on the Mono Lake alkali fly. (Photo by Gerda S. Mathan)

This story has been told, but told always secondhand. No one seems to have sat before that fire. What we have here is a foundation myth, a metaphor for what indeed occurred, but in a more gradual, less tidy way. Certainly no one in the original student group felt like organizing a campaign. Most of them were headed back to campuses that fall. But four do figure largely in the continuing story of Mono Lake.

Two of the four, Gayle Dana and David Herbst, pursued their interest strictly as researchers. Over the next few years Dana would make herself the preeminent expert on the Mono Lake brine shrimp, and David "Bug" Herbst would become the scientific proprietor of *Ephydra hians.*

David Winkler would follow them into pure research, but first he, with David Gaines, would launch the Mono Lake Committee.

Back at U.C. Davis, Winkler spent much of his senior year pulling together the ecological study results; Gaines helped get them into print at the Institute of Ecology there. Late in 1977, David Gaines and Sally Judy moved to the redwood region of northern California to serve as naturalists on a Nature Conservancy preserve; Winkler spent a season doing fieldwork for the California Department of Fish and Game.

In November of 1977, when the lake surface was approaching 6,375 feet above sea level, Winkler made another visit to Mono. There he did something no one could have done in over seven hundred years: traversing the freshly exposed land bridge, he *walked* to Negit Island. "I didn't even get very muddy doing it." The gulls had returned to the ocean for the year, but what would await them in May, when they next came inland to breed?

That was the real "moment by the fire." Winkler felt impelled to get something going, and "it wasn't going to happen," he remembers thinking, "unless we could get David Gaines out of the woods." He trekked north to the Northern California Coast Range Preserve. Gaines agreed to see what he could do.

The land bridge to Negit Island, with some of the Negit islets in the foreground. The largest islet is Twain, a key gull habitat; Java lies above it to the right. (Photo by Betty Shannon)

But Gaines and Winkler still hoped to be spared the task of founding an organization. Instead, they turned to existing outfits: Lajoie's Sierra Club Mono Lake Task Force; Friends of the Earth; and the Natural Resources Defense Council. There was a meeting at David Brower's home. All were sympathetic. But Lajoie was now pulling back from this particular fight, and no other party thought it wise, just then, to take up the Mono cause. They would cheer; they would give advice and even some money; but they wouldn't be the ones to pick up and carry the load. There was nothing for it: the new Mono advocates would have to organize on their own.

To ease into corporate existence, David Gaines approached friends at the Audubon chapter in Santa Monica. In March 1978, the Santa Monica Bay Audubon Society sprouted a subsidiary Mono Lake Committee. Its first address was a printshop in Oakland that belonged to David Gaines's longtime friend Mark Ross.

Winkler, meanwhile, had been on the road, whipping up concern about the Negit land bridge and the waiting coyotes. With support from another layer of the Audubon organization, the Western Regional Office, he lobbied the state and the Bureau of Land Management to try a radical temporary solution to the land bridge: blasting a moat across it.

In March 1978, twenty members of the California National Guard turned out with trucks, helicopters, a pontoon bridge, and high explosives. The blasts, on March 17 and 18, made a satisfying noise (and a good media show). Though the resulting moat was

In 1978 the National Guard made the first of two attempts to blast a moat across the Negit land bridge. (Photo courtesy Mono Lake Committee)

more ragged than had been hoped, the first issue of the committee's *Mono Lake News-letter* reported, "It will probably assure the gulls a safe nesting this year."

So the Mono Lake Committee began, literally, with a bang.

6,378' OR FIGHT   This first publication announced a platform. It called for restoring the surface of Mono Lake to its 1976 elevation: 6,378 feet above sea level.

Here the new committee took an unusual approach. Many campaigners would have sought a higher lake and still less diversion, either because they thought this the right outcome or in order to have something to concede at the bargaining table. Kenneth Lajoie urged the committee to follow the Sierra Club Mono Lake Task Force and demand an *end* to diversions. But the committee chose quite deliberately to ask for exactly the lake level they thought to be the minimum necessary. "We were twenty-year-old idealists," Sally (Judy) Gaines recalls, "and we were going to do things differently."

Minimum or not, the proposal would apparently require the city to cut its diversion by three-quarters. Not surprisingly, the Department of Water and Power, already embroiled in the Owens Valley, wasn't inclined even to acknowledge the new challenge.

The amazing fact, looking back, is this: the city would have done well to accept that opening offer, however brash it seemed, however unsupported by political or legal power. A better proposal, from the city's point of view, was never to come. But who could have dreamed such a thing at the outset of what appeared an absurdly unequal battle?

In this corner: the Department of Water and Power of the City of Los Angeles. Its annual budget, over one billion dollars at the time, made up nearly half the total expenditures of the municipal government. The department had a single, clear mission: to provide the best and cheapest water to the citizens of one great city. It had armies of lawyers, armies of engineers, armies of lobbyists. Its right to the waters it had tapped, however much resented by people in the source regions, seemed unassailable; it was anchored in a system of state water law that every water supplier in the state could be counted on to defend.

And in the other corner: the upstart Mono Lake Committee. It spent, in 1978, $4,867.15. In the early days it could not be reached by phone. Its leaders worked out of "homes and tents scattered hither and yon," as a newsletter put it. Bill Kahrl, in his Owens Valley history *Water and Power*, described the group as "a small band of bird-watchers and graduate students . . . activated by nothing more complex than their deep affection for a place few Californians will ever see."

It is easy to overlook, as Kahrl did, the power in such an affection.

Until about 1960, the biggest towns in Mono County, settlements like Bridgeport and Lee Vining, June Lake and Benton, were not very big at all. Then the Mammoth Mountain ski resort went up near the town of Mammoth Lakes, on the western edge of Long Valley. By 1970, Mammoth Lakes would account for half the county's population.

That rapid growth brought problems. It also brought to Mono County people with urban backgrounds and environmentalist inclinations. People like Mortimer and Edith Gaines, the parents of David Gaines, who had a summer condo there. Like Genny Smith, publisher of books on the eastern Sierra and a Mono Lake Committee board member. And like Andrea Lawrence.

Lawrence is, to put it mildly, a skier: in the 1952 Oslo Olympics she swept the gold medals in women's downhill racing. She got to know Mono County in the middle 1960s, fell in love with the region, and in 1968 moved up from southern California with her five children.

At that time the growth of Mammoth Lakes was entering a controversial phase. A developer was proposing to build an anomalous phalanx of six condominium towers. Several local people asked the energetic Lawrence to organize an opposition. "I had a houseful of little kids, but it never occurred to me to say no." The group she founded was called Friends of Mammoth.

When the Mono County Board of Supervisors approved the high-rise project, Friends of Mammoth went to court. Their weapon was the recently-passed California Environmental Quality Act of 1970 (CEQA). CEQA required government agencies to assess the effects of their actions or projects by writing Environmental Impact Reports. But did private projects subject to government planning permission, like the Mammoth condos, require such analysis? Friends of Mammoth said yes, and in 1973 the California Supreme Court agreed, setting a major statewide precedent.

The offending project in Mammoth Lakes fell through, and the citizens turned their energies toward producing a sophisticated local plan.

Andrea Lawrence was well aware of Mono Lake and knew instantly which side she was on. She met limnologist David Mason and invited him to give his slide show to the Friends. In 1976 she sat at the campfire with the Ecological Study crew. In 1979 she took part in the original Bucket Walk.

In 1982, Lawrence won a seat on the Mono County Board of Supervisors and has served there ever since. There she came to understand the clout Los Angeles Water and Power, as a dominant landowner, has in Mono County affairs. Sometimes, she feels, they have used this leverage crudely. "I have a word for that: tyranny."

Andrea Lawrence

Mono County Supervisor Andrea Lawrence, gold-medallist skier, was the first local government official in modern times to speak for Mono Lake. (Photo by Gerda S. Mathan)

What would the strategy be? Not knowing which might open, the committee resolved to knock on every available door.

It would publicize the situation at the lake and try to sway public opinion.

It would work to draw visitors to the lake.

It would encourage research and publicize the results.

It would lobby the legislature to enact laws protecting Mono Lake.

It would draw attention to the growing dust-storm problem and seek recourse through the air pollution laws.

It would, if it could find a basis, take Los Angeles to court.

The committee also made two fundamental decisions that were by no means self-evidently wise. The first, already noted, was to ask only for the lake level it thought was the real minimum. The second was to put itself in the shoes of the Los Angeles water user and to address a question it might instead have ducked: just how could Los Angeles replace the water it would lose in saving Mono Lake—estimated at 12 percent or more of the city's existing supply?

Water and Power, of course, had its own answer. Deprived of Mono water, the city would simply suck harder on its other sources. As its other sources were much more expensive, the department would demand compensation, $30 million a year or more, to match. There would be, moreover, an environmental cost to any alternate supply. Reliance on State Water Project water, drawn from the Sacramento/San Joaquin Delta, would be particularly harmful: the delta, deprived of its natural freshwater inflows, was already in serious biological trouble.

For years the department had met every challenge to its policies with a devastating counter-question. Which place, they asked their critics, would you *rather* destroy? When the Toiyabe chapter of the Sierra Club took an interest in Mono Lake in 1973, it fell neatly into this trap and found itself advocating more delta pumping, a position it quickly had to abandon.

During the administration of Governor Jerry Brown, though, establishment views of water were starting to change. Planners were realizing just how much waste there was in the contemporary water system and how much could be, even rather painlessly, conserved. During the drought of 1976–77, water users around the state proved that they could save dramatically in a pinch: in Los Angeles, which made a good but not outstanding effort, water use fell by 19 percent. That was more than the amount the committee calculated was needed to save Mono Lake.

The Mono Lake Committee seized on this new information. Los Angeles, it argued, would not have to raid any region whatsoever to replace Mono water—it could simply get by on less. The city could reduce water use by nearly one-quarter, without sacrifice, by installing more efficient plumbing fixtures, irrigating lawns and gardens more carefully, encouraging use of drought-tolerant plants, allowing higher residential densities, and slightly reducing the water pressure in its mains.

Some of these notions were practical, some less so. The committee was to become much more sophisticated in this field. Water reclamation—the use of highly treated wastewater for mostly nondomestic purposes—would come to seem the most important option of all. The basic message, however, would never change. From the beginning, the Mono Lake Committee refused to countenance any solution to the Mono problem that would shift the burden to some other source region.

One region that seemed a candidate to be burdened, if the Mono Basin kept more of its water, was its neighbor down the Los Angeles Aqueduct, the Owens Valley. Reduced exports from the Mono Basin, Water and Power pointed out, could only strengthen its case for higher pumping rates in the valley. (Which place would you *rather* ruin?) But the Owens Valley and Mono Lake advocates were in touch from the start, keeping any disagreements private, refusing to be cast as opponents. That, each party knew, would be fatal.

THE DAVID
GAINES ERA

After helping to found the Mono Lake Committee, David Winkler made a decision to concentrate on his scientific career, pursuing a doctorate from U.C. Berkeley. David Gaines took up the slack. In the next several years he and companion Sally Judy would have many co-workers but no co-leaders. The Mono Lake Committee would be, fundamentally, his.

In the fall of 1978, using a small inheritance, Gaines and Judy bought a pair of run-down houses in Lee Vining. "It cost more to fix them up," Sally recalls, "than it did to buy them." Soon the committee opened a storefront office in town. At last the Mono Lake Committee had a genuine home base. For Gaines and Judy, too, it was the end of years of wandering.

But not quite yet, for David. Before settling in, Gaines wanted to make sure that everyone in California had heard about Mono Lake—if possible, straight from him. For eighteen months, from late 1978 to early 1980, he spent more than half his days on the road with a Mono Lake slide show. He hit schools and colleges. He hit every Sierra Club and Audubon chapter in the state, and every Lions Club that would have him. He paid special attention to Sacramento, where the legislators were, and to his home town of Los Angeles, where the water went. No Californian who even glanced at the environmental press could have failed to get the message, by 1980, that Mono Lake was in trouble—and that someone was offering to save it.

One of Gaines's early stops was the blandly imposing building on Hope Street in downtown Los Angeles that houses the Department of Water and Power. (Sally Judy

David Gaines

Mono Lake Committee founder
David Gaines. (Photo by Jim
Stroup)

*The long-shot effort on behalf of Mono Lake
took more than knowledge, more than good-
will, more than commitment. It took a fanati-
cal, self-sacrificing dedication. That dedication
came from David Gaines.*

*What kind of a man was Gaines? People
who remember him use three adjectives: char-
ismatic; romantic; and maddening.*

*Gaines came from a cultured Jewish family
in Los Angeles. At various times in his life he
played the piano, the clarinet, the guitar, the
mandolin, and the hammer dulcimer. He
loved the music of Beethoven and Gustav
Mahler, and the songs of the Grateful Dead.
In high school he belonged to a philosophy
club. In college he drifted into a major in
German literature, spent his junior year in
Göttingen, Germany, and won a prestigious
fellowship to continue his studies at Stanford.*

*But there was another element in Gaines's
life. With his childhood friend Mark Ross
("We met in the sandbox") he had roamed the
mountains around Los Angeles, bird-watching
and collecting. "We'd sell insects to the kids
who had to collect ten species for their science
classes," Ross recalls. He had read* Silent
Spring *by Rachel Carson and Genny Smith's*
Deepest Valley, *the standard portrait of the
Owens Valley, including the Los Angeles Aqueduct story.*

*After almost a year at Stanford, Gaines re-
alized that his ecological interests were stronger
than his literary ones. He switched to the University of California at Davis and to a program that would allow him to earn a Master's
in ecology without conventional preparation.
From that all else would follow.*

*"The Mono Lake battle," says Mark Ross,
"gave Dave a focus he had never had before."
He grew into the role. By all accounts he had a
gift of persuasion, a power to move audiences,
that was almost unmatched. George Peyton of
the Audubon Society recalls one pitch he gave:
"He started hesitantly, shyly. It was almost
painful to listen to him in the early days. But
after ten minutes you were sucked in. I've
never been so touched and inspired in all
my life."*

*David Gaines was no politician. Naturally
aloof and visibly aware of a certain superiority,
he didn't sugarcoat things he thought needed
saying. "It could go beyond frankness," says
Mark Ross. "He could actually hurt." Nor was
Gaines much of an administrator: "If you were
to pick someone to run an organization, you
wouldn't pick David Gaines." Sally Judy, says
Ross, was the practical half of the team:
"Without Sally, he couldn't have done it."*

*And without David Gaines, it couldn't
have been done at all.*

Sally Gaines, co-founder of the Mono Lake Committee. (Photo by Gerda S. Mathan)

compared it to a stack of cafeteria trays.) Here Gaines had an audience of sorts with the Board of Water and Power Commissioners, nominal bosses of departmental affairs. The winter of 1978–79 was turning out to be a wet one, with lots of snowfall in the Sierra. Gaines suggested, in carefully measured terms, that in such a period Los Angeles could afford to interrupt diversions from the Mono Basin and give the lake a chance to rise. His address was met, he reported, "with neither appreciative applause nor critical questions, but with a stony silence." *Intake*, the department's house organ, did not acknowledge the meeting at all.

If the Mono Lake Committee seemed out of its league in most respects, it had, from the first, one key advantage. Its cause was not an abstraction but a vivid, compelling *place*, a landscape that seemed itself a character in the play. Arranging publicity hardly involved more than giving directions—the media came unasked. Once on the scene, reporters usually got to talk to David Gaines, called by Bob Jones of the *Los Angeles Times* "the most quotable person I ever met." Beginning in 1978 and picking up speed in 1979, the articles began to flow: *Audubon, Outside, Smithsonian, Sports Illustrated, National Geographic*, even in time the *Frankfurter Allgemeine Zeitung*.

The committee was also lucky, for PR purposes, in its opponent. The Department of Water and Power, typecast as the villain since the days of the first Owens Valley war, was peculiarly clumsy at making its case. Stingy with information, heavy-handed in its propaganda, somnolent in its power, the department seems to have felt too secure to need friends. "DWP," Congressman John Seiberling was to remark, "gives arrogance a bad name."

In 1979, San Francisco photographer Stephen Johnson approached the Mono advocates with a plan for a major photo exhibition to be called "At Mono Lake." "After a little research," says Johnson, "it became clear that practically every major landscape photographer in the history of the western United States had been to the Mono Basin; we have photographs from as early as 1868." When complete, the show represented forty-one photographers, including Ansel Adams, Phillip Hyde, and Brett Weston, as well as many whose names were then unfamiliar. No propaganda was attached. "I didn't think we had to say *Save Mono Lake*," Johnson remarks. "The great and strange beauty talks for itself." Seen by millions on its long travels, "At Mono Lake" is now housed at the U.S. Forest Service visitor center in Lee Vining.

One way or another, images of Mono Lake were everywhere in the next few years. In 1981 a picture of Mono tufa towers would drive the marriage of Prince Charles and Lady Diana off the cover of *Life*. Soon there were calendars, published by a separate group of Monophiles in the San Francisco Bay Area, the Mono Lake Coalition. Tufa trunks and swooping gulls, storm clouds and lakescapes turned up on the office walls of Congresspeople, key bureaucrats, and (eventually) members of the Los Angeles City Council. At an important hearing many years later, a citizen of Los Angeles would say, "I've never been to Mono Lake, but I know that it is beautiful." The camera did that.

Along with the parade of photographers and reporters, a growing parade of researchers was now walking the shores of the lake. David Herbst was comparing alkali flies from Mono and from Abert Lake, Oregon. Gayle Dana and Petra Lenz were studying shrimp populations. David Winkler was working on plovers and phalaropes (but would soon shift back to gulls). Geomorphologist Scott Stine was beginning an exhaustive exploration of landscape processes around the lake. Limnologist John Melack was launching a decade of research. In a few years Mono Lake would be one of the most studied waters in the world.

The scientific front was not necessarily calm. Seldom has a public policy battle focused on science, and on the latest research, as intensely as the Mono battle did. From the beginning, each new finding, each new set of data, has been seized on by one side or another for use in the skirmish of the moment. Complexities have been simplified, partial results headlined as final truths, false impressions cultivated. Scholars have found themselves aligned, willy-nilly sometimes, with one camp or the other. David Winkler would later speak of the joy of "studying something nobody cared about." At Mono Lake, that luxury was never to be had.

The *Mono Lake Newsletter* tried to juggle science and advocacy. At the beginning, many articles were footnoted. Later, research notes, including notes provided by Los Angeles Water and Power, were published. Both the committee and the department claimed that their positions were based on the facts and only the facts, but each party saw those facts with a highly selective eye.

THE COLORS OF MONO

THE MOUNTAINS. THE DESERT. THE SEACOAST. In all these places we come to the edge of our everyday world and look outward. We can stand there diminished and exhilarated, faced with a strangeness that even long acquaintance doesn't render trivial. The mountain is always the Mountain. The desert is always the Desert. The sea is always the Sea.

In the Mono Basin, strangeness upon strangeness, we get all three at once: a rim of peaks 12,000 feet and higher, a valley floor of sagebrush and bitterbrush and desert poppy and desert peach, and an expanse of water that, if less than an ocean, seems something more than just a lake. Mono Lake is more than marine in its saltiness; it has its squalls and far-off shorelines, its volcanic archipelagoes, its reefs and sea stacks of tufa; it is even equipped with gulls.

Whichever light you want, you find it here: the sharp, chilly light among the peaks; the broad and overbearing valley sky; the lively, watchable light off the water. You can have the drifted colors of aspen or of sunrise, the smoke of storm and of steaming fumaroles, the whiteness of snow and the whiteness of alkali.

What you won't find here much, out of doors, is coziness. Even when it's hot, it's getting ready to be cold. And this big, high-energy country, steep and young, somehow smells of danger. It has avalanches, flash floods, windstorms, shipwrecks, and at longer intervals earthquakes and eruptions. The faults and volcanoes that built this land have not finished building it. The great geologic shoulders are ready to shrug, perhaps to shrug us off, at any moment. There is something bracing about all that.

Indeed the whole region seems designed for stress, not comfort—seems to promise a test, a revelation. This is the sort of place a new religion might come from. Who can stand on the lakeshore at twilight, with lightning glittering along the hills, and not have the fantasy that some compelling Word is waiting to be spoken?

We know better, in a way. Nobody here is talking to *us*. This country is minding its own stupendous business. Any lessons we derive are taught by ourselves to ourselves.

"Our ability to perceive quality in nature begins, as in art, with the pretty," wrote Aldo Leopold half a century ago. "It expands through successive stages of the beautiful to values as yet uncaptured by language." He wasn't writing about the Mono Basin, but he might well have been. Certainly "pretty" is not the word that comes often to mind in these parts. The admixture of strangeness is too large.

To learn to love this landscape took some expansion of our grasp of "quality in nature," and it took some time. The serious push to "save Mono Lake" came almost a century after the push to preserve the adjacent, classically alpine region, Yosemite. We learned the lesson very nearly too late. But we seem to have learned it well.

The revelation is the place itself.

Provided we don't turn back, the test is passed.

Paoha Island fumaroles. (Photo by Jim Stimson)

Lifting fog at sunrise, Mono Craters. (Photo by Elaine M. Straub)

Twilight at Tufa Reserve. (Photo by Barbara A. Brundege)

South Tufa at sunset. (Photo by Marjorie Anderson)

Mono Lake from Mount Dana, 1990. (Photo by James Sano)

California gulls. (Photo by Ernest Braun)

Some birds of Mono Lake. Left: California gull feeding on brine flies; right (top to bottom): Wilson's phalarope; American avocet; eared grebe. (Photos by Betty Randall)

Left: Snowy plover on nest. (Photo by Mark A. Chappell)
Bottom: Brine shrimp. (Photo by Joan Rosen)

Winter fog, the "poconip," over Mono Lake. (Photo by Dwight G. Straub)

Winter at Mono Lake, looking south from Lee Vining to the Mono Craters. (Photo by Barbara A. Brundege)

Old Mono cemetery. (Photo by Jim Stimson)

View through the barn at the old Dechambeau Ranch, north shore. (Photo by David Sanger)

Hot springs, south shore. (Photo by James Sano)

Sand tufa. (Photo by Galen Rowell/Mountain Light)

Counting gulls on Negit Island. (Photo by Daniel D'Agostini)

Sheep near Conway Summit. (Photo by Ken Carlson)

Animal tracks in the sand. (Photo by Jeff Gnass)

Incoming storm. (Photo by Kennan Ward)

Alkali wasteland. (Photo by Claude Fiddler)

Cinder landscape near Black Point. (Photo by Greg Gnesios)

A landscape starts to recover: lupine along Lee Vining Creek. (Photo by Daniel D'Agostini)

Yellow aspen: autumn in the Mono Basin. (Photo by Richard Knepp)

Shore with cattails and sedges. (Photo by Allen Kuhlow)

Winter sunset. (Photo by Allen Kuhlow)

Dawn at Mono Lake. (Photo by Frank Moore)

Anvil cloud over tufa. (Photo © Don Jackson/Don Jackson Photography)

Mono Lake expanse. (Photo by Jim Edgar)

An Audubon Society chapter was already helping the committee by providing a temporary organizational home. Early in 1979, Audubon's role became central.

In January, representatives of all the Audubon chapters in California met in Sacramento to agree on priorities. After a presentation by David Gaines, the group chose Mono Lake as an issue of highest concern. (Mono shared the top spot with the California condor.) Present was George Peyton, a member of the board of the *national* Audubon organization. Would the chapters like to see Mono Lake get the same high priority nationally, he asked? They would. Peyton's board had a meeting coming up, as it happened, in San Diego.

But Peyton wasn't at all sure his fellow national board members could be persuaded to take on what might be seen as a merely regional issue. He needed the expert salesman, David Gaines. "Come down," Peyton invited Gaines. Gaines, exhausted from three months of nonstop appearances, very nearly, but not quite, declined.

When Peyton drove down to San Diego from his Bay Area home, he brought with him not only Gaines but also a trunkload of fine wines and chocolate truffles. A tasting was on the program, and Peyton, an aficionado, was in charge. After pouring the dry whites and reds, he brought the tasting to a halt and sent the crowd off to hear Gaines. By the time they came back for the featured late-harvest dessert wines and the truffles, they were sold.

At the board meeting the following day, the Audubon directors agreed unanimously to call for lake protection. But, they cautioned, most of the money for the campaign would have to be raised by the California chapters. For the next fifteen years and more, Audubon fund-raising work all around the state funneled money into the Mono Lake campaign.

It wasn't clear at the outset what form of action this hard-raised money would be supporting. Soon, however, it became obvious that the legal front was key. It is at this point that legal researcher Tim Such comes back into the story.

By 1978 Such was deeply discouraged and too broke to pay the storage rental for his twenty boxes of public-trust research files. But one of his final contacts paid off. He went to David Brower of Friends of the Earth, who referred him to Friends lawyer Andy Baldwin, who in turn put in a call to a contact at a major San Francisco law firm called Morrison & Foerster, MoFo for short. That contact was Palmer Madden.

In October, Such walked into the MoFo eyrie, on the fortieth floor of the Spear Street Tower at the foot of Market Street, to face the selling challenge of his life. His job was not just to convince the firm of the merits of the issue. Since no likely Mono advocate had any real money, he had to persuade MoFo to take the case pro bono, without charge.

Attorney Palmer Madden carried the load in Audubon v. Los Angeles, *the original public trust lawsuit. (Photo by Gerda S. Mathan)*

Palmer Madden sparked at the idea. Even with Madden's backing, however, the Morrison & Foerster pro bono committee said no to Mono. So did the firm's executive committee. It was Bruce Dodge, a full partner in the firm and thus a member of its elite, who got his colleagues together and persuaded them to accept the case after all. In the end, MoFo agreed to contribute unpaid time to the tune of a quarter of a million dollars, one of the largest such commitments on record for an environmental case. Nobody guessed that the limit would be reached within a year.

In January of 1979, Such signed on as an investigator with Morrison & Foerster and spent hectic months working with Madden to sort out possible approaches—again. Now that the attorneys were on board, the legal labyrinth Such had traced had to be recharted. But the exit point was the same. Though several arguments would be offered, as is standard practice in legal cases, the public trust doctrine would be central. The state, through the courts, would be called upon to do its duty in defending a public water. As Palmer Madden put it, "If under the Public Trust Doctrine it would be illegal to fill Mono Lake, it must also be illegal to drain it."

It was at this point that the Mono Lake Committee met the MoFo staff. Participant Gray Brechin recalls, "That meeting was like the Children's Crusade at the court of some Eastern potentate. Trail mix and backwoods idealism confronted pinstripes across a corporate table 40 floors up." The gulf can be exaggerated, though—in those days Palmer Madden wore both pinstripes and a ponytail.

On whose behalf would the suit be brought? Friends of the Earth, which had sent Tim Such to MoFo, had an obvious interest. So did the Mono Lake Committee. So did Audubon. All three would be "on the case," but only one could be listed first and thus get a plug every time the lawsuit was mentioned in the usual abbreviated form. *National Audubon Society v. Los Angeles* sounded somehow a little more mainstream than *Friends of the Earth* or *Mono Lake Committee v. Los Angeles.* Audubon was certainly a much more substantial organization than either ally and, most important, it had a check, so to speak, in hand.

Despite Morrison & Foerster's pro bono generosity, the incidentals would mount up. The National Audubon Society, its Los Angeles chapter, and Friends of the Earth each agreed to contribute $10,000. That, they thought, should about take care of it.

The Department of Water and Power had other thoughts. On May 5, the opponents met in the Water and Power office building for a pre-trial conference, just to make sure no chance for a settlement was missed. "It was a very genteel meeting," Bruce Dodge recalls. Not surprisingly, no last-minute deal emerged. But no one forgot the small exchange with which the meeting concluded. In a tone of friendly warning, Water chief Paul Lane remarked to Dodge, "The last lawsuit we had like this took forty-three years." Glancing at his cohorts left and right, Dodge responded, "Fortunately, we're young."

When the suit was filed at Bridgeport, county seat of Mono County, Los Angeles understandably asked for a change of venue. The proceeding was shifted to little Alpine County, north along the Sierra. The lawyers began the preliminary dances of "discovery": serving and answering "interrogatories," deposing witnesses, and so on. The Mono Lake Committee hoped that the trial could begin early in 1980. "An early trial date is crucial if the issue is to be resolved before the next gull breeding season," said their newsletter.

That belongs in some collection of Famous Last Words.

6

THE PUBLIC TRUST

---

*The human and environmental uses of Mono
Lake—uses protected by the public trust
doctrine—deserve to be taken into account.
Such uses should not be destroyed because the*
*state mistakenly thought itself powerless to
protect them.*

California Supreme Court, February 17, 1983

THERE WAS A MOMENT, in the spring of 1979, when the Mono Lake advocates
seemed to be sweeping all before them. The lawsuit was under way. The Mono Lake
Committee had a thousand members and was ready to incorporate in its own name.
The National Guard was about to blast a second moat in the land bridge. A task force
of government agencies was wrestling with the Mono problem, and in Sacramento a
legislator had introduced a save-the-lake bill.

In January Assemblyman Norman Waters, the Democrat whose district included
Mono Lake, called for a halt to streamflow diversions until the lake surface returned to
6,390 feet. Because this first-ever Mono Lake bill did not outline any solution to the
water needs of Los Angeles, the Mono Lake Committee declined to endorse it. Still, the
Mono advocates had to be encouraged.

"It was primitive, heady days," recalls hydrologist Peter Vorster, who went to work
for the committee in March. For a little while it actually seemed that the Mono Lake
issue might he headed for swift resolution. Vorster finds this worth a chuckle now: "We
were pretty naive."

What was clear instead by the end of the year was just how long the road was going
to be.

Huey Johnson, a veteran conservationist and Secretary of Resources in the Jerry Brown administration, had been aware of Mono Lake's predicament for years. Late in 1978, he judged the moment right to try to make something happen. On December 20, Johnson called a summit meeting of bureaucrats in Sacramento. The upshot: formation of an Interagency Task Force on Mono Lake. The blandly inclusive charge: to "develop and recommend a plan of action to preserve and protect the natural resources in Mono Basin, considering economic and social factors."

Task force members came from two state departments, Water Resources and Fish and Game; two federal agencies with land in the Mono Basin, the Forest Service and the Bureau of Land Management; the U.S. Fish and Wildlife Service; the County of Mono; and of course the Los Angeles Department of Water and Power. A nonvoting Inyo County representative sat in; otherwise, during six early working meetings, the public was excluded. The Mono Lake Committee lobbed in packets of data and encouraged a barrage of public opinion letters, as did the League of Women Voters of the Eastern Sierra.

The early focus in the task force was all on finding replacement water for Los Angeles—from the Sacramento/San Joaquin Delta, from the Owens Valley, from wherever. Water conservation got little play. The group talked about such notions as diverting the East Walker River, which lies north of the Mono Basin, southward into the lake. Target lake levels under discussion ranged from 6,350 feet above sea level to 6,406.

In May of 1979, in Lee Vining, Los Angeles, and Palo Alto, the group presented its nineteen alternatives for public response. (In Palo Alto, Ken Lajoie called attention to several unidentified Water and Power employees who had somehow joined the crowd.) The result was a lopsided public endorsement of fairly high lake levels. Almost a quarter of the participants favored a 6,378-foot lake elevation. Well over half, however, asked that the lake be allowed to rise to 6,388, the level it had last occupied in 1970, and most of the rest wanted Mono kept at a higher level still.

At this point the Mono Lake Committee abandoned "6,378′ or Fight" and joined in the push for 6,388. It felt free to do that because of some new information about the lake's history. This change in policy, however, was not so large as it appeared.

With a lake like Mono, in a constant state of natural fluctuation, it's a tricky business to predict a future level and trickier still to establish a lake-level "target." Definitions are critical. The committee, in asking for a 6,378-foot lake, had been speaking of a floor: the lake should *never* fall below that level, even in a prolonged drought; most of the time it would be much higher. The task force, in suggesting a 6,388-foot lake, was talking as though a single nonfluctuating level could be maintained. In fact, the lake would fluctuate around 6,388 feet, being lower than that a good deal of the time. Allowing for the clashing definitions, the real difference between the new and old committee positions was probably closer to five feet than to ten. Nonetheless, it was real.

Scott Stine
and the Lake Levels

Biographer of a landscape:
geomorphologist Scott Stine.
(Photo by Gerda S. Mathan)

One piece of information, accepted as fact, tended to mock all this concern about the health of Mono Lake. It was reported in the technical literature, and reluctantly repeated even by Gaines and the committee, that Mono Lake had been very low in the middle 1800s. "Only recently," the Ecological Study report conceded, "has the lake dropped below its 1860 level." The lake had been just as salty as it currently was; Negit Island had been a peninsula. The streamflow diversions seemed merely to mimic a natural variation in level. This certainly weakened the case for instant alarm.

In March of 1979, Berkeley graduate student Scott Stine was passing through the Mono Basin. He stopped off to meet David Gaines and got the tour. As they stood on Panum Crater and gazed across at Paoha Island, Gaines mentioned the conventional wisdom about the low lake of the 1850s. Stine got an itch. He had been researching historic and prehistoric climate fluctuations, and he knew that the decades before 1860 in California had by no means been exceptionally dry. If the lake was low in 1857, he reasoned, it must have been rising from a still lower level; and that still lower level could only have been produced by a very severe and prolonged drought sometime after 1700. Stine knew no evidence for such a drought. It just didn't seem to add up.

So Stine went back to the oldest available source: the township maps made in the late 1850s by Colonel Alexis Waldemar von Schmidt. Though von Schmidt hadn't known what the lake's elevation actually was, he had

surveyed its outline with scrupulous care, a process called "meandering." Comparing von Schmidt's outline with later maps, Stine found that it very nearly matched the one traced by the U.S. Geological Survey in 1953. But in 1953 the lake surface had stood at 6,409 feet above sea level. Going into greater detail, comparing inlet to inlet, point to point, Stine was able to show that, in 1857, Mono Lake had had a surface elevation of 6,407, thirty vertical feet higher than the long-accepted figure.

In other words, mid-nineteenth-century Mono Lake had contained 60 percent more water than had been supposed. It had been 60 percent less saline than had been supposed. And it had protected a Negit Island that stood well offshore.

Stine also found where the misinformation had come from. The sources were consultants for southern California water interests, which used the erroneous findings to build the case for higher water imports.

Like so many before him, Stine was now thoroughly hooked on the landscape and politics surrounding Mono Lake. After publishing his lake-level findings separately, he expanded them into a chapter of a doctoral thesis titled "Mono Lake: The Last 4,000 Years." Since those days he has never ceased to study the basin, having logged over 450 days of fieldwork there by the end of 1993. The general understanding of recent changes in the Mono Basin landscape, including the complex effects of stream diversion and lake level decline, is quite largely the creation of Scott Stine.

In 1977 a young hydrologist named Peter Vorster snagged an ill-paid state job helping to develop a book called The California Water Atlas. This magnificent reference work was to lay out and illustrate the state's natural water supplies, its reservoirs and aqueducts, its water dilemmas and controversies. The Mono Lake issue was not hot yet, but Vorster was aware of it; he persuaded project boss William L. Kahrl to give it space in the form of a photograph taken by Vorster's friend Scott Stine.

As the atlas project wound down, Vorster applied for a job with one of the most prestigious outfits in his field: the Los Angeles Department of Water and Power. The position was that of hydrologist for the Mono Basin. He did well on the written test, but a schedule conflict kept him from getting to the oral interview. It's tempting to see a kind of fate in that. It was soon after, at a Sacramento conference on river preservation, that Vorster wandered up to a booth labeled "Save Mono Lake" and met David Gaines and Sally Judy. "I was kind of surprised by the home-grown nature of the operation," says Vorster. "But something hit me." He put himself forward to help.

After a short and difficult stint on the committee staff (he clashed with Gaines and Judy), Vorster decided that his talents were better used on the technical side. From then on he served Audubon and the Mono Lake Committee as their chief guide through the intricate world of water and water supply. He gained an understanding of the operations of the Los Angeles aqueduct that few of Water and Power's own engineers could match. He calculated means by which the city could

compensate for a smaller Mono export. And he built a new and more sophisticated water-balance model for Mono Lake itself.

Here Vorster faced the traditional problems of describing the behavior of a fluctuating body of water, along with some added problems of faulty and lacking data. "I could have cobbled something together pretty fast," he says. But he wanted his model to be unshakable, definitive. Audubon could not be expected to buy that amount of work, so Vorster made it his Master's thesis at Hayward State. He pursued every branching question, followed out every detail. His final equation contained nineteen terms, supported by several hundred pages of text.

Even before its official publication in 1985, Vorster's water-balance model for Mono Lake was becoming the recognized standard. It contained good news: the lake needed less water income than formerly believed in order to maintain itself at any given level. Putting it the other way around, the city could divert somewhat more. Take, for example, the goal of a 6,388-foot average lake level. The 1979 Interagency Task Force had thought this level would be maintained if Los Angeles diverted 15,000 acre-feet a year, but according to Vorster's calculations 25,000 acre-feet could actually be taken. Vorster's findings made the Mono problem seem just a little less intractable.

Like other scientists at Mono Lake, Vorster had to guard his objectivity while studying a place he loved. As a paid consultant to the Audubon side, he had an additional concern about appearances, for he could readily be cast as "hired gun." His work, however, seems to have resisted serious challenge.

Peter Vorster and the Water Balance

Hydrologist and early Mono Lake activist Peter Vorster giving the lake a drink of mineral water, 1980. (Photo by Michael Beaucage)

Such problems of definition were to come up continually over the next fifteen years. In all the years of the Mono Lake debate, whenever someone endorsed or discussed a lake level, it would be necessary to say, "Stop. Is that a median, a minimum, a maximum, an average? What are your assumptions? What is your water balance model? What do you *mean*?"

After the May hearings, the task force forgot about the lower lake-level options and concentrated on ways and means of getting the lake to 6,388 feet. The plan finally chosen was expected to cut the city's exports from the Mono Basin to 15,000 acre-feet a year. The task force spelled out how the city, through conservation and reclamation of wastewater, could compensate for the loss. With lessened flows in the aqueduct, it acknowledged, the city would also lose electric power. But the task force report suggested that water conservation measures, by reducing the amount of *hot* water wasted, would overcome this deficit.

The plan carried some sweeteners for Los Angeles. The state and federal governments would pay two-thirds of the cost of replacement water for the first two years, at which point conservation programs were supposed to make subsidy unnecessary, and these governments would also pay seven-eighths of the cost of water reclamation plants. Moreover, the city would be allowed to take more Mono water in a drought.

The task force report was a powerful endorsement, at the highest levels, of the Mono Lake Committee's positions.

REALITY HITS
By early 1980, though, reality had set in, and the lake, despite all the talk on its behalf, was falling as fast as ever.

In April 1979, a second attempt had been made to breach the land bridge with dynamite. As a media event, the blasting was even more successful than the 1978 attempt; the Department of Fish and Game estimated that fifty million people saw it on the news. As a practical solution, it was a failure. Impressive geysers of mud fell right back where they came from. No moat was formed. On May 27, researchers starting their annual gull census found coyote tracks, empty nests, and scattered shells. Water and Power argued that the gulls had only moved to other nesting sites, and many of them had, but at the end of the breeding season the balance was grim. Three-quarters of the gulls at Mono failed to nest at all that year.

In Sacramento, the water establishment lobby swarmed over Norman Waters's AB 367. This first crude save-the-lake bill was diluted into a noncontroversial measure authorizing $250,000 for another attempt at moat-building. The money would eventually be spent instead on a chain-link fence, which would prove no more effective.

The Interagency Task Force recommendations, too, came to nothing. The group, for all its prestige, was in fact an advisory body only. In developing proposals it had worked by majority rule. But to carry them out there was only one vote that mattered, that of the Department of Water and Power. In a stinging letter published as part of the final report, aqueduct chief Duane Georgeson cast his veto.

As for the lawsuit, the Audubon side had badly underestimated its opponent and its task. No one would ever better Water and Power at the art of delay. Dissatisfied with the new Alpine County venue, the department first petitioned, unsuccessfully, for another move. Next, it filed cross-complaints against 117 other Mono Basin land-owners, arguing that each of them used some water and thus contributed to Mono Lake's decline. All rights and uses, the city said, must now be balanced against one another and against the alleged public trust. Alpine County Judge J. Hilary Cook permitted this tactic to proceed. In a further complication, the state of California cross-complained against Audubon and the Mono Lake Committee, claiming that the plaintiffs should have taken their grievance first not to the courts but to the State Water Resources Control Board.

So much for a resolution by the next nesting season.

The battle over Mono Lake was clearly going to last awhile. There was always the real possibility that Water and Power would simply outlast and outspend its underfunded, amateurish opponents. So for Mono advocates another battle began, incessant, stressful, and occasionally desperate: the campaign to keep the money flowing in.

Audubon chapters dug deep. In Fresno County, for instance, the local society once skipped a newsletter, mailing instead a postcard explaining that the money saved had gone to the Mono effort. The Point Reyes Bird Observatory, a separate organization based near San Francisco, pitched in with bird-watching marathons or "birdathons." On November 27, 1979, birders up and down the state turned out to count bird varieties in their regions, receiving money from sponsors for each species spotted; most of the receipts were Mono-bound. The birdathons, later sponsored by the National Audubon Society and various chapters, have continued ever since.

In 1980 the "birdathons" were joined by the "bikeathons." On August 27, the first of many annual cohorts of cyclists gathered at the foot of the department's building on Hope Street in Los Angeles. Kneeling at the reflecting pool that wraps around the building's base, they dipped up tiny samples of water, strapped the vials to their spidery bicycles, and swooped out into the traffic. More or less following the route taken by William Mulholland and Fred Eaton in 1903, they carried the water back up the long slope it had descended, "home" to the eastern Sierra. Six days later and a vertical mile

FUND-RAISING: THE
LONG UPHILL RIDE

higher, they arrived at Mono Lake and joined the Bucket Walkers by the shore in the second annual "rehydration ceremony." Like the birders, the cyclists raised money and received a lot of press.

The inventiveness of the fund-raisers seemed inexhaustible. In the San Francisco Bay Area, Mono Lake Committee board member Grace de Laet tried to top herself yearly. Two of the most extravagant ventures were a luxury bus tour to the Mono Basin and a picnic on Angel Island in San Francisco Bay, complete with transportation by yacht. After a number of such experiments, the annual de Laet event became a wine drawing. George Peyton of Audubon, naturally, saw to the wines.

1980–82:
MARKING TIME

After the great flurry of action in 1979, the pace slowed. The committee prodded; the department stood its ground and began a counterattack in the propaganda war, with official speeches, lakeshore tours, and a polished film presenting its side of the story. Water and Power also began serious funding of lake research. Scientists filled in a few more corners of the Mono picture. The legislative wheels whirred with limited result. And the mills of the courts ground on.

Legislators whose districts included the lake—Norman Waters in the Assembly, John Garamendi in the State Senate, Norman Shumway back east in the House of Representatives—carried bills to implement the recommendations of the interagency task force. Each bill, after passing through a succession of attenuated versions, died. The Waters bill made it furthest; in a final form, it purported to cut the department's diversions enough to slow but not to halt the lake's decline. The bill got a majority on the Assembly floor, but not the two-thirds required (since it contained an appropriation). No one knew whether it could have been enforced.

And the legal duel proceeded. The department's strategy of involving other Mono Basin landowners backfired badly. Because federal agencies were among the new defendants, the federal government now had the right to move the proceedings to federal court, if it chose. It did choose, and in April of 1980 the case came before U.S. District Court Judge Lawrence Karlton in Sacramento. Karlton was known for his sympathy with environmental causes. The Department of Water and Power fought for the rest of 1980 to get out of his courtroom; Audubon fought just as hard to stay in it. To this end, MoFo lawyers Dodge and Madden developed a new cause of action, arguing that damage to the lake affected other states and was thus a federal concern. (Dust storms reach Nevada; waterfowl cross state lines; so do tourists; so do brine shrimp, packaged as fish food at a plant on the west.) In January of 1981, Karlton decided to keep the case.

Before proceeding, though, Karlton felt he needed the answers to two questions, answers that only a state court could provide. First, should the plaintiffs indeed have

Since the 1970s, Harrison C. Dunning has been a leading voice for California water law reform. In 1980 he organized a two-day conference at the University of California at Davis on the implications of the public trust doctrine. (Photo by Gerda S. Mathan)

taken their case to the state administrative authorities before coming to any court at all? Second, and far more fundamental, just how did the public trust doctrine fit in with that other body of state law, the well-developed system of water rights? When the two doctrines came into conflict, as they seemed to do at Mono Lake, which one should rule? Alpine County Superior Court Judge Cook was asked to advise.

This very question was meanwhile getting some timely attention on campus. In September of 1980, 650 people had gathered at U.C. Davis for a two-day conference on "The Public Trust Doctrine in Natural Resources Law and Management." A major session applied the idea to streams and lakes in general and to Mono Lake in particular. "The public trust doctrine and the appropriative water rights system are on a collision course in the West," said Ralph W. Johnson, a law professor from the University of Washington. In an important paper, he sketched various ways in which the two might be integrated by legislatures or by courts. Bruce Dodge of MoFo and Assistant City Attorney Ken Downey gave their views on *Audubon v. Los Angeles*. This conference, organized by Davis law professor Harrison C. Dunning, did much to put the issue on the intellectual map.

Plainly, the legislatures were not going to force a solution. Plainly, the courts were not going to produce one anytime soon. Mono advocates turned now to a more modest strategy. Without directly challenging Los Angeles, they would try to increase the pressure in two ways. First, they would seek to engage the state and federal governments in Mono Lake research. Second, they would seek park status for the lands surrounding the lake.

THE TUFA RESERVE AND THE NATIONAL MONUMENT CAMPAIGN

The Mono Lake Committee took up this second idea with reluctance. Everyone remembered the time when the shores of Mono were unknown, unvisited, remote. ("Remember when God owned Mono Lake?" a bumper sticker later asked.) But the committee had to face the price of its own success. The campaign had undeniably succeeded in one goal—it had attracted attention to the lake, and visitors to its shores in unprecedented numbers. Most behaved themselves, but some did not. Jeep tracks and campfire scars proliferated. Vandals, souvenir collectors, and youthful scramblers swarmed over the landlocked tufa towers. Some structures were carted off entire. It was time for some control.

After the election of November 1980, the committee asked lame-duck President Jimmy Carter to declare the federal lands around Mono Lake a national monument. He declined. The following January, State Senator Garamendi introduced a bill in Sacramento to protect the state-owned lands around Mono Lake, consisting of lakebed exposed since 1941, in a park to be called the Mono Lake Tufa State Reserve. In June, Congressman Shumway revived the national monument plan in a congressional bill.

The tufa reserve idea, though resisted at first by Los Angeles, moved quickly; Governor Brown signed it into law in September 1981. The national monument was another matter. Water and Power understood quite well that national recognition for the Mono Basin landscape could only increase pressure to cut streamflow diversions. The department not only opposed the national monument proposal vigorously but also mounted a counterattack. In those young days of the Reagan administration, Interior Secretary James Watt was inviting all comers to acquire chunks of federal land; the department lost no time in filing an application for 23,850 acres of National Forest and Bureau of Land Management property around the lake. In so doing, the department could cite not only Watt's invitation but also a federal law, passed in 1936, allowing the city to select additional lands for its use from the public domain at a price of $1.25 per acre. Now Shumway introduced an additional bill removing the department's land preference, and Congressman Jerry Patterson countered with one giving federal blessing to Los Angeles's water rights.

THE CRASH OF '81   What was happening to the lake itself during all these efforts on its behalf? Seemingly, nothing good.

The late 1970s had been wet but not too wet. From the standpoint of Los Angeles, they were perfect. The Mono Lake and Owens River watersheds produced just about the amount of water the department's facilities could store and carry. Mono diversions reached levels in this period that they had never attained before, nor have they since.

Plaintively the Mono Lake Committee suggested that, in such years, the department could well spare some flow for the lake, but not a drop was voluntarily spared.

And the lake inched, or footed, downward. On June 21, 1981, it stood at 6,372.8 feet. Negit Island was solidly fused to the mainland and the gulls, not reassured by the gleaming new chain-link fence intended to keep out predators, continued to stay away. But, just as the department had predicted, the birds had found refuge elsewhere. All nested now on two clusters of islets, one northeast of Negit and the other, recently exposed by the falling lake, just west of Paoha. Some 12,000 chicks were fledged in 1980, less than half the recent number, but more than had been expected.

Then, in the spring of 1981, the lake went through changes that looked, at the time, like the beginning of an unexpectedly early ecological collapse.

The spring hatch of brine shrimp—the generation that comes from overwintering cysts—was extremely small. "The lake, usually clear and swarming with shrimp by June, was still green and choked with algae," the *Mono Lake Newsletter* reported. "There were not enough shrimp to graze the algae away." In July the second generation of shrimp, live-born rather than egg-hatched, arrived; it was huge, making up for the shortfall. What was going on?

On July 6, David Winkler and his crew headed out from the base camp on Krakatoa islet for the annual gull census, now done in cooperation with Water and Power. They found only fifteen chicks on Negit and 11,698 on the islets, making it a very poor year. Worse was to come. On August 2, they found that most of the chicks seen earlier— 90 percent or more—had died. David Gaines raked together a pile of feathered bodies and posed with it, looking tragic. The department, for its part, at first refused to acknowledge how many birds had died; thereafter it denied that the falling lake level could have had anything to do with the deaths. Chief Aqueduct Engineer Duane Georgeson told reporters, "I don't think there's any connection."

As would happen more than once at Mono, a scientific question—what happened here?—could not be separated from the political one.

Two explanations for the die-off suggested themselves. The obvious one was a food shortage resulting from the low first hatch of brine shrimp; maybe the gulls had starved. Not quite so obvious was the weather: the spring of 1981 had been a hot one, with an unusual number of days over 90 degrees Fahrenheit; maybe the heat had been too much for the birds.

David Winkler at first hung his hat on the food hypothesis. "The increased chick mortality is probably due to the collapse of the early season food supply," he wrote in a report to the Department of Fish and Game. Water and Power, predictably, blamed the weather. "It was the unusual heat that caused the gull deaths," water chief Paul Lane told the *Los Angeles Times*.

The matter would never be resolved, but the department got somewhat the better of

When thousands of fledgling gulls died in 1981, David Gaines blamed the falling lake—and the Department of Water and Power. (Photo courtesy Mono Lake Committee)

Duane Georgeson, chief of Water and Power's aqueduct division and later assistant general manager for water, was the department's Mono Basin spokesman throughout the 1980s. (Photo courtesy Duane L. Georgeson)

this scientific skirmish. David Winkler was later to concede that a food crunch alone could not account for the gull deaths and that heat stress must have had a lot to do with it. However, the Mono Lake Committee continued to publish the unmodified food hypothesis as fact.

No wonder that the next season, 1982, was closely watched. But it left matters no clearer. The two most important of the gull islets, Twain and Java in the Negit group, were now themselves practically land-bridged. Sure enough, when the gulls arrived there, so did the coyotes, chasing the birds away. Again the spring brine-shrimp hatch was low, the summer generation large. The early chick count was even lower than in 1981, about 5,000, but this year most of them survived. As it happened, 1982 was a peak year in the Mono Basin for cicadas, "seventeen-year locusts." Had this alternative food source not arrived, Winkler suggested, 1982 might have been even worse for the gulls than 1981. But Water and Power again credited success solely to the cooler weather.

After all these years, it still is not clear what happened at Mono Lake in the early 1980s. We know that the lake was at or near its historic low. We know that the brine shrimp population was unusually small in the spring of several years. We know that the gulls died massively in one of those years. The combination is suggestive, but the connections among these events simply cannot be known.

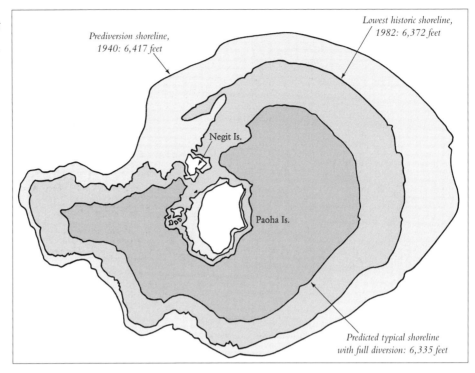

The Low Point

Prediversion shoreline,
1940: 6,417 feet

Lowest historic shoreline,
1982: 6,372 feet

Negit Is.

Paoha Is.

Predicted typical shoreline
with full diversion: 6,335 feet

Historical outlines of Mono Lake, 1940 and 1982, and a projected ultimate outline under full diver-
sion, using Peter Vorster's water balance model.

With a little cooperation from the weather, Mono Lake should never again fall below the level it reached early in 1982. On January 1 of that year, the lake surface stood at 6,372.0 feet. Since diversions had begun in 1940, it had fallen forty-six feet. Lake area had declined from 55,000 acres to 37,000 acres. Lake volume had shrunk by half, from 4.3 million acre-feet to 2.1 million. Salt content had more than doubled, from 48 grams to the liter to 102 grams to the liter; put another way, the fluid in the lake was now about 10 percent salt.

As it happened, the United States Geological Survey was preparing new maps of the region at just this time. If you buy any of the current 7.5-minute USGS quadrangles that include a slice of Mono Lake—Lee Vining, Mount Dana, Lundy, Negit Island, Sulphur Pond, Mono Mills—you will see the lake depicted very near its lowest ebb. One hopes.

Joseph R. Jehl, Jr. (left) and colleague Hugh Ellis dip-net grebes for banding. (Photo courtesy Joseph R. Jehl, Jr.)

Wrangles about *Larus californicus* would continue for years. More or less on the Audubon side would be Winkler and David Shuford of the Point Reyes Bird Observatory, which began work at the lake in 1983. The Department of Water and Power was to draw increasingly on the findings of ornithologist Joseph Jehl, author of numerous articles on Mono grebes and phalaropes. These scientists could be counted on to arrive at opposite conclusions about gulls past, present, and future.

Jehl pointed to reports indicating that gull populations at Mono had increased after 1950. He suggested that the drop in Mono Lake had in fact permitted this increase by producing new islands for nesting. Negit Island, he argued, had no special importance; the concentration of gulls there in 1976 was a fluke. Given a choice, he maintained, gulls actually prefer barren sites to shrubby ones like Negit. Jehl singled out the new islets west of Paoha Island as his special object of study.

Shuford and Winkler felt that the gull population had increased after 1950 despite, not because of, the lake's decline. What was going on, they believed, was continued recovery of a population almost wiped out by human egg-taking (which continued into the twentieth century). Citing historical accounts, they argued that most of the birds, most of the time, had been on Negit, drawn there, perhaps, by available shade. All researchers, however, agreed that nationwide the population of gulls was now on the rise.

David Shuford of the Point Reyes Bird Observatory, banding a gull chick. (Photo by Daniel D'Agostini)

On November 9, 1981, Alpine County Superior Court Judge Hilary Cook had given Mono Lake supporters a stiff dose of bad news. Responding to federal Judge Karlton's request for elucidation of state law, Cook ruled that Audubon should indeed have taken its case to the State Water Resources Control Board before ever coming to court. He ruled, too, that the public trust doctrine was "subsumed within the California water rights system." This implied that when Los Angeles received its license to divert, the trust had already gotten whatever consideration it had coming.

Audubon, of course, appealed. Normal procedure would have sent it first to the Third District State Court of Appeal, with a further appeal to the California Supreme Court a certainty. Claiming imminent risk to the lake, Audubon's lawyers asked the Supreme Court to take the case directly. The high court not only accepted the case but also placed it first on its 1982 calendar.

On May 3, 1982, oral arguments were heard. Palmer Madden and Bruce Dodge spoke

From 1980, Adolph Moskovitz headed the Department of Water and Power legal team. (Photo by Gerda S. Mathan)

for Audubon; the department's lead counsel was now Adolph Moskovitz of Kronik, Moskovitz in Sacramento, one of the preeminent water law firms in the state. Questions and comments from Chief Justice Rose Bird gave the Audubon side considerable hope. Then the court sat down to think for nine months.

In the spring of 1982 there was something of a revolution in the Mono Lake Committee. When it was over the organization had its first full-time executive director, a man named Ed Grosswiler.

A number of people had held that title before him; none had lasted long; all had been overshadowed by David Gaines. Several had reported that the founder was impossible to work with. (The feeling tended to be mutual.) Gaines, the superb propagandist, took little pleasure in administration, but he could not bring himself to step out of the center. Finally his board of directors gave him a push. With mingled resentment and relief, he moved into the role of a youthful elder statesman.

That status was hardly retirement. Gaines was now writing books— *The Mono Lake Guidebook*; *Birds of Yosemite and the East Slope.* As Artemisia Press, in partnership with Sally, he was also publishing them. And it was about this time that David and Sally got married. Soon there were children, Sage and Vireo. Kids and deadlines: enough to occupy the energies of the most ardent activist.

So Ed Grosswiler, a former congressional aide and Associated Press reporter, was in a position to lead. Very significantly, he would do that leading from an office in Los Angeles.

Enemy territory? The Mono Lake Committee had never looked at it that way. Gaines himself was an Angeleno; the committee got much of its support from the south and was careful never to cast itself as a northern group opposed to southern interests.

ED GROSSWILER

Indeed, if there was one place in the state where the Mono campaigners *had* to have a presence, it was there, at the downstream end of the aqueduct. It was there that the committee wanted policies changed, there that it asked for some small sacrifice, there that its hopes for a solution ultimately lay. It had had a Los Angeles office for several years, but now that office would be at least the peer of the Lee Vining headquarters. This was indeed a change.

It was Grosswiler's task to engineer a larger transition at the Mono Lake Committee. What had been a group of amateurs, pouring themselves into a cause without stint or serious compensation, would now become far more businesslike. To keep on fighting, it had to.

THE CREEKS GO OUT OF CONTROL

On July 6, 1982, Mayor Tom Bradley of Los Angeles, alluding to requests from the legislature and from the Brown administration, made an announcement. Los Angeles, he promised, would reduce its water diversions enough to halt, for the moment, Mono Lake's decline. State Senator John Garamendi spoke of a "basic, fundamental policy change." But what had changed was the weather.

After a succession of years just wet enough for the water managers, the winter of 1981–82 had been entirely too wet. The following summer, the Sierra creeks were pouring more water than the aqueduct could handle. Down the ravaged streambeds, into the lake, some of it would have to go.

It was in everyone's interest to make this necessity seem a choice. Mayor Bradley was running for governor that season: here was a chance to strike a pleasant pose for northern Californians. Water and Power had no objection to seeming flexible when its rights were not at stake. As for the Mono advocates, they made a considered decision to play along. By praising the city for its unavoidable actions, they hoped to induce it to do the same thing again, sometime, on purpose.

Nature had done what laws and lobbying could not. The water flowed. And flowed. And flowed. An unusually strong September storm forced Water and Power to stop Mono exports altogether. For the first time since the wet years at the end of the 1960s, the lake level began a significant rise. In the fall, Twain and Java islets regained their isolation. The winter of 1982–83 was the wettest of the century in this region. The following summer, aqueduct brimming with Owens River water, the department took not a gallon out of the Mono Basin. In April, Negit became an island again, though the gulls stayed away. Only in 1984 did the deluge abate enough so that Water and Power could move to shut off the streams again—but that belongs to a later chapter of this story, when far more than the weather had changed.

So researchers puzzling over the behavior of shrimp and gulls in 1981 and 1982 did not have a third year of similar conditions to observe. Instead they faced a rapidly rising lake and the strange condition called meromixis. In ordinary years, fresh water pouring into the lake with the summer snowmelt mixes, a few months later, with the colder and saltier water beneath, producing a fairly uniform brew. This yearly cycling is called monomixis. But the huge fresh flows entering now proved too much for the lake to digest; the fresh water remained stubbornly on the surface. In the winter of 1982–83 this upper layer froze, and the whole western embayment of the lake became an ice sheet. Ice skaters and cross-country skiers turned out. This separation of layers, this meromixis, would persist for six years.

A fascinating phenomenon accompanied the freshwater input: there was a great pulse of tufa formation, a "bloom." In 1983, in 1984, and again in 1986, springs beneath the lake grew milky as calcium carbonate precipitated. Researchers saw tufa taking shape, in several forms, before their eyes. At the mouth of little Dechambeau Creek, Scott Stine observed tufa building up on underwater surfaces to thicknesses of several feet, and later eroding off again. The Mono Lake tufas, it became clear, were more than a fixed set of objects, inherited scenic bric-a-brac; they were part of an ongoing though intermittent process, a life process almost, a dance.

On February 17, 1983, the California Supreme Court broke its silence. The plaintiffs found it had been worth the wait. In a six-to-one decision written by Justice Alan Broussard, the court declared that the public trust existed at Mono Lake; that it had not been properly considered in the past; that it should be considered now; and that Los Angeles's water rights were subject to revision.

THE PUBLIC
TRUST DECISION

It was not quite a total victory for Audubon. The court rejected the plaintiffs' view that the public trust values at the lake were paramount and must be protected, no matter what. The court directed, rather, that the authorities "consider" those values and "attempt, so far as feasible, to avoid or minimize any harm" to them.

The justices saw the needs of the lake and the needs of the city as competing interests, both legitimate. "Mono Lake is a scenic and ecological treasure of national significance imperiled by continued diversions of water; yet, the need of Los Angeles for water is apparent, its reliance on rights granted by the [state water] board evident, the cost of curtailing diversions substantial."

The Supreme Court laid great weight on two recent sources. One was the report of Huey Johnson's Interagency Task Force on Mono Lake in 1979. The second was the record of Harrison Dunning's public trust conference at Davis in 1980. On questions of law, the court often cited the conference papers; on questions of fact, it deferred to the task force, calling it "objective." Two exercises that had seemed academic—a term that can mean either "scholarly" or "futile"—turned out to have a tremendous influence after all.

The court went on, "It is clear that some responsible body ought to reconsider the allocation of the waters of the Mono Basin." As to what body that should be, the court refused to shut out either the lower courts or the State Water Resources Control Board; they had "concurrent jurisdiction." (This was the point on which one judge disagreed.)

Not many court decisions break as much new ground as the Supreme Court's public trust opinion of 1983. The typical court looks at the specifics of one case and generalizes only so far as it must to support the verdict. But this decision, written in response to general theoretical questions from federal Judge Karlton, did just the opposite: it started with broad principles and moved to the Mono Lake specifics. Thus it established a broad new doctrine overnight. The public trust must be taken into account and preserved "so far as feasible," not just at Mono but in *all* water allocations. And *any* water rights that affect public trust waters might have to be reconsidered in the light of changing conceptions of the trust.

It was a judicial earthquake. The court put life into the traditional teaching that water really belongs to the people and that diverters enjoy only use rights or "usufruct." Before 1983, this notion was a nearly meaningless formality; water users and their lawyers had succeeded in establishing water rights as the functional equivalent of property. But in 1983 the provisional nature of such rights, at least in certain circumstances, was reasserted. The decision "poses a serious threat to Los Angeles' water supply, and could have far-reaching implications for all state water rights," said *Intake*, the department's in-house magazine.

There was only one place to go to challenge the new doctrine: the U.S. Supreme Court. The Los Angeles Department of Water and Power went there, charging that the public trust decision threatened to confiscate its property. Without prejudging that issue, the highest court in the land refused to hear the case.

It was now established for all time that, in taking Los Angeles to court, Audubon and the Mono Lake Committee had had a very muscular leg to stand on. What the decision did not do was to dictate any outcome or put any specific limit on the city's diversions.

The Mono Lake advocates now tried to take the next step. Returning in July 1983 to Judge Karlton's federal court, they asked him for an injunction ordering Water and Power to release enough water into the lake to keep it at a level of 6,378 feet through August 1, 1984. Depending on runoff, this might cost the department as much as 20,000 acre-feet of export water, or none at all.

But Water and Power had its own ideas, and it had some new allies. As a result of the November 1982 election, Governor Jerry Brown had been replaced by George Deukmejian. In 1983 new people were sitting behind the biggest desks in Sacramento. New Resources Agency chief Gordon Van Vleck remarked that he knew nothing about Mono but understood that Los Angeles had ironclad rights there. The state of California now joined the department in asking once more that the case be sent back to state court.

When the California Supreme Court ruled that diversions from the Mono Basin could be limited by the public trust doctrine, Ken Alexander drew this cartoon for the San Francisco Examiner. *(Courtesy Grace A. de Laet)*

Audubon successfully resisted this shift, still thinking that Karlton, with his record of sympathy with environmental causes, would give them a better deal. The Mono advocates had no wish to find themselves again before Superior Court Judge Hilary Cook or a water board appointed by George Deukmejian.

Karlton, feeling that the wet winters had given him leeway, was in no hurry to rule. In fact, eighteen months after the public trust decision came down, the case had moved no further.

On March 29, 1983, the House Subcommittee on Public Lands and National Parks came to Lee Vining to take testimony about the National Monument idea. That plan had been through several versions since 1981; it now had a new champion, Representative Richard Lehman, who had just replaced Norman Shumway as the local Congressman. Until now, the Department of Water and Power had easily turned aside monument legislation; this time the issue had more momentum. Lehman's version called for the monument to be administered by the U.S. Forest Service.

The local community was torn between the desire to see the lake saved and a dislike of government intrusion. Though the Mono County Board of Supervisors endorsed the latest monument plan by a vote of 3–2, in the Mono Basin itself the nays appeared to have it. Locals worried that the bill would bring crowds and restrictions without helping the lake. "We need water, not people," said one Lee Vining man. Another remarked, "We don't need a ranger breathing down our necks every time somebody loads a shotgun or pulls out camping gear or locks their vehicles into four-wheel drive."

The Mono Lake Committee took a conciliatory line. David Gaines, speaking for himself, supported boundary adjustments, protection for private lands, continued snowmobiling and hunting, and other provisions designed to reassure local opinion. En-

TOWARD A
NATIONAL
MONUMENT

vironmental groups other than Audubon and the committee wanted a monument administered by the National Park Service and covering more ground, perhaps the entire watershed.

The central issue, though, was—naturally—water. Technically the proposal had no effect on Los Angeles's diversions, but the city feared an indirect effect in court. "We are deeply concerned," said Water and Power's Duane Georgeson, "that the bill . . . would seriously jeopardize the city's position as we head back into Federal court to balance the city's long-standing water rights against the new public trust doctrine." If there must be a Mono Lake reserve, Georgeson averred, the establishment law should proclaim "the intent of Congress that . . . export continue."

The next eighteen months saw a tug-of-war, mostly behind the scenes, about the exact form of language to be placed in the bill regarding the city's water rights.

BLOWING IN
THE WIND

While all this was going on, Mono dust storms had been coming in for some separate attention. Back in 1979, the Great Basin Unified Air Pollution Control District had placed two air samplers on the north shore of the lake. Though primitive by later standards, the gadgets immediately began showing violations of both state and federal standards for suspended particles.

But were those standards really applicable? Did air pollution laws, written with smokestacks and tailpipes in mind, extend to this peculiar case? "Dust storms are natural phenomena, not air pollution," a city consultant averred. The Department of Water and Power could point to other dry lakebeds, to other and even larger dust clouds, produced by nature alone. It denied that the air pollution controllers had jurisdiction.

In 1982, when Water and Power had to go before the Great Basin district on another matter, the district refused the permit being requested, on the grounds that the city was out of compliance on Mono and Owens Lake dust. That sent the department to the legislature in search of "emergency" legislation exempting its activities from the air pollution laws. The League of Women Voters of the Eastern Sierra led the charge against the bill. Under a compromise passed in 1983, the department was indeed excused from seeking state pollution permits for its water-gathering operations, but it was required to pay for projects to be aimed at reducing the dust problem, for instance by binding down the alkali with salt-tolerant plants. As a result, Los Angeles became a major funder of the Great Basin Unified Air Pollution Control District.

Nature, meanwhile, appeared to be staging a "mitigation" experiment of its own. As the lake continued to rise and cover some of the alkali, the dust abated.

If the public trust decision did not end the Mono Lake debate, it certainly altered it. Water and Power had until now been asserting an absolute right; any evidence of damage done to the lake was irrelevant. That argument had lost some of its respectability. The *Los Angeles Times* said in a November 1983 editorial, "Obviously, a prudent balance must be struck and it is better to strive for it through good-faith negotiations than through a renewal of long and contentious actions in the courts." Said Mono Lake Committee Executive Director Ed Grosswiler, "The time to resolve the controversy is now, when Mono Lake is not in crisis and Los Angeles is not confronting a drought."

At the University of California at Los Angeles is an office called the Public Policy Program; it exists to help decision-makers explore thorny issues in a neutral setting and with the best of expert advice. Grosswiler contacted director LeRoy Graymer to see about tapping this resource for the Mono controversy. In March of 1984, the program brought the parties together in a day-long conference, titled "Mono Lake: Beyond the Public Trust Doctrine" and jointly sponsored and paid for by the contending parties. Until now they had always met—in the courts, in legislative hearing rooms, in the press—as adversaries seeking an immediate result; at the conference, there would be no vote or decision at the end of the day, nothing immediate at stake. The lawyers would be there, but as experts, not as counsel. People could relax a bit and, it was hoped, identify some common ground.

They didn't, really. The positions of the parties, courteously stated, did not change. But the atmosphere gave rise to a vague hope. Committee and department agreed to keep on meeting, exploring Mono problems and solutions away from the courtroom and out of the public eye.

At this time the directorship of the Mono Lake Committee was passing to a woman trained at Yale in just this kind of nonconfrontational problem-solving. She believed that conflicts should be settled, whenever possible, by something more than a mere test of strength; more, too, than mere mechanical compromise. The key, she felt, was to look beyond what disputants say they want and to ask what in truth they *need*—and then to see whether those needs can be met without either side feeling itself the loser.

Somewhat oddly, given this background, Davis found her first environmental job at Greenpeace, an organization known for dramatizing issues, not for defusing them. Greenpeace was thinking of mounting one of its confrontational "direct actions" at the lake, and asked Davis to coordinate with the Mono Lake Committee. (One idea bruited was to install a huge siphon over the Lee Vining Creek diversion dam, symbolically rewatering the streambed below.) But when Davis met Grosswiler in the summer of 1983, they didn't talk about siphons. She asked him boldly why the committee wasn't looking harder for a solution that Los Angeles could accept.

Intrigued, Grosswiler invited her onto the staff. In November 1983 she signed on with the Mono Lake Committee as a lobbyist. Just three months later, Grosswiler was unexpectedly obliged to step down. Would Davis be interested in replacing him? She wouldn't, didn't feel capable. Would she stand in for him while the board searched for a permanent new person? She would. To her great surprise, she found herself enjoying her temporary role and thinking, "I could do this, couldn't I?" She added her name to the list and, in July, was chosen by the board. Martha Davis would spend the next decade and more trying to put her problem-solving ideas into practice on behalf of Mono Lake.

THE SCENIC AREA AND THE STATE STUDY BILL

At about this time, two bills, promoted by Mono advocates for four years or more, became law.

In May of 1984, the legislature approved Norman Waters's AB 1614, ordering a $250,000 state study of Mono Lake, its ecosystem, and its future. It was a sign of improved relations that the two sides jointly supported this measure.

And a few months later the long campaign for a Mono Lake National Monument finally bore a somewhat hybridized fruit. As passed, the park became something called the Mono Basin National Forest Scenic Area. The name change indicated a less exalted status; it also deemphasized the lake itself. A carefully drafted paragraph in the law provided that nothing in it should be construed to affect Los Angeles's water rights one way or the other. These provisions, along with sheer political momentum, persuaded Water and Power to abandon its long fight against the bill. The Mono law was packaged with many other items in the California Wilderness Act of 1984. Republican Senator Pete Wilson urged President Reagan to sign the bill, which he did on September 28, 1984. The new scenic area's boundaries enclosed 118,000 acres of land and water, including substantial strips west, north, and east of the lake and a projection south along the Mono Craters. Nearer the lake, the Tufa State Reserve remained as an inner ring.

In addition, the scenic area law authorized a second major study of the lake, to be coordinated by the National Academy of Sciences.

Modest steps, indeed. But each, in retrospect, was a significant setback for the Department of Water and Power. Though the city had been supporting research since 1980, it was truly not in the department's interest to have a great deal more known about Mono Lake. No independent scholar, however friendly, would ever assert that the ecosystem would survive unlimited diversions indefinitely. Nor was it really in the city's interest to have further attention drawn to the strange beauty of the Mono landscape. But parks and the acquisition of knowledge are two things hard to oppose.

THE UPSHOT

The scenic area enactment marks an important break in the story. By 1984 the Mono Lake Committee had existed for six years; *Audubon v. Los Angeles* had been in the courts for five. The Mono issue had truly been put on the map. An apparent eco-logical crisis had loomed and receded. Parks encircled the lake, and it was known to a larger public than ever before. The public trust decision—if ever it could be turned into action—pointed the way to a permanent solution.

But the leaders of the Department of Water and Power could take some satisfaction, too. True, they had taken some marginal losses; true, the climate of opinion was shifting in a way they could not welcome. Yet on the essential point the city had not had to budge an inch, or a gallon. On September 28, 1984, Mono Lake had the same guaranteed water supply, from Rush and Lee Vining creeks, that it had had in 1977: zero.

7

THE REVENGE OF THE ANGLERS

*Injustices, particularly those that have been
fueled by powerful political interests, do not die
easily, and then usually in unexpected ways.*

From the pleadings, *Dahlgren v. Los Angeles*

IN WAGNER'S MYTH-BASED OPERA *SIEGFRIED*, the traditional dragon
guards the traditional hoard. Someone warns the creature that a hero is approaching
with designs on the treasure. The dragon Fafner answers, basso profundo, "I lie here
and possess. Let me sleep."

"Let me sleep." That more or less sums up the attitude of the Los Angeles Department of Water and Power after the Supreme Court's public trust decision called into
question its long-established rights in the Mono Basin. Deploring the decision, the department made no effort to adjust to it. Neither did the state authorities, the Department of Water Resources and the State Water Resources Control Board, whose ways of
doing business were also implicitly challenged. Nothing had yet actually changed due to
the new interpretation, and a whole industry united in the hope that nothing really
would.

In April 1984, as the Mono Lake Committee and the Department of Water and Power
met in Santa Monica to look for common ground, the department resumed diversions
from the Mono Basin. Lee Vining Creek dried up, and so did Walker Creek and Parker
Creek, small tributaries of Rush Creek. A flow remained, however, in Rush Creek itself.
This time, someone besides the Mono Lake Committee and the Department of Water
and Power was watching. A new player was about to enter the game—one who would
wrest some treasure from the slumbering powers.

In the wet years of the early 1980s, more than water was swept over the brimming spill-way of Grant Lake reservoir. Some brown trout and rainbow trout made it over the barrier as well. Reproducing successfully in the stream below, they reestablished a population gone since the 1960s.

On a cool, bright day in October of 1984, fly fisherman Dick Dahlgren, a realtor in Mammoth Lakes, took a notion to go north to the Mono Basin and explore the banks of Rush Creek. From the top of a bluff above the mouth of the creek, he saw something that amazed him. "I couldn't believe it," he recalls. "Fourteen-inch brown trout were coming down to within a few yards of Mono Lake to eat brine shrimp."

Dahlgren ran back to his car for his flyrod and started casting. "I caught an eight-inch rainbow on the first cast." He kept on angling, in the name of research, and had fifty trout take his barbless hook. In the next days, walking up and down the creek, he sampled segment after segment in this manner. He estimated that Rush Creek now contained some 20,000 brown and rainbow trout. (A Department of Fish and Game census would find that estimate low.) He also learned, from a fish and game warden, that the stream was due to be "turned off" November 1.

Going over to the Mono Lake Committee, Dahlgren talked to David Gaines. Gaines was impressed by the news, but, as Dahlgren recalls, not initially very optimistic about what might be made of the presence of fish in Rush Creek.

On October 8, Dahlgren wrote to Los Angeles Mayor Bradley. He congratulated the city "for restoring one of the finest brown trout fisheries in the country" and, tongue in cheek, asked Bradley to keep up the good work. The mayor made no useful response, but Dahlgren's letter, with copies to the media, served to launch a national publicity campaign.

One of Dahlgren's first contacts was Barrett McInerney, a Los Angeles lawyer with ties to Bradley's political camp. McInerney was also on the board of directors of California Trout, an organization that exists to promote the management of streams for "wild," self-sustaining trout populations.

Dahlgren, CalTrout, and, presently, the Mono Lake Committee set about bringing whatever pressure they could. "We begged just about every elected official in the state to spare the fish until spring," McInerney says. "They were interested only until they heard the initials DWP, and then the phone calls weren't returned." But State Senator John Garamendi, whose district included Mono County, called Los Angeles Council-man John Ferraro, chairman of the Energy and Natural Resources Committee, and asked him to hold a hearing. Ferraro scheduled it for November 13 and prevailed on the department to keep Rush Creek flowing in the meantime.

At the hearing, for the first time lake advocates and fish advocates turned out in the same cause. With them appeared various environmental groups and also Mono County

*November 14, 1984: The Department of Water and Power leaves a
trickle in Rush Creek to allow a trout rescue by the Department of
Fish and Game. (Photo by Larry Ford)*

Supervisor Andrea Lawrence. Ferraro asked Duane Georgeson, chief of the department's
water operations, to "consider" leaving water in the stream until spring, when the new
snowpack measurements would be in. The thought was that another wet winter would
buy time, obviating diversions in 1985. Ferraro also called for a trout study and formation of a citizens' advisory committee.

Outside the hearing room, Dahlgren and McInerney asked Georgeson what he had
in mind to do. He had already considered the council's requests, Georgeson responded.
There would be a study; there would be a citizens' group; but there would be no water.
The stream would be shut down in forty-eight hours. Paul H. Lane, general manager
and chief engineer, confirmed by letter the next day: "Pending the development of a
resolution of the issue, the City's release of water down lower Rush Creek is being
shut off."

An outsider, imagining that the Department of Water and Power took orders from
the Los Angeles City Council, might have been puzzled at this defiance. It wasn't defiance at all. By provision of the city charter, Water and Power was a nearly independent
house of government. Councilman Ferraro acknowledged, "DWP does not have to
come to the council for permission for their actions."

On Wednesday the 14th, the department cut the creek to a trickle, leaving enough
water to sustain the stranded trout while the Department of Fish and Game began
a rescue operation. (Less than 3 percent of the trout were saved.) Total shutoff would

follow at the end of the next day. The brief new life of Rush Creek and its fishery was coming to an end.

But Dahlgren and Barrett McInerney had not relied solely on political pressure. McInerney had also developed a legal theory. It was based on section 5937 of the Fish and Game Code, the long-neglected provision that forbids the dewatering of creeks below dams.

On Thursday, November 15, the allies moved. Dahlgren put in a call to Bridgeport and reached Assistant District Attorney Stan Eller. Dahlgren transmitted McInerney's arguments about the Fish and Game Code. "You know, Dick," said Eller, "it looks like this might work." He agreed to step in to prevent the fatal turning of the valve. He sent two sheriff's deputies to the Mono Wastegate to tell the workers there that anyone touching the valve would be arrested. Calling Los Angeles, Eller gave the same word to Assistant City Attorney Ken Downey, who, Eller recalls, was "shocked and surprised and amazed."

David Gaines, meanwhile, had organized a roadside demonstration on Highway 395 at the Rush Creek bridge. Stan Eller appeared there, muffled against the cold November evening, and repeated his warning for the cameras of KABC TV, Los Angeles.

At the same time, Barrett McInerney was on the phone with local attorney Edward Forstenzer of Mammoth Lakes. On the afternoon of Friday the 16th, Forstenzer filed the case known as *Dahlgren v. Los Angeles*. California Trout and Mammoth Flyrodders were additional plaintiffs. The Superior Court judgeship in Mono County was vacant at the moment, so Forstenzer drove south to Independence and presented the brief to Inyo County Judge Donald Chapman, who was filling in.

As it happened, high winds aloft made air travel to the region impossible that day. Long-distance, Ken Downey asked Judge Chapman to dismiss the suit out of hand. When Chapman declined, Downey agreed that the stream would be kept flowing over the weekend.

The following Tuesday, the 20th, with all the lawyers on hand, Judge Chapman issued a temporary restraining order requiring a flow of 19 cubic feet per second. (This rate was based on a quick estimate provided by a local Fish and Game biologist.) A few days later, the parties agreed to extend the order for six weeks and to take up the fight in the new year.

A flow of 19 cubic feet per second would fill nineteen standard garbage cans in five seconds. Maintained for a day, it would fill a one-acre pool thirty-eight feet deep. Maintained year-round, it would put about 14,000 acre-feet into Mono Lake. That was not nearly enough to stabilize the lake. But it was, as the Mono Lake Committee newsletter put it, "the first real crack in the dam."

November 15, 1984: At a demonstration organized by the Mono Lake Committee, Assistant District Attorney Stan Eller warns Water and Power not to touch the valve that would turn off the Rush Creek flow. (Photo by Larry Ford)

It was not the gulls, phalaropes, or invertebrates indigenous to Mono Lake that first forced the department to release water, but, ironically, some fish that were not even native to the Sierra.

A LAW REBORN   But what had happened? How had the anglers found the key that Audubon and the Mono Lake Committee, for all their court achievements, had missed?

The state has had stream protection laws since the 1800s. In 1937, the legislature wrote the language now found in the Fish and Game Code at section 5937: "The owner of any dam shall allow sufficient water at all times . . . to pass over, around or through the dam, to keep in good condition any fish that may be planted or exist below the dam."

This directive seems perfectly clear. But in fact, from the moment of its passage the law was evaded, interpreted almost out of existence, and simply ignored.

An early blow to 5937 occurred in 1940, with the signing of the Hot Creek Agreement between the Department of Water and Power and the California Department (formerly Division) of Fish and Game. This agreement, we recall, seemed to permit the drying-up of the Mono Basin creeks and also the Owens River below the new Long Valley dam, exempting those streams from the requirements of the code.

A second blow fell in 1951. A big new federal dam had just gone up on one of California's major rivers, the San Joaquin. The Friant dam blocked the river where it leaves the foothills of the central Sierra Nevada to meander through the flat San Joaquin Valley. The dam operator, the U.S. Bureau of Reclamation, proposed to let only the merest trickle of river pass the dam; fifty-six miles of the San Joaquin would go nearly or entirely dry. Downstream landowners sued in state court, charging that the federal bureau must obey the state Fish and Game Code.

The state made a move to support the landowners, then withdrew in confusion: its wildlife and water bureaucrats disagreed. They bucked the question up to the attorney general of the day, a bright young man (and future governor), Edmund G. "Pat" Brown. Brown could have sidestepped the issue by disclaiming state authority over a federal dam. Instead, he took dead aim at 5937. The legislature, he said, could not possibly have meant what it said in that law. Other statutes, he pointed out, seemed to contradict it. It could only, he suggested, apply to streams where there was water to spare; it did not affect a dam-builder whose water rights included the entire flow. In other words, 5937 applied only where it was not needed.

After the Brown opinion, section 5937 fell into a kind of dormancy. The law was not a secret: environmentalists were aware of it; it was cited in government documents; a few brave local fish and game officials, unaware of the chilling opinion, even enforced it. But whenever the top brass heard about such enforcement, it was stopped.

In 1974 another attorney general, Evelle Younger, overrode Pat Brown's interpretation. Even after that, though, the code was not enforced. The concern seems to have been that the law, taken literally, was too strong. It was feared that rigorous stream protection would inconvenience water projects up and down the state, enrage the water lobby, and lead to outright repeal. One might ask what good a dead-letter statute was doing; but Fish and Game people felt they got some mileage out of 5937 by using it as a lever in negotiations with water users.

In 1971 California Trout was formed. Executive Director Richard May was well aware of 5937. He encountered the "Use it and lose it" argument but thought, "What's to lose if we can't use it?" He was itching for a test case. Then Dick Dahlgren came forward.

Rush Creek, a nationally known fishing stream in the 1930s, seemed a splendid test site physically but a difficult one legally, due to the Hot Creek Agreement. Richard May and Barrett McInerney, however, weren't at all sure that this well-known emperor was wearing clothes. Could the Fish and Game Commission so casually set aside the legislature's will?

When McInerney contacted Assistant City Attorney Ken Downey, Downey sent him a copy of the Hot Creek Agreement. The agreement stated that it was merely implementing an earlier action of the Fish and Game Commission. But that earlier action was not attached. When McInerney dug up this missing link, he felt like Dahlgren seeing trout in Rush Creek: he couldn't believe what he had stumbled onto.

For the agreement signed by Fish and Game Commission Chairman Nate Milnor in

Barrett McInerney organized the second major legal attack on the Los Angeles Department of Water and Power's Mono Basin diversions. (Photo by Gerda S. Mathan)

November of 1940 was radically different from the one agreed to by the full commission in August. The earlier action had relieved Los Angeles of building a fishway; Milnor, acting on his own nonexistent authority, had relieved it of making any water releases whatever. Even if there were no question as to basic legality, this action would be void.

McInerney found, in short, a stronger case than he had dared imagine.

Why had the Morrison & Foerster lawyers not found this gap in the city's defenses? The Audubon legal team, says Bruce Dodge, had simply been too closely focused on the lake and the public trust doctrine to consider the creeks and the Fish and Game Code at all. And one might ask, "What creeks?" In 1979, when the MoFo staff was setting strategy, Rush Creek had contained neither fish nor water.

JOINING FORCES   In the weeks that followed the temporary restraining order of November 20, 1984, the old and the new campaigners in the Mono Basin tried to coordinate.

The coalition brought together two magnificently single-purpose movements. California Trout cared for one thing: wild trout and their salmonid relatives. Streams mattered because trout mattered. As for the lake at the bottom of the hill, CalTrout attitudes toward it ranged from friendly indifference to outright contempt. Barrett McInerney makes no secret of having seen the lake as "an ugly little saline sump."

The Mono Lake advocates seemed only a little less monomaniacal. True, key people were aware of lost streams and riparian habitat; Scott Stine, David Gaines, and Peter Vorster had discussed these losses in a 1980 paper. But the positions of the Mono Lake Committee as an organization made little of these values.

Back in 1982, the committee had offered a proposal for lake management called the Wet Year/Dry Year Plan. Under that plan, the city would take little or no water from the

Mono Basin streams in wet years but would divert freely in dry ones. In water-supply terms it made sense, for it is in dry years that the Mono Basin's contribution means most to Los Angeles. But the plan contained no provision for guaranteed minimum streamflows and would, in effect, have perpetuated the artificial drought/flood cycles that had so damaged the streambeds in the past.

Now the committee quickly broadened its view, seeing the streams as "the arteries of this land, nurturing trout, dippers and ospreys, willows and cottonwoods, brine shrimp and birds—and the human spirit." Between them, lake advocates and stream advocates would do a fair job of speaking for an entire landscape. In court, they would be effective, if sometimes contentious, allies.

At meetings late in 1984, the two parties hammered out a common program for the next phase. The National Audubon Society and the Mono Lake Committee would come into *Dahlgren* as supporting plaintiffs, "friends of the court." Bruce Dodge and Palmer Madden would pursue an expansion of the public trust angle. In addition, Antonio Rossmann, who had represented Inyo County in its dispute with Los Angeles over groundwater pumping, would join the legal team; pursuing an idea he had backed in the 1970s, he would call for preparation of an Environmental Impact Report on the Mono Basin diversions.

In the original *Audubon v. Los Angeles*, the public trust had been invoked on the grounds that the navigable lake and lakebed were public property. The streams were involved only as feeders to that lake, not in their own right. Now Audubon sought to apply the public trust doctrine to Rush Creek directly.

How? First, the lawyers would argue that Rush Creek was itself a navigable water. The committee had found a commercial rafter who had floated the last mile of channel in 1980. Second, they would argue for what might be called public trust by contagion: because the Supreme Court had found the feeder streams important to the public trust lake, they were now public trust streams to be protected in their own right.

The third and most powerful argument had to do with fish.

Though submerged land is the classic object of the public trust, it is not the only resource that is held to be public, nor is it the only resource for which the government is held to have an automatic duty of care. In California, fish and wildlife have long been held to be subject to the trust, yet, before 1984, few practical consequences had been drawn from this idea. Audubon was now ready to draw some. Public trust fish, the lawyers would aver, make for a public trust stream.

Meanwhile, Water and Power had requested a change of venue and had gotten, if not that, at least a change of judge. The case would resume in Bridgeport before a visiting jurist, David Otis of Siskiyou County.

In February 1985, a massive filing by Water and Power gave attorney Ed Forstenzer "about a yard" of paper to digest on a tight schedule. Forstenzer, whose contribution had been volunteer, lugged the load to the Greyhound station and sent it, and the responsibility for the case, down to Los Angeles and Barrett McInerney.

THE DAHLGREN
DECISION On May 3, Judge Otis heard the arguments. Bruce Dodge spoke for invoking the public trust. McInerney talked about the Fish and Game Code. To the contention that the Department of Water and Power could not now be challenged on actions taken long ago, McInerney responded with the analogy of theft. "The fact it has been stealing successfully for 45 years, the fact that it has convinced several state agencies . . . to condone its violation of the law, or even the fact that the criminal conduct has been incredibly lucrative is quite irrelevant." Tony Rossmann presented the case for an Environmental Impact Report. To do an EIR, he argued, would merely be to begin the reconsideration required by the Supreme Court in the 1983 Mono Lake public trust decision. Until an acceptable report was completed, the department should be required to release enough water to keep Mono Lake from declining below 6,380 feet.

Water and Power countered that the Fish and Game Code could not be interpreted "to require the maintenance of current fish population in every reach of every major or minor stream in this state," but only required "that total fishery resources in an area or region be reasonably maintained." The Hot Creek hatchery accomplished that for the Mono region. If any further public-trust balancing was required, the water board should do it. As for the law that required environmental reports, it was far too recent to be applicable.

The state attorney general's office filed an amicus brief staking out a position of its own. It agreed that the duty to release water through dams was not absolute, but it demanded for Rush Creek the same kind of "study and reconsideration" under the public trust that the Supreme Court had mandated for Mono Lake itself.

On August 23, 1985, Judge Otis made his decisions. He postponed consideration of the Fish and Game Code argument. He turned down Rossmann's request for an EIR. He declined to hand the matter over to the water board. But he agreed with the Mono Lake Committee and the state that the public trust did in fact apply to the fish in Rush Creek, and he proposed to base the rest of the trial on public trust balancing. So *Dahlgren*, launched in literal reliance on the Fish and Game Code, came instead to center on the deeper but less definite ground of the public trust.

To do that expanded balancing, Otis needed information on what flows the fish in Rush Creek actually required. He suggested that the parties jointly select a consultant to carry out the necessary studies, but they could not agree. In the end, the Department of Fish and Game selected a primary consultant, and Water and Power hired a firm of its own choosing to provide a second opinion.

Such studies cannot be accomplished overnight; many months of data, under many different stream flow conditions, must be gathered. Otis told the parties to come back in about one year. Nobody dreamed that the task would actually drag on for six.

The Rush Creek coalition appealed some of Judge Otis's decisions to higher courts. These moves were unsuccessful. To make a long story short, *Dahlgren v. Los Angeles* dozed off—but Rush Creek continued to flow.

A NEW TARGET

Before 1985 was over, the plaintiffs had leapfrogged *Dahlgren* with a new and much more dramatic legal challenge. *Dahlgren* asked only that the city be ordered to release water; the new suit, dubbed *California Trout v. State Water Resources Control Board*, asked for much more. It asked that the licenses given Los Angeles for the diversion of water from the Mono Basin be ruled illegal and void. It applied to all streams, not one. And it was based, not on Fish and Game Code section 5937, but on a second and later code provision, section 5946.

And here the story has to backtrack once more, to the moment in 1953 when another famous eastern Sierra fishing stream disappeared from the recreation map.

After wandering through Long Valley, the Owens River cuts its way south to lower ground through the rugged defile called the Owens Gorge. In the 1930s and 1940s, the gorge was known as a magnificent trout water. But, like Rush Creek to the north, it was doomed. The Long Valley dam plugged its upper entrance; as soon as the city had completed work on penstocks and power plants, the entire flow was to be diverted through them, leaving the canyon dry.

The Owens Gorge facilities lagged behind the rest of the Mono Extension engineering. In 1952 they were still only nearing completion. Eastern Sierra citizens' groups, alarmed at the impending loss of the Owens Gorge fishery, sought help from the state. A state senate committee asked the city to allow some water to continue flowing through the gorge. Such releases would not cost Los Angeles any water; the river was ultimately headed there, however it traveled those few miles. But some electrical generation would be lost. The city refused to let any water escape.

In August 1953, the legislature responded by enacting Fish and Game Code Section 5946. Section 5946 was, in a sense, the enforcement clause that 5937 had lacked. It gave its instructions, not to Los Angeles directly, but to the state water regulators. Any time the state granted a preliminary permit or a final license for the diversion of water, that document now had to include the requirement that water be released according to 5937. The new law applied only to Inyo and Mono counties, the Los Angeles watershed.

A few weeks after the passage of the bill, in late summer of 1953, Water and Power turned the Owens River into its pipes and dried up sixteen miles of the Owens Gorge.

Fish and Game officials turned to the office of Attorney General Pat Brown. Did the new law provide any leverage? A Brown deputy assured them that it didn't: the city's

1940 permit, protected by the Hot Creek Agreement, could not be affected by a 1953 law. Two years later, in 1955, the same office supplied a further key interpretation: the permanent licenses that would eventually be derived from the 1940 permits *would inherit the same immunity.*

This ramshackle structure of doctrine stood unchallenged for thirty more years. In due course Pat Brown became governor, and he used the office to launch the State Water Project. His son, Jerry Brown, took the same office in 1974 and partially unmade his father's policies. Water battles rose and raged. But in the eastern Sierra old interpretations, dating back to the elder Brown's days as attorney general, ruled.

Then CalTrout and Audubon touched the airy castle with cold iron. It vanished into mist. The Hot Creek Agreement was void; the notion that license, as well as permit, was exempt from the fish-flow law seemed to be the independent invention of a minor functionary. Though Los Angeles had its diversion *permits* in 1940, it received its final *licenses* only in 1974, after completion of the aqueduct's second barrel. At that time, the State Water Resources Control Board had regarded the conversion of permit to license as a mere technicality. In this, the plaintiffs' lawyers were sure, the board had erred.

Why base the new attack, not on section 5937, but on the more limited ground of 5946? Though McInerney had broken the ancient taboo against invoking 5937 in court, both he and Audubon's Bruce Dodge were still wary of its power. A strict application of the statute might lead to a campaign for its repeal. Section 5946 applied to one region, not statewide. It threatened one great power in the water world, not many. Moreover, it provided a new target: not Los Angeles directly, but the state regulators who had failed to do their job.

After some preliminary maneuvers, the new case wound up in Sacramento County Superior Court under Judge Lloyd A. Phillips, Jr. On July 30, 1986, Phillips ruled that Water and Power's rights were immune from challenge because the city had received its permits before the passage of section 5946. So CalTrout and Audubon took the matter to the Third District Court of Appeal. Up to this point, each organization had technically carried its own lawsuit; now the actions were merged under the title *California Trout v. SWRCB.*

LAWSUIT NO. 4:
LEE VINING CREEK

One more in the series of creek lawsuits remained to be filed. Lee Vining Creek had not yet entered much into these debates. It had carried no water since the spring of 1984. But 1986 turned out to be another wet year. Avalanches so plagued Mono County that President Reagan declared it a disaster area. In May, when an early heat wave brought a sudden thaw and a rush of runoff, the Los Angeles Department of Water and Power had to release a hefty flow down Lee Vining Creek.

And suddenly trout were reported there as well. Some suggest they had help getting

The count of active lawsuits, now up to four, would go no higher. At the end of 1986, here's where they stood.

Dahlgren v. Los Angeles was on hold pending fish studies in Rush Creek.

Mono Lake Committee v. Los Angeles, the Lee Vining Creek case, was on hold pending appointment of a new judge. (Edward Denton had retired.)

California Trout v. State Water Resources Control Board, the attack on the department's licenses, was before the Third District appeal panel.

And what about the original granddaddy case, the public trust suit, Audubon v. Los Angeles? It was stuck in the mud. The legal expertise of Morrison & Foerster had a lot to do with keeping it there.

Back in November 1984, Federal District Court Judge Lawrence Karlton had ruled that the public trust issue belonged in state court and had sent it back to Alpine County. But he retained jurisdiction over one of the secondary claims Audubon had concocted with a view toward staying in federal court: the charge that dust storms, sweeping across state lines, constituted an interstate nuisance of federal concern. The adversaries then trooped up to the Ninth Circuit Court of Appeals. The Mono advocates wanted both halves of the case in the federal courts; Water and Power wanted the nuisance suit dismissed; the state wanted the whole controversy turned over to the water board. The circuit court did nothing at all for a while.

---

there. This seems unnecessary. In fact the stretch of the creek immediately below the diversion dam had never gone completely dry, and a few fish had survived there all along. When higher flows extended downstream, those trout could simply go along for the ride.

The Mono Lake Committee, sensing a second *Dahlgren*, went to court. This time it went without its ally. California Trout was not much interested in Lee Vining Creek. Though included in the general legal challenge to the diversion licenses, this lesser creek wasn't a featured attraction. It had been a good fishing stream in its time, but never a trophy water like Rush Creek; moreover, the streambed was now so damaged as to offer minimal habitat. Barrett McInerney feared it would seem ridiculous to want to release expensive water for the benefit of a very few fish. Breaking ranks with the Mono Lake Committee, he joined the new case on the side of Water and Power.

Nevertheless, on August 12, 1986, Mono County Superior Court Judge Edward Denton granted a temporary restraining order that forced the department to release 10 cubic feet per second down Lee Vining Creek, enough water to keep trout alive until the case was tried.

Los Angeles City Councilman Zev Yaroslavsky.
(Photo by Gerda S. Mathan)

Meanwhile, the politics of the Mono issue had been subtly changing where it counted most. At the beginning of the fight, the Los Angeles mayor and city council had been of one mind with the Department of Water and Power. But gradually, in the middle 1980s, the elected leadership of the city began to respond to the proddings of the courts, the media, and public opinion. Increasingly it became incorrect to speak of "Los Angeles" as one character in the story. Increasingly the city was one player, the Department of Water and Power quite another. Again and again the independence, indeed the willfulness, of the department was made sharply clear.

The hearings Councilman John Ferraro had held in 1984 concerning Rush Creek marked the beginning of the change. After that it accelerated. Several councilmembers became cautious Monophiles. Councilman Zev Yaroslavsky, who had earlier suggested that gulls and shrimp could adapt to a dwindling Mono Lake with "American ingenuity," was by 1986 an outright advocate of preservation. And even Mayor Bradley began to soften.

In 1986 Bradley was running for governor a second time. He needed to cut a good figure before northern California voters. The Mono question began to dog him; at one campaign appearance, he found himself facing solid rows of "Save Mono Lake" T-shirts. On August 27, 1986, Bradley issued a statement calling the lake "a rare environmental jewel" and promising that the city would do its part to keep it "in a healthy environmental state." But if Los Angeles was to give up water, he suggested, the rest of the state, and indeed the nation, should help replace the loss.

On August 28 Tony Rossmann, a long-distance runner as well as an attorney, started a hundred-mile lope from the Owens Valley to Mono Lake, carrying some water taken from the Los Angeles aqueduct intake. As is customary in such events, he asked people to pledge money, at a given rate per mile, to the cause of his choice: the Mono Lake Committee. Among his sponsors were Mayor Bradley and four councilmembers. The times, they seemed to be a-changin'.

The exploratory meetings of the parties, begun after the 1984 conference in Santa Monica, were meanwhile continuing. Executive Director Martha Davis attended for the Mono Lake Committee; Duane Georgeson, head of the water branch, for the Los Angeles Department of Water and Power; representatives of the L.A. Water and Power Commissioners and of Mayor Bradley also took part. LeRoy Graymer, head of the UCLA Public Policy Program, "facilitated." After locking horns briefly on the question of desirable lake level, the members turned in a more fruitful direction. They began to explore hypothetical solutions: *if* Los Angeles lost access to some of its Mono Basin water, where might replacement water come from, and how might it be paid for?

Progress was slow and frustrations were many. At one point David Gaines wrote an editorial for the committee newsletter denouncing this incremental, undramatic, rather expensive process; Davis vetoed publication of the piece.

MEANWHILE, BACK AT THE LAKE

For five years in the 1980s, from mid-1983 to mid-1988, the surface of Mono Lake stood at 6,377 feet above sea level or higher. The high point occurred in 1986, when the lake reached 6,381 feet, nine feet above the low stand of 1982. This little "transgression"—to use the geologist's term—had puzzling effects.

In 1983 the flood of fresh water had produced a split-level lake, brackish on top and hypersaline underneath, with little mixing between layers. This meromixis, never seen here before, complicated all observations about the health of the lake. The lower salinities near the surface should have been good for algae, alkali flies, brine shrimp, and birds, but much of the system's sustaining nitrogen was trapped in the cold, dark lower layer, out of reach of the algae that nourished the rest of the food chain. These effects seem to have balanced out, leaving the system neither more nor less productive than before.

One species did notably well in these years: the California gull. Year by year the number of fledglings climbed. In 1987 David Shuford tallied almost 26,000 chicks on the islands, the same number found in the 1976 Ecological Study. The distribution of birds remained different, however. Negit Island had at last been recolonized in 1985 and supported more birds each year, but it was slow to regain its former importance. Twain islet, where half the population now converged, appeared to be the current key site.

It was by now pretty clear that the earlier concern about Negit Island had been overblown—at first, out of genuine ignorance; later, no doubt, for reasons of propaganda. The gulls needed sufficient nesting space, on some combination of islands; they certainly had more habitat available to them with Negit than without it; at lake levels near the historic low, their territory was getting skimpy. But Negit was only part of a complex story.

One component of the gull habitat actually suffered from the lake rise. In the early

1980s, the newly emerged Paoha islets had helped to compensate for the loss of Negit, Java, and Twain. But unlike the older islets, made up of chunky lava rock, the Paoha group was formed of soft sediments. As the waves of a rising lake climbed up their slopes, the new islets crumbled. Clearly, whatever their value might be in a steadily sinking Mono Lake, these specks of land would not survive in a fluctuating one.

The rising water also attacked one of the great lakeshore attractions, the towers at South Tufa, where the structures are unusually shallow-rooted. As waves and currents undermined their bases, several hundred of the less massive towers toppled. Other tufa groves, however, and the larger structures at South Tufa, were not harmed.

The next lake fluctuation was already under way. As 1986 turned into 1987, precipitation once more dropped below normal; California was entering what would turn out to be a six-year drought.

8

LOSSES AND GAINS

And late man, listening through his latter grief,
Hears, close or far, the oldest of his joys,
Exactly as it was, the water noise.

W. H. Auden, "Bucolics: II Woods"

JANUARY 11, 1988, WAS A TRICKY DAY on the roads of the eastern Sierra. It was snowing, sometimes heavily, and a wind was blowing the white stuff flat at your eyes. A small Toyota wagon cautiously began the climb on U.S. 395 out of Long Valley to Deadman Summit and Mono Lake. Behind the wheel was Sally Gaines; her passengers were David, children Sage and Vireo, and committee staffer Don Oberlin.

Coming the other way in a pickup truck, a local man made a fatal decision to overtake and pass. Pulling into the northbound lane, he struck the Gaines car head on. Sally was injured slightly, daughter Vireo badly, son Sage not at all. Don Oberlin and David Gaines died in the crash.

Bad news travels fast. A worker from the California Department of Transportation recognized the victims. Someone in Lee Vining heard of the accident on a police scanner. At committee headquarters, staff member Ilene Mandelbaum and several colleagues were sitting around the potbellied stove, chatting. Then came the knock at the door.

So Gaines would not see the success of the campaign he had done so much to launch. But in their shock his friends could take some comfort in the thought that he had died expecting good news. The week before the accident, this inveterate pessimist told Martha Davis he believed the tide had genuinely turned. By 1988, the reasons for believing that were multiplying.

In 1984, the legislature and Congress had each ordered a study of the Mono Lake ecosystem. These efforts progressed almost as slowly as the lawsuits.

The National Academy of Sciences report appeared first, in August of 1987, under the title *The Mono Basin Ecosystem: Effects of Changing Lake Level*. On too tight a budget to produce much original research, the team mostly pulled together and analyzed work already done—and gave it a weighty stamp of approval.

The academy confirmed that maximum diversions would end by killing the lake ecosystem. Flies and the birds that feed on flies would begin to suffer as the lake surface sank below 6,370 feet; at 6,360 the effects would become acute. For shrimp and the shrimp-eaters, the effects would set in about ten feet lower: at 6,350 feet, the lake would be in serious trouble. At that level, too, virtually no protected nesting areas for gulls would remain.

Though the academy study did not recommend a lake level, it implied that the lake surface should be kept above 6,370 feet at all times. It suggested, too, that a ten-foot buffer should be added to any lake level chosen, as insurance against droughts. In wet and normal years, then, the lake should be maintained at 6,380 feet—just about what it was, in fact, when the report appeared.

Duncan Patten, the chairman of the study committee, emphasized the uncertainties involved. "The best experiment would be to let [the lake] go all the way [down] to see if we're right," he said, "but you can say the same thing about the consequences of nuclear war."

Eight months later, in April of 1988, the state-funded lake study appeared. Titled *The Future of Mono Lake*, it is usually known as the CORI report after its sponsor, the Community and Organization Research Institute (at the University of California at Santa Barbara). Unlike the National Academy of Sciences, CORI underwrote some fresh research—by limnologist John Melack, ornithologists Joseph Jehl and David Winkler, geomorphologist Scott Stine, and air pollution researcher Thomas A. Cahill. The new report took a marginally dimmer view of the lake's future than its predecessor had. It saw decreases in algae, flies, and shrimp below 6,375 feet, and death of the ecosystem by 6,352 feet.

The CORI report proclaimed another reason, not yet much remarked upon, for stemming the lake's decline. At the beginning of the 1980s, Scott Stine had already noted the existence, clear around the lake, of a submerged terrace; this feature had been cut by the lake at its record low stand of 6,368 feet, reached about A.D. 150. At the lakeward edge of this terrace the slope of the lakebed dramatically steepened. If the lake now fell below this "nick point," all its feeder streams, even intermittent ones, would begin a new cycle of downcutting, further damaging stream habitats and making a sort of badlands of the shore. If the lake dipped below 6,368 feet and then rose again, the consequences would be hardly less severe; a rising lake mauls and reshapes its shores, and a lake rebounding from so low a stand would devastate many of the tufa groves.

To prevent the lake from ever touching the nick point, CORI recommended that it be kept at 6,382 feet or higher in normal runoff years.

Everybody, including Duane Georgeson of the Department of Water and Power, seems to have accepted these two studies as victories for the Mono advocates. At the time the department was still denying that its activities could or would hurt Mono Lake; this position was now branded as nonsense by authorities much harder to dismiss than the hasty Interagency Task Force of 1979. The department reacted defensively, especially attacking Stine's "nick point" theory (a challenge it was forced to withdraw).

As the committee newsletter acknowledged, however, the two reports also contained some unwelcome thoughts for the Mono Lake Committee. Each held that the lake surface could sink a bit below its historic low of 6,372 feet without drastic biological effects. Neither attached much importance to the gull crash of 1981. The management levels endorsed would not protect Negit Island, or even Twain and Java islets, all the time. Certainly neither report came anywhere near endorsing the committee's preferred management level of 6,388 feet.

It does appear that Water and Power missed a strategic opportunity here. Suppose the department had had the foresight to cut its losses and embrace these results? Suppose it had offered to cut diversions just enough to maintain the lake always above 6,368 feet (protecting the "nick point") or above 6,372 feet (protecting Twain and Java)? Taking such a stand, it might well have cast as unreasonable anyone who asked for more. But its leaders remained stuck on their old policy of maximum diversion. As a result, they allowed the new findings to pass into the record as additional blows against a crumbling position.

During these years a third study, one with more immediate practical application, was pending. The Forest Service was taking stock of its new domain around Mono Lake and preparing to write a general management plan for the Mono Basin National Forest Scenic Area.

At the outset the agency faced this question: should it, or should it not, comment on a desirable lake level? The law authorizing the scenic area was carefully ambiguous. It required the agency "to protect geologic, ecologic and cultural resources," but "in a manner consistent with the protection of the water rights of . . . the city of Los Angeles." The Department of Water and Power argued that this language blocked the Forest Service from so much as stating an opinion on lake level.

In 1986, Inyo Forest Supervisor Dennis Martin decided that the Forest Service should and would define the lake level "that would best meet the overall management objectives

THE SCENIC
AREA PLAN

The Federal Interest

The legal campaign to protect Mono Lake has centered on state laws and doctrines: the public trust, the Fish and Game Code. But as this line of cases was proceeding, another lawyer was prodding the federal government, the largest landowner in the Mono Basin, to do some lake-protecting of its own.

Tim Such enters this story, too. In the late 1970s, when he was besieging all parties to take action at Mono, one of his targets was Laurens Silver at the Sierra Club Legal Defense Fund. "Tim was a prodder," Silver recalls. "How often he called me I don't know. He called me lots. Tim may have started me up."

In 1977, as the sinking lake exposed the Negit Island land bridge, the Sierra Club petitioned the secretary of the interior to take action to protect the federally owned island. (Negit was then controlled by the Bureau of Land Management, an agency within Interior.) Getting nowhere, Silver went in 1979 to the Sacramento federal district court of Lawrence Karlton. The federal government, Silver alleged, had water rights of its own and should be asserting them to protect its property on Negit. On this and other grounds, he asked Judge Karlton to direct Interior to tackle the Los Angeles Department of Water and Power. Federal water rights? This is a tricky area of law. Under our system of government, water matters are basically left to the states. Yet the federal government has a limited claim to water for use on federal lands that have been singled out for some special purpose through what is called withdrawal. Federal land in the Mono Basin had indeed been withdrawn—for the benefit of Los Angeles. But in

1931, when Congress gave its blessing to the Mono withdrawals, local congressmen won a concession. Rather than citing the city's watershed as the sole reason for the action, the withdrawal law listed wildlife and recreation as well. Aha, said Silver. That created a federal right to the water needed for these other purposes, even at the expense of Los Angeles's claims.

Intriguing thought. But soon the legal spotlight was shifting to the public trust theory, and Silver didn't push his case very hard. Early in 1984 Judge Karlton dismissed it, saying that the Mono issue was now in the hands of the state: if the Sierra Club later felt the state had dropped the ball, it was welcome to come back to him.

Under California law, there was a second basis on which the federal government might theoretically claim water at and for Mono Lake: as a riparian owner, one with lakeshore land. But did it indeed possess any lakeshore land? In the early 1980s, the state and federal governments were debating who owned the "relicted lands," the lakebed exposed since 1940 by the falling water level. If the state's ownership claim was valid, the federal government had no shoreline property at all.

Silver surprised many of his conservation colleagues by joining the case on behalf of the federal government. Because Judge Karlton was already involved in Mono matters, the dispute was assigned to him. In 1985 Karlton ruled that relicted lands belonged to the federal government wherever they lay downslope from other, recognized federal property. That meant that 70 percent of the dryland acreage of the

Mono Lake Tufa State Reserve changed hands and became, instead, part of the new Mono Lake National Forest Scenic Area.

The federal government's status as a lakeside landowner was now clear. It was not yet so clear whether it could actually claim water rights as a riparian owner under California law. As it happened, this possibility was just then being tested in court for the very first time. The State Water Resources Control Board was apportioning the flows of little Hallett Creek in the Plumas National Forest in northeastern California, and the U.S. Forest Service had submitted a small claim for watering troughs for deer. The board refused the water; the federal government sued; and Silver once again brought the Sierra Club in on the federal side. In February 1988, the California Supreme Court ruled that the Forest Service did indeed have water rights as a riparian owner, sufficient to serve the purposes for

which the federal land had been set aside. At Hallett Creek, that meant (for instance) deer. At Mono Lake, it could include alkali flies, phalaropes, and scenery.

After creation of the Mono Basin National Forest Scenic Area, the Sierra Club and other groups urged the Forest Service, on legal grounds, to take a stand regarding lake level: failure to do so might compromise emerging federal water rights. Whether or not this argument influenced the service in its lake-level endorsement, the agency has since been careful to proclaim its "latent" water rights, not to be asserted directly unless the state should fall down on the job of protecting Mono Lake on the basis of the public trust.

Some charge that Larry Silver, in his campaign to strengthen the federal government's hand at Mono Lake, has weakened the state's. So far, at least, the two forces seem to be complementary.

of the Scenic Area." In November 1987, three months before the plan was due, Water and Power officials went to Washington, D.C., to ask the top brass of the Forest Service to overrule Martin's decision. A counterforce of lobbyists from Mono County, the Mono Lake Committee, and other conservation groups strove to undo the department's work. In the end, Martin's decision was allowed to stand.

On September 20, 1988, the draft scenic area management plan appeared. It recommended that the lake surface be maintained in the range between 6,377 and 6,390 feet. After several more stages of planning, public comment, and Water and Power protests, this position became policy. Though without immediate legal force, this opinion was surely one the Department of Water and Power would have preferred not to have on the record.

The scenic area plan had another provision that would be important to the debate. It called for maintaining the shores of Mono Lake in a primitive, natural-appearing condition. This would rule out some of the more heroic options for curbing air pollution—for example, the armoring of alkali flats with crushed rock quarried from Black Point.

It was also in 1988 that Congress allocated $4.3 million to the building of a scenic area visitor center. This striking, indeed dominating, structure was to rise on a bluff just north of town, overlooking the lake and the canyon of Lee Vining Creek. It would be an architectural message about the future of Mono Lake. How in the world could the government spend so much on a building celebrating the lake and then permit that body of water to dwindle to a puddle in a bowl of alkali?

CALTROUT I   Meanwhile, the CalTrout/Audubon challenge to Los Angeles's Mono Basin water rights was prospering. On October 20, 1987, the Third District Court of Appeal heard arguments. Two weeks later, Barrett McInerney quietly offered Water and Power a deal, to go into effect if the department came out on the losing side in the pending decision. Under the McInerney plan, the department would provide adequate flows in Rush Creek, rewater little Walker Creek, send some water down the Owens Gorge, and take several steps to improve the management of other streams on its vast watershed lands. In return, CalTrout would sanction full diversion of Parker and Lee Vining creeks and would join the department in backing a bill in Sacramento adopting these arrangements as law. "I did not mention this," McInerney observes, "to the Mono Lake Committee." Adolph Moskovitz responded for Water and Power. His client did not believe the time was right for settlement.

On May 23, 1988, the Third District Court of Appeal ruled that the licenses held by the department for the diversion of water from the Mono Basin were flatly illegal. Neither the Hot Creek Agreement nor the passage of time had made them less so. The court ordered the State Water Resources Control Board to revoke the licenses and instead issue ones that were in compliance with the Fish and Game Code. "What this means," said McInerney, "is that before Los Angeles gets a drop of water from those dams the fish have to be taken care of. We are going to turn the clock back 48 years and do it right this time." "The pieces are falling into place," Martha Davis commented. "This signals that it is time to sit down and hammer out a solution."

The Department of Water and Power asked for and received a rehearing, arguing that it was entitled at least to untroubled possession of the amount of water it had diverted in the wettest year before the passage of Fish and Game Code section 5946. The court took little notice of this argument and instead probed into another aspect of the story: the unprecedented thirty-year gap between the granting of the initial permit in 1940 and the completion of the second aqueduct in 1970. Only the second aqueduct allowed the city to move water on the scale originally contemplated.

On January 28, 1989, the revised ruling came down. In one respect it was an improvement for the Department of Water and Power. Rather than yanking Los Angeles's rights entirely, it merely ordered that the licenses be modified to require the necessary stream-flows. But a new and powerful section took the department to task for its long failure to exploit fully the water to which it had staked its claim. The city had received so many casual extensions on the completion of the second barrel, the court declared, that the second barrel must in truth be considered a new project, subject to a separate approval and unmistakably subject to the fish-flow requirements of 5946. This decision came to be known as CalTrout I.

After the State Supreme Court declined to hear the department's appeal, the matter was passed back to the Sacramento County Superior Court, a bench now occupied by Judge Cecily Bond, with instructions to make sure the water board did as it had just been told.

CalTrout I changed the Mono debate. Under the Supreme Court's public trust decision of 1983, Water and Power was served notice that it would have to protect the value of the lake "as far as feasible," taking into account the other uses served by the water. The planning process envisioned came to be spoken of as a "balancing." Under the Fish and Game Code, however, there was no such balancing to be done. Adequate fish flows were, quite simply, required. Only after that requirement had been met could the public trust balancing even begin.

Before CalTrout I, the Los Angeles Department of Water and Power could well be seen as the victim of a necessary but burdensome alteration in society's rules. But CalTrout I, especially as revised, changed that. The department had failed to play fairly by the old, well-understood rules of water appropriation. It was now cast as a scofflaw, pure and simple.

Up to this point, the department's strongest argument had been expense: it would have to pay $300 or more per acre-foot to replace the water and power lost if Mono exports were curtailed. Once it became clear that much of the water at stake did not properly belong to the city *and never had*, the cost issue acquired a second edge. It could now be argued that the city had been stealing water; the greater the value attributed to the water, the higher the total value of the theft.

In this same period the legal story took another decisive turn. In October 1988, the United States Court of Appeals for the Ninth Circuit dismissed the federal air-pollution nuisance claim in *Audubon v. Los Angeles*. This action ended Audubon's eight-year fight to stay in the federal court of Judge Lawrence Karlton. The original public trust lawsuit could now move ahead—as a state matter purely.

That put the case back in the hands of the very jurist the plaintiffs had been seeking to avoid: Alpine County Superior Court Judge Hilary Cook, who had never made a

THE PUBLIC TRUST
LOGJAM BREAKS

In 1989, all the Mono Lake and creek cases converged in the courtroom of Eldorado County Superior Court Judge Terrence Finney. (Photo by Gerda S. Mathan)

significant ruling in Audubon's favor. But there was an out. Three closely related cases now centered on the public trust in the Mono Basin: *Audubon, Dahlgren v. Los Angeles* (the original Rush Creek case), and *Mono Lake Committee v. Los Angeles* (the Lee Vining Creek case). It was only logical that they be combined or, as the jargon has it, "coordinated." The Department of Water and Power, in fact, beat Audubon to the punch in filing for coordination.

Following such a request, the chief justice of the California Supreme Court appoints an interim "coordination judge" to decide whether the cases should be merged and to whose court the compound case should be assigned. After some rather comical false starts—at one point it appeared that Judge Cook himself might be in charge of coordination—the choice fell on a jurist known to neither side: Judge Terrence Finney of the Eldorado County Superior Court in South Lake Tahoe.

Judge Finney might have been simply a transitional character. But he made himself a central one. In the manner of scholars before him, he grew fascinated with the Mono story. Approving coordination, as trial judge he nominated himself—and received the appointment.

Immediately Finney faced a request from Audubon: that he halt all export of water out of the Mono Basin until the lake had once more risen safely above 6,377 feet. It was the third time that Bruce Dodge had asked a court for such relief, and three times turned out to be a charm. On June 15, 1989, Judge Finney issued a temporary restraining order. The flow of the waters southward out of the Mono Basin ceased at last.

The next step was to convert the temporary restraining order into a longer-lasting order called a preliminary injunction. In arguing against this step, Water and Power proposed what it called the Mono Lake Trial Operation Plan. Under the plan, the department would continue diversions while the lake was drawn down to a "minimum operating level" of 6,372.5 feet. As it fell, researchers would watch it and learn as much as possible from the changes that took place. Judge Finney disallowed this. On August 29, 1989, he issued an injunction "prohibiting respondent DWP from causing the level of Mono Lake to fall below 6,377 feet as a result of its diversions for the remainder of the current run-off year, ending March 30, 1990." But Finney also did something else.

From the beginning the State of California had sought to move the Mono Lake controversy out of the courts and put it before the State Water Resources Control Board, a quasi-judicial body whose members are appointed by the governor. In the spring of 1989, the board announced its intention to hold hearings on the issue. That summer, the attorney general renewed his request that the board be assigned primary responsibility for the case. On August 29, even as he granted the preliminary injunction halting exports, Judge Finney agreed to the assignment. He asked the water board to review Los Angeles's Mono Basin water rights and to perform, at long last, the balancing of domestic water needs and natural values called for in 1983 by the California Supreme Court.

The Audubon Society and the Mono Lake Committee opposed this shift. They argued that the court could work faster than the board and would be less subject to political pressure. In truth, the plaintiffs feared that the water board would be a far chillier spot for them than the courts had been, a friendlier place for the Department of Water and Power. The department plainly thought so, too.

You could not tell it from public and courtroom pronouncements, but behind the scenes the Mono Lake Committee and the Department of Water and Power were still probing gently for accommodation. In the summer of 1987, their regular discussions were expanded to include the Forest Service and the government of Mono County; the participants now called themselves the Mono Lake Group. At the end of the year, the group hired Thomas J. Graff of the Environmental Defense Fund to look for possible replacements for Mono export water. Graff was becoming known as an advocate of the idea called water marketing, which, in simplest terms, promises to stretch available water supplies by swapping them around. Within six months he had located two small irrigation districts in the San Joaquin Valley that were interested in dealing. Using city funds, the districts would improve their facilities so that they could grow the same crops with less water. The surplus thus created would travel down the state aqueduct to Los Angeles, replacing some Mono Basin water.

At the end of 1988 the Board of Water and Power Commissioners declared, for the first time ever, that Mono Lake was indeed an ecosystem worth saving. They acknowledged the department's "responsibility to do what it reasonably can to maintain the lake in an environmentally healthy condition." They conceded that streamflow diversions from the basin would have to be curtailed—to some unspecified degree. Architect of the new policy was commissioner Walter Zelman, who had represented his board on the Mono Lake Group.

Like Mayor Bradley two years earlier, the department underlined the need for replacement water and asked for state and federal help in finding it. Barrett McInerney was unimpressed. "This means the [Water and Power] board won't stand in the way of anybody else solving their problem," he quipped. But Martha Davis had quite another viewpoint. She wanted very much to help the department solve its problem; indeed, that aid had been part of her strategy from the beginning.

Having apparently located a water source, the Mono Lake Group now sought state and federal subsidies to help Los Angeles pay for it. The state was to come through first.

Early in 1989, assemblyman Phillip Isenberg, Democrat from Sacramento, was casting around for a way of helping to resolve the Mono matter. A bond issue, perhaps, to develop replacement water? He took the idea up with Davis and soon with the entire Mono Lake Group. In the next few months the idea took various shapes. Instead of floating a bond issue, a relatively painless funding source was found: a debt owed to the state by contractors to the State Water Project. Assemblyman Bill Baker, a conservative Republican from Danville, had his own bill pending to resolve this debt. Baker and Isenberg got together, a potent political odd couple, to link their issues. Assemblyman Richard Katz, a Los Angeles Democrat and a veteran worker in the cause of water law reform, cheered them on. For the first time, legislators who did not themselves represent Mono County were taking the lead.

Isenberg's bill, AB 444, ran a gauntlet of objections, changing considerably on the way to passage. The state Department of Water Resources grumbled about bailing Los Angeles out (a sentiment shared by a few on the Mono Lake Committee board and by commentator Bill Kahrl of the *Sacramento Bee*). The Metropolitan Water District of Southern California insisted on language stating that the fund would not be used simply to buy replacement water, gallon for gallon, from them. Water and Power itself had various objections, but finally, after strong prodding from the *Los Angeles Times*, swung around into support. Senator Pete Wilson urged a skeptical Governor Deukmejian to sign AB 444, and on September 22, 1989, he did, praising it as a "win-win situation for all Californians."

In final form, AB 444 allocated $60 million in state money to help Water and Power get along without some of its Mono Basin supply. At the department's insistence, the bill did not specify a lake level or other terms of a Mono Lake agreement. But there was a catch: this money could be granted *only on a joint application by the Department of*

Assemblyman Phillip Isenberg, author of the Environmental Water Act of 1989 (AB 444). Among other things, this bill offered funding to help Los Angeles find environment-friendly replacement sources for Mono Basin water. (Photo by Gerda S. Mathan)

Water and Power and the Mono Lake Committee. The money was dangled in front of the participants. To reach for it, they somehow had to agree to agree.

The balance of power had indeed shifted in eleven years. Now the scruffy band of rebels was placed, by the legislature itself, on an equal footing with the mighty southern bureaucracy.

At this same moment the legislature came through in another manner, granting $750,000 to the Department of Fish and Game for studies of the flows needed for fish in various Mono Basin streams and in the upper Owens River. Staff biologist Gary Smith now had some hope of producing the answers he knew would soon be urgently required.

On the lake, too, changes were in motion. Throughout 1988, researchers saw signs that the six-year interlude of meromixis, when fresh water lay on the surface of salt, was approaching its end. Gases trapped in the lower layer began to bubble to the surface. On calm days in mid-November the basin stank of ammonium. As algae blossomed, the lake turned an unusually dark shade of green.

In the spring of 1989, the first generation of brine shrimp was very sparse, a phenomenon not seen since the early 1980s. In that earlier period, and especially in 1981, the gulls had done very poorly; scientists still argued over the reasons why. In 1989, however, the gulls did well. Did they find something besides shrimp to eat? Did they survive some degree of hunger because the weather, this time, was not so hot as to stress them further? Or had the low shrimp hatch in fact never mattered to them at all? Here

THE LAKE
TURNS OVER

was a chance to take another look at the old debate, but apparently the necessary research was not conducted.

The water surface that year stood near 6,375 feet above sea level—almost exactly where it had been when the battle began. The political and legal weather was shifting in favor of Mono Lake, but the weather of the world was not. It continued stubbornly dry.

9

EVE OF DECISION

My lord, you do not well in obstinacy
To cavil in the course of this contract:
If once it be neglected, ten to one
We shall not find like opportunity.

Shakespeare, *Henry VI, Part 1*

AS THE 1980S TURNED INTO THE 1990S, the Mono Lake action came to focus more and more on the coming confrontation before the State Water Resources Control Board.

In Sacramento, the water board and its consultants were launching a vast project of information-gathering and analysis that would culminate in a Draft Environmental Impact Report 1,700 pages long.

In Los Angeles, the Mono Lake Committee and the city were struggling to come together on a plan to harvest the $60 million promised by AB 444.

In the Mono Basin, consultants and engineers were beginning the process of repairing some of the damage done to the creeks by fifty years of diversion.

The courts, in Sacramento and in South Lake Tahoe where Judge Finney presided, were busy as usual with Mono matters.

And in Bishop, California, and Washington, D.C., like a reserve squadron mustering, the dust pollution issue was taking actionable form.

After June 15, 1989, Los Angeles exported not a drop from the Mono Basin. Starved by a purely natural drought, the lake nonetheless continued to drop. Negit Island once more became a peninsula and lost its nesting gulls. In another replay, the Forest Service built a fence—electrified, this time—across the land bridge (this one didn't work, either). As it had in the late 1970s and early 1980s (but with rather less justification) the Mono Lake Committee beat the drums of alarm. The word *catastrophe* was used.

For anyone familiar with the recent history of the lake, it was hard to work up much of a sweat about the new drop in the water level. The higher salinities probably cost the ecosystem some of its productivity, yet experience suggested that it was nowhere near collapse. The gulls, for their part, obstinately continued to prosper.

But it is worth recalling just how much further the lake might have fallen if Judge Finney had not blocked Mono Basin exports. If Water and Power's "trial operation plan" of 1990 had been carried out, the lake would have sunk below its previous historic nadir. Twain islet, which now appeared to be the key gull rookery, would have become a peninsula and have stayed that way, with unknown effects. And the lake would have turned saltier than ever before.

What happened in Los Angeles as the drought deepened and Mono water remained out of reach? In a way this is the biggest story of all, for what happened was . . . nothing much. Some serious conservation efforts worked and the Metropolitan Water District played its intended role as backup source. The city lived without Mono water almost as though Mono water had never existed. Of the long-feared backlash—the public political wrath that would sweep away the consensus for saving the lake and the streams—there was no sign.

At a key hearing later on, a Los Angeles citizen was to announce his willingness to pay higher water rates to save Mono Lake. The hearing officer would then point out, "If you were going to feel it on your water bill, you would have felt it by now."

THE WATER BOARD TAKES OVER

When Judge Finney handed the Mono issue to the water board, he temporarily relegated his own court to the sidelines. For the next several years the real action would take place behind the scenes at the water board and in the offices of Jones & Stokes of Sacramento, the consulting firm selected to write an Environmental Impact Report (EIR) setting out the effects of various possible management plans for the lake and the feeder streams.

An EIR has an almost ritual format. It begins by describing, in great detail, the place where a proposed project is to be built or carried out. Then it sketches a number of alternative courses of action, including the option of doing nothing at all, and describes how each choice will affect the place and the wider world. On this basis, one alternative is identified as environmentally the best. EIRs are supposed to be complete and honest in their presentation of effects; if they are not, court challenges can be brought. But the agency making the final decision does not necessarily have to adopt the option that looks best in the EIR.

In the case of the Mono Basin, this standard process had to work around several thorny problems. First, what was the "project"? It was not the Mono Extension of 1940, nor was it the city's past diversions. Rather, the "project" was the current effort to rewrite the rules governing the activities of Los Angeles at Mono Lake.

What, in that case, was the "environment," the "before" picture, the pre-project scene? More accurately, *when* was it? Jim Canaday, the project manager on the water board staff, chose a baseline in the summer of 1989, just before the moment when Judge Finney stopped exports and handed the issue to his agency. That choice had its logic, but it also had a very obvious drawback. If 1989 was taken as the basis of comparison, the vast changes that had occurred since 1940 would drop out of the picture; a future of low lake levels and low streamflows would look better than it ought to.

To solve this problem, Canaday ordered the team to add a second starting point, a second measuring stick. The effects of possible actions would be judged not only against 1989 conditions but also against those of 1940. This binocular approach was a novelty in the EIR trade. Neither the L.A. Department of Water and Power nor the growing list of Mono advocates liked it much. The department wanted less concentration on 1940 conditions; the Mono Lake Committee, the Audubon Society, and the Department of Fish and Game wanted much more. Yet Canaday's awkward solution was probably the best that could be had.

As the work plan unfolded, the parties continued to lobby for ground rules each thought favorable to its cause. According to Canaday, Water and Power sought to direct attention to alternative plans with a low lake and a lot of water export, while lake advocates tried to focus on high lakes and low exports. Canaday resisted both tilts: Jones & Stokes would study a wide range of levels (though none below 6,372 feet).

What about the dust problem? The department wanted the issue left out entirely, on the grounds that the legislature had exempted them from state air pollution laws (in 1983). They argued—unsuccessfully, however—that what the federal government might do or might force the state to do was outside the water board's jurisdiction.

Again, how much attention should be paid to the effects of different Mono policies on fishing and recreation spots elsewhere along the line of the aqueduct? Grant Lake reservoir was itself an attraction. Much more so was Crowley Lake, the reservoir behind the Long Valley dam. (On the opening day of fishing season Crowley's shores resemble a stadium parking lot.) These bodies of water, the department liked to point out, received hundreds of times more use than the controversial Mono Basin streams ever had or ever would. Different amounts of Mono diversion might mean different amounts of water in the two reservoirs.

Then there was the upper Owens River, the wandering stream that has served since 1941 as a natural conduit for Mono export water between East Portal and Crowley Lake. The river had been a trout stream of national note in the 1930s. After the Mono water poured into it, the stream adjusted to the larger and much more variable flow by widening and straightening its course. As long as flows remained artificially high, fishing remained excellent. But if Mono export were permanently decreased, it seemed likely that the fishing in the upper Owens would suffer, at least for a time.

The Audubon Society and the Mono Lake Committee were sympathetic to these "downstream issues" but wanted them kept out of the EIR. So did the Forest Service. Again, though, the wider view was chosen.

What followed was a vast, compound research project that stitched together everything already learned about the lake and added a great deal more besides. Most of the veterans of Mono Lake studies launched into another round.

David Herbst took another look at the effects of salinity on alkali flies, using what he called "microcosm studies." He set up twenty 130-gallon tanks containing sediments, algae, flies, and lakewater of different concentrations and watched them for numerous fly generations. Besides confirming that high salinities were harmful, Herbst's microcosms showed that the fly population responded to very low salinities with an increase in vigor.

Margaret Rubega studied red-necked phalaropes and made an accidental discovery. Trying to maintain captive birds in the lab on a diet of brine shrimp (convenient for the staff) she found that the animals wouldn't touch *Artemia monica* unless they were near starvation. (She changed the food.) Her work in the lab and on the lake confirmed that this phalarope depends on the alkali fly absolutely—and suggested that present fly crops in the lake were already less than optimal for this bird.

Scott Stine produced no fewer than five special reports, discussing historic vegetation along the streams; wetlands fringing the lake; the distribution of pumice blocks and other hard substrates important to the alkali fly; and the effects of different lake levels on tufa displays and on the configuration of the islands.

This being the 1990s, computer models were made of several aspects of the case. Herbst and others designed one for flies; Gayle Dana, John Melack, and Bob Jellison did one for shrimp. There were models to predict dust storms, models for water and energy supply and demand, and very important hydrologic models called LAAMP and LAASM (Los Angeles Aqueduct Monthly Program and Los Angeles Aqueduct Simulation Model). Here Peter Vorster was heavily involved.

On the low-tech side, the Mono Lake Committee took the lead in scaring up information about the pre-diversion days. Ilene Mandelbaum and others interviewed old-timers, combed ragged archives, and put out a call for historic photographs. One valuable collection turned up scattered around an abandoned house in Chatsworth, California. The committee secured access to hundreds of photos, postcards, and films made in the 1920s by local photographer Burton Frasher: early images of gulls on Negit, crater lakes on Paoha, tourists on excursion boats, bathing beauty contests, speedboat races, and Paiute basketmakers.

And it all poured into the office of Jones & Stokes in Sacramento, a river of paper that at times could probably have been measured, like Mono Basin streamflows, in cubic feet per second.

After the 1989 court decision known as CalTrout I, the State Water Resources Control Board was expected to modify Los Angeles's water diversion licenses to guarantee adequate streamflows in the Mono Basin creeks. But the board was now settling in to consider all the Mono Basin issues together and at leisure. It proposed to add streamflow requirements to the licenses at the end of this multi-year process, not at the beginning. In the meantime, the board alleged, it had no authority to impose higher interim flows. The Department of Water and Power, understandably, agreed, arguing that although its diversions were officially stamped unlawful, any further interference with them must await due process. In July of 1989, Sacramento Superior Court Judge Cecily Bond agreed to the delay.

But Audubon and CalTrout weren't willing to wait to cash in their chips. Back they went to the Third District Court of Appeal. On February 23, 1990, the appellate court, angered at the stalling, gave them what they asked. It jerked the case out of Judge Bond's hands and handed it to Judge Finney for final action. Via Finney, it directed the water board to add the following specific language to the department's diversion licenses: "The licensee shall release sufficient water into the streams from its dams to reestablish and maintain the fisheries which existed in them prior to its diversion of water." This provision applied by implication not only to Rush and Lee Vining creeks but to Parker and Walker creeks as well.

This was remarkable language. For this time the court did not speak of maintaining some fish in the streams; it did not speak of maintaining fish "in good condition," the language of the Fish and Game Code. Rather, it required *the restoration of the fish resource that had been there in 1940.*

Given the punishment the streams had taken since that year, such a restoration might well require more than water. Water and Power lawyers had unwisely called this fact to the judges' attention; in opposing stream releases for Parker and Walker creeks, they had stated that the degraded channels "may or may not be capable, in their present condition, to [*sic*] sustain any fish life at all." In that case, the judges snapped, it was up to the department to make repairs. The principle applied to all the creeks: if recovering the historic fishery meant doing restoration work on the streams themselves, so be it.

Implementation was now in Judge Finney's hands. He transmitted the appeal court's instructions to the water board, which added the specified language to the city's permits. In June of 1990, after lengthy hearings, Finney also set flow rules specifying the minimum amount of water to be released down each creek in each month of the year. His schedule approximately doubled the existing flow in Rush Creek and increased the puny allotment for Lee Vining Creek sevenfold. The authoritative fish-flow studies—the Rush Creek ones ordered by Judge Otis back in 1986, and others begun on its own initiative by the Department of Fish and Game—were still incomplete, so Finney's numbers were interim rules only. By themselves, these flows would guarantee about 60,000 acre-feet of water per year for Mono Lake, enough to maintain the lake surface in a range between 6,368 and 6,375 feet.

Finney also instructed the Los Angeles Department of Water and Power, the Mono Lake Committee, the Audubon Society, CalTrout, and the Department of Fish and Game to sit down together and begin planning for stream restoration, beginning with Parker and Walker creeks.

When water and fish reappeared in Rush Creek, CalTrout and the Mono Lake Committee had emphasized how good the renewed fish habitat was. The committee newsletter once referred to lower Rush Creek as "a paradise for trout and anglers." The message seemed to be: just provide the right amount of water, and everything else will be fine.

But everything else was not fine. In fact, Rush Creek and Lee Vining Creek were in terrible shape. Decades of too little water, punctuated by occasional doses of far too much, had turned them into wrecks of the streams old-timers remembered.

Biologist Elden Vestal could testify to that. It was Vestal who, back in 1941, had first protested the shutting off of flows. Not long after *Dahlgren* began, the lawyers had sought him out. In September of 1986 Vestal had visited Rush Creek. "I wasn't prepared," he says, "for what I found. In all my years as a fisheries biologist I've never seen a scene that was so devastating. The terrible incision, the frightful effects of flooding, erosion. And I thought . . . it took thousands of years to build this habitat but just a short time in the life of man to destroy all this. I was a little choked."

When stream restoration was ordered, it suddenly became vital to determine what the pre-diversion conditions had been. The Department of Water and Power argued that no one could really say what the streams had been like before 1941. The recollections of old-timers, who were, after all, not trained observers, didn't count. Neither did the abundant but indirect evidence readable in the land.

It was then that Elden Vestal became the star witness. In depositions and testimony he spelled out what he knew of the creeks, and of Rush Creek in particular. Far from relying on memory alone, he had kept a garageful of detailed, week-by-week reports. (He apologized for having destroyed his *daily* records.) "It's all there in my notes," Vestal said. Recalling the scenes he remembered, he added, "Perhaps it will be like that again."

PARKER AND WALKER CREEKS

"Perhaps it will be like that again." The possibility was tested first at Parker and Walker creeks, the two small streams that come down from the mountains north of Rush Creek and join it on the lakeward side of U.S. 395. In their natural state these streams meandered down a vast, sloping meadow in narrow, sod-bound channels. When flows were high, they spilled over into parallel distributaries. (That water, sinking into the ground,

Ilene Mandelbaum joined the Mono Lake Committee staff in 1984, the year the court fight over Rush Creek started; the streams have been at the center of her job ever since. From 1990 to 1994 she served on the contentious Restoration Technical Committee, the group in charge of stream repairs. (Photo by Gerda S. Mathan)

may have helped to feed the springs along the Rush Creek canyon wall below.) After white settlement, the meadow became a sheep pasture, the chief asset of the Cain Ranch. Irrigators spread water across the grass; after diversion began, Los Angeles, new owner of the ranch, continued to let some irrigation water pass the upstream diversion points. But the creeks, as such, disappeared.

Now it was time to bring them back. Noted restoration consultant Scott English was chosen to do the work; Audubon brought in a second consultant, Woody Trihey, who had helped them before Judge Finney; Peter Vorster and Scott Stine completed the initial team.

That summer the crews excavated the creeks, lifting off the turf that had formed in the dry decades. Ilene Mandelbaum of the Mono Lake Committee recalls the next step: "In places where the original stream channel was crisscrossed by a confusing network of man-made ditches, the work resembled an archeological dig. . . . Backhoe operators, guided by engineers, would dig down and carefully lift out large, intact chunks of sod. . . . Sure enough, underneath the old sod we would find the spawning gravel of the old stream bed."

Below Highway 395 on Parker Creek was another problem, the "Parker Plug." During the dry decades the California Department of Transportation had stored coarse construction gravel (cobble) on the site, shoving huge piles into the abandoned streambed. Now CalTrans crews worked for several weeks to remove some of this cobble and re-establish a channel.

The first water finds its way down the restored bed of Parker Creek. (Photo by Ilene Mandelbaum, courtesy Mono Lake Committee)

On October 9, 1990, water was turned back into Parker Creek. The occasion was something of a festival. Children ran downstream beside the leading edge of the water. Young members of the Los Angeles Conservation Corps, who had helped with the construction, watched proudly. And Judge Finney looked on with visible satisfaction.

Ten days later Walker Creek was rewatered. Along both creeks, fences were built to keep livestock out. In the following spring, high flows ordered by the court would flush out additional silt and push the recovery process along. And in a year or two, people returning to Parker and Walker creeks would stand amazed. The scars of construction quickly vanished in the verdant landscape. To an untrained eye the streams looked as though they had never been altered: deep slots walled with turf, curving and doubling back on themselves, filled with bright water, colored stones, and, to the sharp eye, fish.

But Parker and Walker creeks were the easy cases. Here, a true, simple restoration—a putting back—was almost possible. The bigger creeks would be far bigger challenges.

On November 2, 1990, the parties agreed to undertake the restoration of Rush and Lee Vining creeks. An unwieldy two-level structure was built to manage the work. In overall charge was a misnamed Restoration Technical Committee—by nature, rather, a political body—with one seat each for the L.A. Department of Water and Power, the Mono Lake Committee, the Audubon Society, CalTrout, and the Department of Fish and Game. The Restoration Technical Committee (RTC) was to act only with unanimity; given even one dissent on any issue, that matter would be bucked up to Judge Finney. The actual work would be planned and performed by a planning team led by Woody Trihey. Trihey's expanded role came at the suggestion of the Department of Water and Power: despite his earlier connection with Audubon, Water and Power liked what it saw as his commonsensical, economical "fix-it" approach. Trihey was to take direction from the RTC but to submit his bills to the department.

If it sounds like a recipe for gridlock, it was.

Meanwhile, back in Los Angeles, there was hope that the hostilities might be brought to an end before the legal process had run its course.

Early in 1990, Los Angeles Mayor Tom Bradley appointed two new members to the Board of Water and Power Commissioners. The first was Mike Gage, a former Northern California assemblyman, a whitewater rafter and guide who had recently served as one of Bradley's two deputy mayors. The second appointee was well-known southern California environmental activist Dorothy Green; she had founded the organization Heal the Bay to attack pollution from sewage outfalls and knew water issues from the other end of the pipe, so to speak. Introducing the new members, the *Mono Lake Newsletter* referred to them as "Dorothy" and "Mike."

In July, when the mayor named environmental attorney Mary Nichols to the board, the new outlook seemed to have a majority. The staff was changing to match. General Manager and Chief Engineer Norman Nichols bailed out upon the arrival of Mary Nichols (no kin by blood or attitude); water chief Duane Georgeson, the department's voice on Mono Lake for a decade, had already moved over to the Metropolitan Water District.

Mayor Bradley was trying, belatedly, to get control of a branch of government that had become an ever-increasing embarrassment to his administration. The constant bad news from the Mono Lake legal front was only one cause of the embarrassment, but it was a substantial one.

In September 1990, when the yearly cavalcade of Mono-bound bicyclists dipped their vials into the reflecting pool in front of the Water and Power building in Los Angeles, Mike Gage, now board president, was there to send them off. That year's bicycle marathon was billed as a "victory ride."

But it was too early for celebration—or perhaps it was too late. Behind the scenes, relations between the Mono Lake Committee and the new Water and Power commissioners had already begun to sour.

At this time, LeRoy Graymer's Mono Lake Group was trying to put together a package of federal legislation to help resolve the Mono issue, something similar to Isenberg's AB 444 on the state level. California Senator Wilson was interested in carrying such a bill, but this time the parties could not agree on its contents.

Meanwhile, the Department of Water and Power was mounting a sustained challenge to Judge Finney's lake-level injunction blocking diversion until the lake surface climbed well above 6,377 feet. Finney proposed to extend the injunction until the water board had ruled. Opposing this extension, the department requested an elaborate trial.

When Gage arrived in 1990, it appeared that this exercise might be avoided. It seemed that the Board of Water and Power Commissioners would agree to keep the lake above 6,377 feet on its own initiative, and in return the Mono Lake Committee would agree to let the formal injunction lapse. But the compromise foundered on misunderstandings, and the legal show went on.

TRIAL RUN: THE PRELIMINARY INJUNCTION HEARINGS

In the overall legal scheme of things, the hearings before Judge Finney in the summer of 1990 were actually fairly small potatoes. What was at stake, technically, was merely the extension of an existing preliminary injunction. But in truth the hearings were a major test of strength (and fund-raising ability), and a landmark on the march toward a decision.

For one thing, the cast of characters changed. Up to this point, Audubon had opposed Los Angeles alone, or in somewhat unstable coalition with CalTrout. Now others began to move. The U.S. Forest Service asked to join the case as an amicus curiae, "friend of the court," in support of the 6,377-foot lake minimum (also called for in its Scenic Area management plan). Water and Power hotly objected, but Judge Finney allowed the Forest Service in.

Equally significant was the entry of the California State Lands Commission. This little-known board manages, among other miscellaneous properties, such submerged lands as the bed of Mono Lake. In the early 1980s, the commission had fought the federal government for control of land exposed by lake decline and had lost the bulk of the territory it claimed. Now it stood to lose additional acreage whenever the lake sank; it was unclear whether or not it would regain land when the lake rose. Lieutenant Governor Leo McCarthy, a member of the commission, tipped the balance for intervention in the present case. In this action, as in the earlier turf battle, the commission relied heavily on the findings of Scott Stine.

Suddenly Los Angeles found itself facing, not one or two opponents, but a government-environmentalist phalanx.

What followed was the longest, most expensive courtroom operation since the beginning of the struggle ten years earlier. There were dozens of witnesses, weeks of testimony, cartloads of exhibits. For the first time, actual evidence about the state of the lake was presented in court and subjected to cross-examination. The gull doctors testified, and disagreed in detail. Hydrologists argued about how far the lake might fall and about the state of the city's water supply. Other experts held forth on the needs of flies and shrimp, on recreation, on scenery. The dust problem was the subject of extensive debate that turned on highly technical points about particle size, arsenic levels, and the weather. In pushing to maintain the lake above 6,377 feet, Audubon relied heavily on the findings of the CORI report *The Future of Mono Lake* and on the National Forest Scenic Area Plan. Water and Power cited recent history to argue that letting the lake drop below 6,377 feet would do no lasting harm.

On April 17, 1991, Judge Finney made his decision: the lake-level injunction stood. In July, Judge Finney refused a request from the Department of Water and Power to reopen the matter yet again and ordered them to pay the latest batch of legal costs. According to the house organ *Intake*, the department's investment in the fight, since 1979, was now up to $12 million for outside lawyers and consultants alone.

Meanwhile, the AB 444 negotiations were floundering. Martha Davis and Mike Gage were the principals. It cannot be clear to any outsider what went on between them. What is certain is that they could not agree and that each came to regard the other as an impossible negotiation partner.

As a state legislator in the 1970s, Gage had felt a lot of sympathy for the Mono Lake Committee's opening position: "6,378′ or Fight." In 1990 he still liked that position. He

NEGOTIATIONS
BREAK DOWN

believed that the lake should be maintained at levels high enough to protect Negit Island, even in drought—but not a foot higher. This stance, it should be noted, was considerably more generous than that held by department *staff*.

If Mike Gage's views hadn't changed in fifteen years, the Mono Lake Committee's certainly had. Ever since the days of the Interagency Task Force, the committee had been calling for a lake level of 6,388 feet; with each Los Angeles court defeat, this position was looking another notch less extreme.

The usual confusions of definition were at work here, of course. Gage's suggested lake level (officially 6,377 feet) was a floor; he proposed to limit diversions so that the lake would never sink below that level. The committee's 6,388 feet was the center of a range. The committee's plan would generally keep the lake six to eight feet higher than the one offered by Gage.

In an attempt to move matters along, the committee shifted its position—slightly. It called for a Mono Lake management level of 6,386 rather than 6,388 feet, combined with continued streamflows not less than those established by Judge Finney. With some water flowing into the lake every year, a smaller buffer was now required against drought.

The committee's offer was part of a new package called the Six Point Plan. Like the committee's old Wet Year/Dry Year Plan, this scheme contained some provisions meant to appeal to Los Angeles. Rather than halting diversions outright until the lake reached 6,386 feet, the plan would allow the city to divert 15,000 acre-feet a year during a transition period; after 6,386 feet was reached, it would allow some extra diversion during droughts, even if this caused the lake to sink again.

Gage made it clear that, to interest him, the committee would have to come down a good deal further.

Would a little more flexibility on both sides have produced a lake-level agreement? Perhaps. But Mono advocates, looking back, don't see a near miss in the events of 1990–91; they see a narrow escape. No possible agreement could have matched what was later gained for the lake. For Water and Power, on the other hand, *any* agreement—even simple acceptance of the Six Point Plan—would have been advantageous. The tide was running. Nobody knew with what force.

Gage next proposed setting the lake-level question aside but seeking state money for projects "which, individually, may not provide a permanent solution but would contribute toward a permanent protection for the Mono Lake ecosystem." Davis and the committee found this language uselessly vague. In the spring of 1991, the dispute hit the press and the honeymoon was officially over.

Discussions resumed early in 1992, driven by a political fact of life: the $60 million pot established by AB 444 would not be around forever. The state was heading into a streak of bad budget years, each worse than the last, and the unused Environmental Water Fund of AB 444 was a tempting target. Already a couple of million had been diverted to other purposes, and a bigger bite was looming.

The initiative in 1992 came from Mayor Bradley's office and from Water and Power commissioners Mary Nichols and Dorothy Green. Nichols thought she saw a way around the lake-level impasse. Why not leave that question open, as Gage had suggested, but add a guarantee that Gage had not suggested: a promise to credit any new water developed with state money to a sort of Mono Lake account? In other words, for each acre-foot of annual supply produced with the help of AB 444, the department would give up all claim to an acre-foot of water from the Mono Basin. In addition, Nichols offered a moratorium on diversions, to run until the final resolution of the case. Unlike Judge Finney's preliminary injunction, this freeze would remain in force no matter how high the lake might climb in the interim.

Draft agreement in hand, the negotiators went back to their respective boards. The Mono Lake Committee board, impressed by the moratorium offer, said yes; the Los Angeles Board of Water and Power Commissioners, on June 2, 1992, refused to back the moratorium. After an acrimonious follow-up meeting, negotiations ceased once again. Soon after, the legislature shifted another $12 million of AB 444 money to other purposes.

FEDERAL HELP AND THE RISE OF RECLAMATION

Though Water and Power and the Mono Lake Committee hadn't managed to join forces in seeking federal help to replace Mono water, nothing prevented the committee from lobbying in that direction on its own. In the early 1990s, California Congressman George Miller and New Jersey Senator Bill Bradley were putting together a congressional coalition to reform the operation of various federal water projects (while launching several new ones). Their major and most controversial reform target was the Central Valley Project in California. But when the Reclamation Projects Authorization and Adjustment Act (HR 429) finally passed in September 1992, it included a federal counterpart to California's AB 444. The new law authorized the U.S. Bureau of Reclamation to pay one-quarter of the cost of some water recycling projects in southern California, which were "expected to offset water diversions from the environmentally sensitive Mono Lake Basin." The bill was tailored for two applicants: the Department of Water and Power, and the West Basin Municipal Water District, which serves eighteen cities in the South Bay region of Los Angeles County.

This sudden zeroing-in on reclamation as a way of stretching the water supply reflects a change of thinking. Over the years, various sources had been looked to as substitutes for eastern Sierra water. Water and Power, of course, had never ceased eyeing the Sacramento/San Joaquin Delta, making scary sucking sounds (take away Mono, and here we come!). Its critics sought answers that would harm neither the delta nor any other source region. Conservation—which might better be called simply efficiency— was always part of the formula. In the late 1980s, attention turned to a form of water marketing in which Los Angeles would pay for conservation measures in certain farm districts and would receive the water the farmers could then spare. During the 1991 negotiations, a water market scheme had again been the talking point. It involved retiring from agriculture some lands in the Central Valley where the soil is tainted with toxic selenium—lands that should not, in fact, be farmed—and shifting that irrigation water to the southern city.

By 1992, however, attention had turned back to a more traditional idea whose hour seemed at last to have come. Over a period of years, the metropolitan region had been under increasing pressure to improve sewage treatment and reduce pollution of the nearby ocean; the effluent local plants produced was now approaching potable quality. Plans for wider use of this reclaimed water were maturing, both within the city limits of Los Angeles and, much more rapidly, in jurisdictions outside it. Though some of these plans would go ahead regardless, the state and federal subventions of AB 444 and HR 429 could be of critical help in the costly startup phase.

One local leader was the West Basin Municipal Water District. West Basin was about to begin building a major reclamation plant in El Segundo to produce 100,000 acre-feet of water a year, destined mainly for injection into the ground to form a barrier against encroaching seawater. That would be 100,000 acre-feet the district would no longer need to buy from the Metropolitan Water District, 100,000 acre-feet that would be available for someone else, perhaps for Los Angeles proper. In 1991, Martha Davis and district manager Rich Atwater got together to seek money for West Basin in the pending federal water bill.

Within Los Angeles, the comparable venture was the East San Fernando Valley Project. In that case, the city already had the reclaimed water. What it needed was the pipes to distribute it. Part of the supply would be used for irrigation and other nonpotable purposes; most of it would be allowed to percolate into groundwater basins, adding indirectly to the supply of drinking water. Total output was estimated at 35,000 acre-feet or more. If the Department of Water and Power could ever get together with the Mono Lake Committee on an application for AB 444 money from the state, East Valley would be the project to benefit; the federal bill was written to benefit it as well. Water and Power was slow to apply, but on a 1993 lobbying trip Davis took the liberty of soliciting a small grant for East Valley. It came through, and much more was to come.

And so it was that the Mono Lake campaign led to the state and federal funding of water reclamation projects on a scale never before seen in California or, indeed, anywhere in the United States.

THE OTHER MONO LAKE COMMITTEE

By this time the Mono Lake Committee had made itself a presence in local and statewide water policy debates that went well beyond its primary cause. You might say there was a second Mono Lake Committee: a low-budget think tank and advocate concerned above all with the water welfare of—Los Angeles.

That role came to public attention in 1988, when a lengthy drought was tightening its hold. Dissatisfied with what it considered a perfunctory official water conservation campaign, the committee launched its own, livelier ads. For that purpose it joined forces with the anti-pollution group Heal the Bay. "What's the connection between Mono Lake and Santa Monica Bay?" the public service spots asked. "Give up? You are! L.A. takes water from Mono Lake, and pours pollution into Santa Monica Bay. Every drop you save can help the lake, and the bay, and save a bundle on your water bills."

Conservation efforts sputtered along in Los Angeles until 1990, when a mandatory rationing program produced a larger-than-expected drop in water usage. At that point an important, built-in drawback of successful water conservation became apparent. Because the fixed costs of running the system are spread over fewer gallons, there arises what seems a great injustice: consumers who cut their water use wind up paying more for each gallon they use. In the summer of 1991, per capita use actually sank 30 percent, and Water and Power, in the manner of water utilities everywhere, proposed a double-digit rate increase. The city council granted only a small increase, but even that caused great consumer anger.

In reaction, Mayor Bradley appointed a Blue Ribbon Committee to restudy water rates from scratch. Mono Lake Committee Associate Director Betsy Reifsnider took extensive part. In February 1993, following Blue Ribbon advice, the city adopted a two-bracket rate structure: users of small or moderate amounts of water would pay rather less per gallon than before and avoid the "conservation penalty"; heavy users would pay a markedly higher amount that reflected the cost of developing new supplies.

Reifsnider served also on a statewide Urban Water Conservation Council, a consortium of governments and conservation groups; in 1991, the council agreed on a list of modest water-saving measures called the Best Management Practices. The most significant "practice" was the subsidized installation of ultra-low-flush toilets. Together, the "practices" were projected to save southern Californians 700,000 acre-feet of water every year.

In July of 1992, after a wet winter, water rationing ended in Los Angeles. What happened then was unexpected and highly significant: people kept right on conserving. The individual "conservation effort," according to the computations of the Department of Water and Power, continued in the range of 15 to 25 percent. Total water use remained well below the peak levels reached in the 1980s. Conservation, once regarded as a short-term sacrifice, seemed on its way to becoming the norm. It was built into the city physically, in such forms as newfangled toilets, and built into citizen habits as well.

Up in Lee Vining, the stream restoration work begun so auspiciously was bogging down.

It wasn't too bad in 1991. The new Restoration Technical Committee got started with one important, obvious, but not uncontroversial step: the exclusion of grazing sheep

Stream restoration expert Woody Trihey up to his knees in Lee Vining Creek. (Photo by Gerda S. Mathan)

from the streambanks. Though the riparian corridors had withstood quite a bit of live-stock use before 1940 without widespread ill effects, they were far more fragile now; trampling by stock was hindering the regrowth of streambank vegetation. When attempts to control the animals failed, Water and Power agreed to lock them out entirely.

In 1992, after some trial runs on less damaged reaches of the streams, the team turned to the first of the really hard cases: Lee Vining Creek below U.S. 395 and the town of Lee Vining.

Lower Lee Vining Creek, we recall, dried up in the 1940s and lost most of its riparian forest to drought and fire. In the late 1960s, floods tore through, reaming out a simplified channel. The torrents also stripped off thousands of tons of fine sediment and carried it into the lake, leaving large areas of sterile cobble. The heavy-runoff years of the 1980s intensified the damage.

Now, the stream ran shallow, straight, and fast. There were few places for fish to escape the current that tended to sweep them into the lake, or for small fish to hide from predatory larger ones. There was little spawning gravel. There was almost no shade.

Tramping up and down this problematic landscape, the planning team saw several things to be done. They proposed to breach cobblebars and nudge some of the streamwater into certain subsidiary channels, now dry, that had retained their original narrow, deep form. With a little more hesitation, they proposed to reshape the ditchlike main channel itself by digging a series of pools and strategically placing some logs and stumps from the burned forest. Finally, they proposed to speed up the natural recovery of streambank vegetation by planting cottonwoods, willows, aspens, and Jeffrey pines.

These measures promised to be expensive, and in 1992 Water and Power began to balk. Challenged to make the case for their plan, Woody Trihey and company produced more studies, more documentation, at more expense. As disagreements multiplied in the Restoration Technical Committee, Judge Finney ordered transcripts kept to establish what had and had not been said, and lawyers for all sides began to hover, usually silent, in the background.

By mid-1992 the department had found another theme, besides expense, for its objections. It began to argue that most of this work was in fact a bad idea, that the best restoration was restoration unaided by human hands. The streams should be allowed to recover on their own. Intervention would only do harm.

Recovery. Restoration. In what might be called the ecosystem-repair business, these are terms with specific and differing meanings.

Recovery is something that just happens. The moment a landscape or natural system ceases to be disturbed, it starts repairing itself through the natural succession of plants. A place undergoing recovery will "green up," look better and better, more and more "natural," with time. Whether it will come to resemble what it was before it was disturbed depends on how large the disturbance was and on how much time has elapsed since then.

Restoration is something else. It means the return to a particular desired condition—in this case, something comparable to what was there in 1940. It implies human assistance. (Some object to the very idea, on the grounds that we can't know enough to do it right and had better not even try.)

The Los Angeles Conservation Corps came north to work on Lee Vining Creek. (Photo by Jane Dove Juneau for Mammoth Times*)*

With water back in the Mono Basin streams and cattle and sheep excluded from their banks, recovery, in the form of a lush band of waterside growth, was evident in many places. But was this automatic rebound sufficient to produce, in a reasonable time, something like the values present in the streams in 1940?

The department's consultants said yes. When the saplings now lining parts of the streambank became large trees and began to topple into the stream, pools would form behind the logs; the banks would narrow and steepen; water would presently find its own way back to the abandoned channels or would find new ones; and fish habitat (the legal object of this exercise) would be remade.

Trihey and most of his advisers were more pessimistic. Scott Stine compared the creeks to a patient with a badly broken leg: the bones will undoubtedly knit together, but if they are not set properly the victim may not walk again.

If no two of the doctors on the case prescribed exactly the same treatment, the consensus was for intervention—in some degree.

Water and Power countered that restoration work was actually holding back the natural recovery process. It complained, for instance, that rock dredged from the creek produced new cobblebars, slow to revegetate, and that heavy equipment crushed young plants. In a rather comical reversal of roles, the city now took a stance of exquisite sensitivity to the ecosystem.

The court verdicts that rewatered the Mono Basin creeks were soon guiding decisions on other streams as well. The first echoes were heard in the eastern Sierra, in the region covered by Fish and Game Code Section 5946.

Just north of Mono lies another spectacular lowland, the Bridgeport Valley, with a vast, vivid meadow spread across its floor. The East Walker River flows across this expanse, through the town of Bridgeport and on out into Nevada. Below the town is a reservoir run by the Walker River Irrigation District. In the dry late-summer of 1988, in order to send the last available drop to downstream ranches the district opened the gates of its dam wide. With the gush of water came a gush of silt; then the stream dried up completely. Aquatic life and habitat were destroyed for miles. This certainly was not maintaining "in good condition" the fish below a dam. Observers from California Trout raised the alarm.

Stan Eller, the official who had once warned Water and Power not to turn off Rush Creek, was now district attorney in Mono County. Edward Forstenzer, who had carried Dahlgren v. Los Angeles *in the early days, was now justice court judge there. Eller took the irrigation district to Forstenzer's court. After a jury found the district guilty of violating the Fish and Game Code, Forstenzer ordered it to provide specified flows. Later, the water board wrote new conditions for the district's*

diversion license, and the Department of Fish and Game went after the district in a civil suit that yielded a restoration program and $250,000 cash for Fish and Game. Once more a diverter had discovered that a water right does not confer absolute ownership of water.

The next outbreak of the new doctrine occurred to the south of the Mono Basin, along the Los Angeles Aqueduct line. On March 5, 1991, on the rim of the Owens Gorge, 1,200 feet of Water and Power's penstock ruptured. Water poured onto the lava tableland and would have made its way into the desiccated gorge below. But the department, not wanting a repeat of the Rush Creek situation, steered the flow the other way, out into the sagebrush. That, however, put them in the position of wasting water, which is forbidden by the state constitution. On April 11, Mono County District Attorney Stan Eller filed a suit in Superior Court to demand that the runaway water be turned into the gorge and that a flow be maintained there from then on.

This time, before the trial began, a settlement was reached. On June 21 a crowd of dignitaries watched water spill from the Upper Gorge Power Plant into a stretch of the gorge that had been dry since 1953. Since the dry streambed could not handle much flow until vegetation came back, the initial releases were small. More was to follow.

The Precedent Spreads

Unresolved paradox: if nature could be counted on to repair the catastrophic damage done to the streambed by decades of desiccation, erosion, and heavy grazing, why could she not be trusted to heal any scratches made by Woody Trihey and Scott English in a few passes with a backhoe?

Judge Finney did not go in much for these philosophical doubts. Though he accepted some of the department's proposed changes of plan, he forced most of the Lee Vining Creek work to proceed. Then, when the promised department work crews showed up, they stayed only a few hours a day. "That's not going to cut it," Finney warned. Finally, in the late summer of 1992, after twenty-two days in court, the bulk of the work was done.

Lower Rush Creek, with its great gash of incision and its dried-up springs, was next on the agenda. Plainly the Restoration Technical Committee as originally designed was not equipped to deal with it. In June of 1993 Judge Finney reorganized the group, expanding it to include three scientists affiliated with none of the parties. He also ended the requirement of unanimity: it would now take three votes of eight, not one of five, to block a majority decision.

The new format looked like an improvement, but it might prove short-lived. For Finney's Restoration Technical Committee, in either version, was an interim body only, a stopgap. The real word on restoration, both its ends and its means, was expected, in due course, from the State Water Resources Control Board.

DUSTY ROADS
Elsewhere, wheels had been turning, ever so slowly, on the dust issue.

The air pollution exemption the Los Angeles Department of Water and Power won in Sacramento in 1983 did not bind the federal government. In 1987, the Environmental Protection Agency (EPA) set a national standard for "fugitive dust," focusing on those particles, 10 micrometers across or smaller, that pass most readily into the lungs. (Pollen grains, by contrast, are 20 to 100 microns.) Like the more general Total Suspended Particulates standard heretofore used by the state, the new PM-10 standard was surpassed in the Mono Basin several days a year. Nonetheless, EPA proposed to label the Mono Basin a "clean air district." In June of 1988, Congressman Richard Lehman prevailed on the agency to give the area instead "unclassified" status. This meant that monitoring would continue and that correction of some sort would eventually be required.

Here the Audubon side almost tripped over its own feet. For years its lawyers had actually argued that the federal Clean Air Act did *not* apply to Mono Lake dust. Why? Because if the act did cover the case, Audubon couldn't sue about dust under the general doctrine of interstate nuisance; instead, the Clean Air Act procedures would take over. And if it couldn't sue under nuisance, it would lose its foothold in the court of its favored jurist, Federal District Judge Lawrence Karlton.

Congressman Richard Lehman pushed legislation to create the Mono Basin National Forest Scenic Area and later made sure that Mono dust was covered by federal air pollution laws. (Photo courtesy Mono Lake Committee)

Then, in October of 1988, the federal Ninth Circuit Court of Appeals dismissed the nuisance suit. But the justices also took occasion to repeat and endorse the old Audubon contention that the Clean Air Act did not apply. In short, the court disclaimed any federal role at all in confronting the problem of alkali dust.

The Morrison & Foerster legal team had other matters on its mind and would have let this language, potentially quite damaging, pass. However, a law professor in Arizona, one Joseph Feller, saw the draft ruling and took alarm at this undermining of federal pollution-control powers. A rare thing happened: Feller wrote a letter to the circuit court stating his disagreement, and the judges revised their decision to remove the prejudicial language.

Congress, meanwhile, was rewriting that Clean Air Act. The Environmental Protection Agency proposed language exempting natural sources from the controls. Eastern Sierra interests wanted it established that Owens and Mono dust storms were not "natural." They got the language they sought—not, to be sure, in the final law itself, but in the reports of the relevant committees, the next best thing. The House Committee on Energy and Commerce, for instance, remarked, "The term anthropogenic source includes sources that are indirectly created by human activity as well as those that are the direct result of such activity. An example of such a source [is] the dust storms that are generated from dry lake beds at Owens and Mono Lakes in California." The lingering question—were the storms just "natural"?—was officially resolved.

The Great Basin Unified Air Pollution Control District, meanwhile, was monitoring away. Finally it felt sure it had enough data to prove the violations beyond cavil, and it so informed the California Air Resources Board. In August 1991, the Air Resources Board asked the EPA to move the basin from its "unclassified" list to the status of "moderate nonattainment."

Once such a declaration of nonattainment becomes official the state must take corrective steps, and on a very firm schedule. If progress is insufficient in five years, the violation is reclassified from "moderate" to "serious" and pressure increases. If the problem still exists in fifteen years, EPA can step in and impose a solution of its own.

The Department of Water and Power naturally sought to delay the onset of this timetable as long as possible. But by the end of 1992 it was clear that the enforcement machinery would soon be in motion. What enforcement might mean in terms of a required lake level was still an open question.

10

THE CLOCK TURNED BACK

---

*Quite long while this talk mixed up—only
today decide it.*

Paiute leader on the resolution of a tribal
dispute, 1901, reported by W. A. Chalfant in
The Story of Inyo

LATE IN MAY OF 1993, after 43,000 hours of preparation, the document everyone
had been waiting for landed with a thump on desks up and down the state of California.
Its full title was *Draft Environmental Impact Report for the Review of the Mono Basin
Water Rights of the City of Los Angeles* (DEIR). Its three volumes and twenty-eight auxiliary reports weighed in at twenty-six pounds. It had cost over three million dollars of
Water and Power's money to prepare. And its contents, on several points, were a mighty
surprise.

Analyzing a range of lake-level alternatives, the DEIR found the best one to be what
it called 6,383.5 feet. Under this option the lake surface would actually fluctuate between
6,378 and 6,389 feet, depending on weather, touching the lower level only during extreme drought. Los Angeles's water exports would be cut to approximately half of the
long-term average, to a mean rate of 44,000 acre-feet a year. This alternative closely
matched what the Forest Service had recommended in its Scenic Area Plan. Allowing
for the usual complexities, it was also quite close to the position of the Mono Lake
Committee.

This 6,383.5-foot alternative was called "environmentally superior" based on a comparison with the situation in 1989. But the staff had also gauged the choices against
another baseline: the lake as it was in 1940. Against this background, they concluded,
the lake level that appeared superior was half a dozen feet higher: 6,390 feet. Under this
alternative, the lake surface would rise as high as 6,395 feet and, in extreme drought,

sink only as low as 6,383 feet. Water exports would be reduced to some 30,000 acre-feet a year.

Why did the choice favored depend on the year chosen for comparison? Chiefly because of the tufa displays exposed since the lake began to fall. If the pre-diversion lake is the basis of comparison, these groves don't count; if the lowered lake is taken as the basis, they count a great deal. The authors of the report concluded that the 6,383.5-foot plan would preserve these newly revealed towers and sand tufa displays; higher levels would topple, erode, or submerge them.

But the 6,390-foot alternative had a powerful advantage of its own. According to the air quality modelers at Jones & Stokes, only a 6,390-foot lake would submerge enough of the alkali rim to put an effective end to dust storms. This was a stunning development. Until now, it had been thought that a level as low as 6,380 feet might suffice.

In other respects the two alternatives seemed about equally attractive. Either would protect Negit Island and the Negit islets (but not the Paoha islets, which would be lost to wave erosion). Under the 6,383.5-foot plan, many pumice boulders and other hard substrates would be just shallowly submerged, providing optimum habitat for alkali fly larvae and pupae; this level, the report concluded, was best for *Ephydra hians*. But the lower salinities under the 6,390-foot plan would be better for *Artemia monica*, the unique local brine shrimp species. An attempt to gauge public preferences found the two options rather evenly matched.

The DEIR disposed of several traditional objections to a high lake level. For example, the National Academy of Sciences team had worried that a high lake, by flooding the alkali ring, might destroy nesting habitat for the snowy plover, but later research had shown that the plover would find plenty of nesting spots almost regardless of lake level.

There had also been worries about the other attractions along the path of Mono water: Grant Lake, the upper Owens River, Crowley Lake, and more distant reaches of the Owens. Would a reduced input of Mono water degrade these places? The DEIR found these effects likely to be minor, easily offset by careful management. As for the Owens Valley, the city's groundwater extraction there was now governed by agreement with Inyo County; no decision concerning Mono would cause pumping to increase.

The late chapters of the DEIR turned to the price: what would a higher lake cost Los Angeles? Here came conclusions unwelcome to the Department of Water and Power. No matter what lake level was chosen, the report claimed, reclamation and conservation could make up for any Mono water lost. Even if Mono Basin diversions were entirely cut off, the shortfall could readily be overcome. As for the energy produced by Mono water on its travels southward, there was hardly any impact to be overcome. Mono water passing through the aqueduct power plants accounted for less than 1 percent of the department's generating capacity—the smallest of small change.

In the weeks after the environmental report appeared the Mono Lake Committee found itself in a most peculiar position. The new report, with its split endorsement of two generous lake levels, left the committee's thinking far behind. In its Six Point Plan of 1991, the committee had chosen a target level of 6,386 feet. As the *Mono Lake Newsletter* editorialized, "DWP rejected that level as much too high, but new data suggests that it may be much too low."

Back in the 1970s, when the lake had appeared doomed to a long and finally fatal decline, merely to stabilize it was goal enough. "Save Mono Lake!" people cried, and they meant, "Save What Is Left!" Researchers did not spend much time estimating what might have already been lost; indeed, they barely guessed what had been lost. Most of their study and debate concerned what was still to lose.

When Congress launched the National Academy of Sciences study in 1984, it confirmed this focus. The authorizing legislation spoke of maintaining *current* wildlife and studying effects of *further declining* lake levels only. Though the Academy report of 1987 spent a few pages looking at higher lake levels, for the most part it fixed its gaze resolutely downward. The state-funded Community and Organization Research Institute "Blue Ribbon Panel" paper, which appeared a few months later, shared that emphasis.

These studies agreed that Mono Lake at 6,376, 6,374, or even perhaps 6,372 feet above sea level was not about to enter ecological collapse. If the purpose was literally to "save" Mono Lake—to continue to have approximately what was there in the days of the 1976 ecological study—a fairly low water level could be tolerated. Only the insurance factor required a decision: how much higher should the lake be kept in normal times to avoid dropping below some critical point in dry cycles?

In the late 1980s the discussion gradually shifted. People were becoming more keenly aware of the richness present at the lake *before* diversion. They were starting to realize that Mono Lake circa 1976 had not been, after all, an Eden, but a Paradise partially lost.

In 1989 the *Mono Lake Newsletter* ran a feature on historic conditions. At that point the picture was painted only for contrast value, to make the committee's actual position seem modest: "We will never swim in Paoha Island's Heart Lake, witness a brine fly band six feet wide, or view flocks of ducks darkening Mono's shores." But even to say this was to invite the question Elden Vestal posed in a letter to Scott Stine: *Why not?*

The stream restoration projects encouraged this subtle change of thinking. For the creeks, at least, the game was now to reimagine and partially to reconstruct an old reality.

Yet until the DEIR came out these ideas had not come sharply into focus. Now that the report had broken the taboo against considering high lake levels, the parties opposed to the Los Angeles position had some fresh thinking to do—in a hurry.

In July of 1993, Patrick Flinn of Morrison & Foerster invited representatives of several parties to a meeting in Lee Vining, together with such scientists as David Herbst, Dave

Shuford, Scott Stine, and air researcher Thomas Cahill. It was a day of lively debate, with many positions argued. At the end of the session, the key question was not whether sights should be raised to 6,390 feet. The question was whether 6,390 feet was high enough.

6,390 FEET — OR HIGHER?

There were really just two powerful arguments in favor of lake levels lower than 6,390 feet. David Herbst took aim at one of them, Scott Stine at the other.

Herbst reported on his latest fly research, not fully reflected in the DEIR. It was now clear, he stated, that the 6,390-foot lake level was preferable for alkali flies as well as for brine shrimp. The lower salinity helped the flies much more than the partial loss of shallow-water substrate harmed them.

Scott Stine discussed tufa effects. The DEIR had found that the 6,383.5-foot alternative, and no higher alternative, would preserve the tufa displays. Though this conclusion was based largely on Stine's background work, he felt that the report had drawn the wrong conclusions.

The waves and longshore currents of a rising lake can indeed cause tufas to fall. Contrary to what you might think, it is not the impact of waves against the flanks of the towers that does the harm; the structures are neither notched at waterline nor knocked over. Rather, the damage comes when waves lap just at the base of the towers, cutting away at the sediments in which they are rooted. During the lake rise of 1982–86, a large number of slender towers were toppled in this way. However, Stine argued, the DEIR had erred in concluding that the 6,383.5-foot lake management plan would avoid this type of damage. Even under that plan the lake would rise high enough during wet periods to undermine the more vulnerable towers.

Wholesale destruction, fortunately, is not in the cards. The most massive and complex architectures are least vulnerable; it is the free-standing, small-diameter tower that falls. And it probably falls at South Tufa. The South Tufa structures, Stine believes, were built over a few decades at the start of the twentieth century. Sediment immediately began to accumulate around their bases, a process that would eventually have anchored and protected the towers—but the falling lake after 1940 exposed them before this reinforcement had progressed very far.

What about sand tufa? Here Stine corrected an error of his own. He had believed, and so had advised the water board, that the 6,383.5-foot option would keep the water's edge away from those fragile structures. On reexamination, he knew better. This lake management alternative, like all the others under study, represented a range of water levels; at the first high stand under the "6,383.5-foot" plan, the present sand tufa displays would be destroyed. As waves cut new embankments, however, other sand tufas would appear, not free-standing and castle-like, but exposed in intricate cross-section, like fossils.

There seemed no reason left for preferring 6,383.5 to 6,390 feet.

The north shore in the 1930s, a tufa grove now high and dry. If the lake surface reached 6,405 feet above sea level, these towers would once more stand on the shore. (Photo by Brett Weston)

What, then, about still higher levels?

When its surface stood higher than about 6,402 feet above the level of the sea, Mono Lake had sandy beaches instead of an alkali rim. It had expansive marshes at the creek mouths and extensive lagoons on the northern shore. It had a million migratory ducks. Much of this richness, Stine maintained, would come back of itself if the lake rose far enough. If the idea was restoration, he argued in Lee Vining, the target lake level should be a median of 6,405 feet.

Again the question of the tufa arises. A lake above 6,400 feet would submerge South Tufa and much of Lee Vining Tufa, respectively the best-known and largest stands. A submerged tufa tower is not destroyed—indeed, it is better preserved than one exposed to the air—but of course it is lost to view. Unacceptable scenic losses? Stine felt the answer was no. Other displays would replace the hidden ones. After all, early visitors who saw the lake at high levels had marveled at the tufa groves. They were simply different tufa groves. With the lake at 6,405 feet, tufa on the north side, now well back from the shore and almost unvisited, would stand at the water's edge. There would be compensation, if not perhaps an even trade.

Stine made a pretty impressive case. Yet the 6,405-foot plan was not one that all could embrace. The drowning of South Tufa seemed a heavy price, and the plan would reduce Los Angeles's water diversions to a mere 20 percent of the historic average, and even less, while the lake was rising. The proposal was, depending on your viewpoint, bold—or overbold.

In the weeks after the Lee Vining conference, the Mono Lake Committee debated within itself whether or not to hang its hat on 6,405 feet, breaking ranks with allies who were just getting used to 6,390 feet. At last the board agreed on a compromise formula: "6,390′ or Higher."

THE DEPARTMENT
OF WATER AND
POWER REPLIES

The DEIR presented the Los Angeles Department of Water and Power with no such pleasant dilemmas.

In June, at a meeting of the City Council's Commerce, Energy, and Natural Resources Committee, chairperson Ruth Galanter asked plaintively, "Why are we still litigating this? I would much rather see us spend ratepayers' money to put in the pipes so we can use reclaimed water than to spend it on more lawyers' time." Water and Power's Mitchell Kodama and department legal advisers repeated old arguments about expense: in the very long term, the cost of replacing Mono water would reach two billion dollars. As for the length of the battle, water rights cases always run long. "This case is still a teenager," an attorney said. Galanter asked if the council could see the department's comments before they were filed with the water board. The response was a courteous No.

So, while its opponents debated whether 6,390 feet was high enough, Water and Power prepared once more to argue that an average level in the 6,370s would suffice to "save Mono Lake." Its *Mono Lake Management Plan*, published later that summer as a handsome booklet, proposed to keep the lake generally fluctuating between 6,374.6 and 6,385.3 feet, with the mean at 6,377.7. In a drought of six years or longer, it could dip lower.

The department's plan aimed to maintain the status quo, to keep the lake fluctuating within the range of recent experience. This, they argued, was the safe and sane solution. They pointed out quite correctly that the lake in this state was appreciated by millions. On the low end, the plan purported to protect Twain and Java islets and to keep the water level above the "nick point," the change in bottom topography below which, it was now agreed, catastrophic erosion would be triggered. On the upper end, the lake would allegedly stay low enough to spare South Tufa and leave intact the Paoha islets, the new gull habitats. (These promises did not stand up to analysis: the predicted lake fluctuations would actually destroy the Paoha islets, topple tufa towers, and let coyotes invade Twain.)

For the larger streams, the department offered flows a bit below those set in 1990 by Judge Finney and far below the emerging recommendations of the Department of Fish and Game. Parker and Walker creeks, however, would be unhitched from the system and allowed to carry whatever water nature provided year by year. Active restoration work on all the streams would be abandoned, or at least deferred.

In the five-month period between the appearance of the DEIR and the beginning of the water board hearings, the parties scrambled to buttress and present their cases. Huge documents were prepared on all sides. Around the offices of Morrison & Foerster the joke ran, "Save the lake, kill a tree."

There also was a scramble to rally public support and, behind the scenes, to gather institutional allies. The latter process, like the first, was very one-sided. The Department of Water and Power had long since lost the public opinion war, and its support in governmental circles had lately been waning as well. Now it saw the powers lining up, one after another, in support of a lake level of 6,390 feet or higher.

On July 7, 1993, the federal Environmental Protection Agency at last proposed listing the Mono Basin for nonattainment of air quality standards under the Clean Air Act. This was one short step from the actual action (which would occur at the following New Year). EPA had not planned to appear at the upcoming hearings, but when Water and Power attempted to exclude the issue from discussion in this forum the agency changed its mind. On July 14, the Great Basin Unified Air Pollution Control District became the first party to endorse a high lake level, raising the bidding to 6,392 feet. The district, running a different computer model from the one used by Jones & Stokes, had arrived at all but identical conclusions about dust.

The Forest Service weighed in. Though it had earlier called for a lake range from 6,377 to 6,390 feet, it now joined the chorus calling for 6,390 feet. The State Lands Commission and the Department of Parks and Recreation, also responsible for Mono lands, did the same.

The federal Fish and Wildlife Service announced that selection of any level lower than 6,390 feet would cause it to seek listing of the brine shrimp *Artemia monica* as a threatened species.

The Department of Fish and Game put the finishing touches on its streamflow recommendations. It proposed flows in the creeks high enough, by themselves, to raise the lake to about 6,390 feet over a long period of time. But this normally cautious bureaucracy went further. In hopes of bringing back the ducks, it flatly endorsed a lake level of 6,405 feet.

The most damaging shift, perhaps, was that of Water and Power's long-standing ally, the Metropolitan Water District of Southern California. The Met, which distributes water from the Colorado Aqueduct and the State Water Project, is Water and Power's fallback source, the spigot from which, it had long been argued, replacement water for Mono must necessarily come. In 1990, Metropolitan Water District General Manager Carl Boronkay had warned, "Increasing demands on Metropolitan caused by reduction of the Mono Basin supply could exacerbate . . . shortages in other areas of California."

But early in 1993 Boronkay was replaced by John "Woody" Wodraska, who saw the water situation in less hackneyed terms. A sharp internal struggle ensued. On the losing end were Duane Georgeson, who in 1990 had moved to the Met from the Department of Water and Power, and Mike Gage, who had also left Water and Power and was now president of the Metropolitan Water District board. So narrow was the balance that the Met issued two statements: the first, its comments on the DEIR, supported Water and Power; the second, its prepared testimony for the water board, was neutral.

In filing the *Aitken* condemnation case, back in the 1930s, the department had asserted its rights "as against the defendants and each of them, and against all the world." That was merely the ripsnorting rhetoric of normal legal combat. Now, though, it came to seem prescient: Water and Power did, indeed, stand against "all the world."

The Mono Lake Committee, meanwhile, was seeking support from the very top—Republican Governor Pete Wilson. As a senator, Wilson had more than once been a key voice for Mono; as governor, he had suffered a series of embarrassments on water policy issues and could use a success before his reelection bid in 1994. And though the water establishment as a whole was still a force to be reckoned with in California politics, the Department of Water and Power itself was now so isolated that its protestations could safely be ignored.

THE SHOW BEGINS   In the fall of 1993 the water board held hearings of two kinds: three days of public sound-off sessions, simply to gather statements of opinion, and what were projected to be twenty-one days of formal evidentiary hearings.

It had been several years since the Mono Lake Committee had last called on members and supporters to speak out for the cause, for the controversy had been proceeding in the courts and in technical study groups. Now that pent-up support could be expressed in a way that really mattered. Some four thousand letters, overwhelmingly in support of high lake levels, poured in to the water board. At the public hearing in Los Angeles on

Marc Del Piero of the State Water Resources Control Board. In 1993 and 1994, he chaired forty-six days of hearings; more often than not he was the sole board member present. (Photo by Gerda S. Mathan)

October 4, all day and through the evening voices spoke the mantra "6,390' or higher." A number of people underlined the "higher." The record shows only three dissents. And it was at this meeting that the governor's representative, California Environmental Protection Agency representative James M. Strock, gave the word insiders had been expecting: Wilson gave his weighty endorsement to 6,390 feet. At sessions in Mammoth Lakes and Sacramento, later in the month, the pro-Mono avalanche continued.

On October 20, 1993, in the plush auditorium at the Resources Building in Sacramento, the State Water Resources Control Board opened its formal evidentiary hearings on the Mono Basin issues. The event had a solemn feel. All the elaborate legal actions up to this point—all the multitudinous courtroom events since 1979—had been in the nature of skirmishes. Only now were the issues truly coming to trial.

In opening statements, MoFo attorney Bruce Dodge could not resist drawing the contrast between these last days and the first. At the beginning, Audubon and the Mono Lake Committee had faced a Department of Water and Power secure in its possessions, supported by the entire water industry and by the state government. Now, of fourteen parties represented, eleven were actually inimical to the department. Technically, each of these parties was entitled to the same amount of time; however, hearing officer Marc Del Piero, recognizing the disadvantage under which the department now labored, would take pains to allow it the fullest presentation of its case.

That case was a pitch for keeping things as they were. The situation that had existed at the lake since 1976 and in the streams since 1984, Water and Power witnesses argued, was quite all right. Higher lake levels would harm tufa. Historic conditions could not be assessed accurately, but, so far as they could be judged, they had not been nearly as good as old-timers remembered. Conservation and reclamation efforts in Los Angeles, already under way, were needed to supply the needs of future growth and should not be counted on to replace Mono water. Replacement water would have to come, ultimately, from the Sacramento/San Joaquin Delta—and it might not be available at all. Responding to criticisms of its lake management plan, the department offered a revision purporting to hold the lake surface within a narrower range, as being better for both tufa and gulls.

Audubon and the Mono Lake Committee urged that the lake be raised to 6,390 feet or, better, to 6,405 feet. In order to meet air quality standards and to minimize the toppling of tufa, the lake should be filled as rapidly as possible, especially in the early years.

CalTrout's main concern was to support the generous streamflow recommendations of the Department of Fish and Game. Counsel Richard Roos-Collins defended the usefulness of historic accounts and sought to show that in the old days the Mono Basin creeks had been not just typical eastern Sierra fishing streams but superior ones. Putting aside some earlier doubts, CalTrout also endorsed an active restoration program on all the creeks.

The Department of Fish and Game made its own lengthy presentation, centering not only on fish but also on ducks. Among the department's witnesses was habitat restoration expert Frederic Reid of Ducks Unlimited; this national organization had been taking an increasing interest in the Mono Basin.

Some key questions were matters of law, not fact. For instance, what did the State Supreme Court mean when it said that public trust values must be protected "as far as feasible"? Los Angeles wanted to interpret "feasible" to mean "reasonable" and "to the minimum necessary degree." But Audubon read the word to mean, literally, "capable of being done." (On this count Los Angeles would prevail.)

On one legal point there was no disagreement. It was clear to all parties that the legally required flows for fish would be set first, and only after that did the public trust "balancing" begin. For this reason, many highly technical days were spent justifying low fish flows, or high ones.

Most of all, the proceedings were one long battle of experts. Some days were fourteen hours long. It was heavy going at times, but there were lively moments, as when the three Davids—fly researcher Herbst, ornithologist Shuford, and Winkler, the gull expert and Mono Lake Committee pioneer—appeared on the same panel. Unfortunately, Winkler never appeared jointly with Joseph R. Jehl, Jr., his long-time sparring partner in the debate over the status of *Larus californicus*.

Often the experts were not so much disagreeing as talking past each other. Water and Power's witnesses insisted that a moderately low lake level was not too bad; its opponents, that a high lake level would be much better. Both positions might be true. Limnologist John Melack, for instance, said that a lake in the 6,370s was "a functioning ecosystem" (what ecosystem is not?) and that it was "healthy" and "vibrant." Yet a higher lake would be healthier and more vibrant still. Melack declined to speculate on levels above 6,381 feet, let alone above 6,400 feet: "That would be a different lake."

Tom Birmingham, counsel for the Department of Water and Power, and Assistant City Attorney Ken Downey (right). Of all the lawyers that have worked on the case, only Downey and Bruce Dodge remember the very beginning. (Photo by Gerda S. Mathan)

Air pollution was a more dangerous area for the department. One day in November, Water and Power counsel Tom Birmingham was trying to get a witness from the Environmental Protection Agency to agree that air quality problems in the Mono Basin were not bad enough to warrant expensive correction. Patrick Flinn took the occasion to read into the record some language that seemed almost fatal to the department's cause. In 1990, during the Clean Air Act debate, congressional committees had explicitly observed that eastern Sierra dust storms were "anthropogenic" and subject to the law. Because these words did not appear in the legislation itself but only in committee reports, they had apparently escaped the notice of Water and Power. Birmingham, in any case, had no response.

The next day, Flinn pinned down a public health witness for the department. Reading a graphic account of a dust storm—"It hurts to breathe"—Flinn more or less dared the hapless expert to deny that this sounded like a threat to health. Faced with a choice between conceding the point and sounding heartless, the witness chose to concede.

Twenty-one days, the board had said. Not half enough. As the testimony trundled on toward Christmas, with no end in sight, a curious thing happened: the contending lawyers and witnesses, board staffers and onlookers, began to form a community, a sort of village. The confrontation came to have its own history, its notable characters, its running jokes. Peter Vorster became known for his habit of passing suggested questions

The Mono Lake brain trust at the water board hearings. Left to right: Scott Stine, David Shuford, David Winkler, Bruce Dodge, Peter Vorster, Patrick Flinn. Water and Power attorney Janet Goldsmith (right) looks on. (Photo by Gerda S. Mathan)

to any attorney who would take them. David Herbst drew laughter, and a reprimand from Del Piero, by demanding of Water and Power's decorous Adolph Moskovitz, "Did you understand what I just told you, though?" The most spectacular attorney was Bruce Dodge, tall, bow-tied, disapproving, bending dangerously over the lectern or pacing in the background, wincing at the ignorance of the world. And beside him was his colleague Patrick Flinn, bouncing up and down at seven in the evening after a long day, trying to get an economic consultant to concede a minor point obvious to all.

THE 444
BREAKTHROUGH

In Los Angeles, 1993 had been a year of city government change. In June, after twenty years of Bradley administrations, Republican Richard Riordan became mayor. Riordan, a businessman not known as an environmentalist, brought to the job an executive's virtues: dislike of waste and unresolved conflict, along with an eye to the budget.

Assemblymen Richard Katz and Phillip Isenberg both wrote to the new mayor, reminding him of the $36 million that remained in the AB 444 fund. Mono Lake Committee board members Ed Manning and Tom Soto followed up. Deputy Mayor Michael

Richard Katz, assemblyman for Van Nuys, a Mono supporter and sponsor of many bills for water law reform. (Photo by Gerda S. Mathan)

Keeley got the parties together again and tried to broker a solution that would include a lake level, perhaps one as high as 6,390 feet. In the weeks before the water board hearings began, rumors flew that a city spokesman might announce an agreement on the opening day. But no agreement was reached.

At this point Martha Davis made a suggestion to councilmember Ruth Galanter: why not go back to the formula developed by Mary Nichols in 1992? Under that plan, the city would renounce an amount of Mono Basin water equal to the quantity developed with state money. Galanter now took this idea to Department of Water and Power General Manager Daniel Waters. Waters agreed in principle, but expressed doubt that the Mono Lake Committee would! It remained to turn all this agreement-in-principle into agreement-in-fact. Galanter shuttled back and forth with drafts of language until a text was arrived at that satisfied both sides.

On December 13, 1993, in crowded press conferences in Los Angeles and Sacramento, the Department of Water and Power and the Mono Lake Committee proclaimed their intent to apply together for the state money. Most of the $36 million would go to the East Valley water reclamation project, with smaller amounts to other reclamation and conservation efforts. In exchange, Water and Power would abandon its claim to at least 41,000 feet per year of Mono Basin water.

It was a jovial moment. The participants, including Mayor Riordan, Governor Wilson, and assorted legislators, passed Mono Lake calendars around, signing them like yearbooks. But the announcement proved to be another beginning, not an end. The process of turning agreement into finished application took months. Obstacles were encountered in Sacramento. The legislature had been shifting the unclaimed Environ-

Announcing the agreement to substitute water reclamation for Mono Basin water. Speaking, Los Angeles Mayor Richard Riordan. At his left: Los Angeles City Councilman Nate Holden; City Council President John Ferraro; California Governor Pete Wilson; Water and Power General Manager Dan Waters; Dennis Tito, president of the Board of Water and Power Commissioners; Councilman Zev Yaroslavsky. At his right (left to right): Mono Lake Committee board member Tom Soto; Assemblyman Richard Katz; Mono Lake Committee Executive Director Martha Davis; State Senator Tim Leslie; Councilwoman Ruth Galanter; Marc Del Piero of the State Water Resources Control Board; Edith and Mortimer Gaines (parents of David). (Photo courtesy Councilwoman Ruth Galanter)

mental Water Fund, bit by bit, to the Department of Water Resources, which had grown accustomed to this income stream and wanted the AB 444 money extracted from some other budgetary pocket. Jim Wickser, head of water operations at Water and Power, made a small bet with Ruth Galanter: if the funds should ever materialize, dinner would be on him. But Assemblyman Richard Katz and State Senator Tim Leslie (the latter representing Mono County) successfully defended the original arrangement. In September, Governor Wilson signed off on the first of four $9 million installments.

Meanwhile, the revolution in the Los Angeles city government rolled on. In March, Daniel Waters, general manager and chief engineer, retired and was replaced by a caretaker. In August, Mayor Riordan announced the appointment of his chief of staff, Bill McCarley, to the top spot. For the first time since its beginning, a nonengineer was running the Los Angeles Department of Water and Power. And for the first time, all the people in ultimate charge of the department were known to favor a rapid settlement at Mono Lake.

But that is getting ahead of the story.

On the morning of February 18, 1994, CalTrout lawyer Richard Roos-Collins walked into the water board hearing room wearing a necktie with a picture of a trout. "This," he said, "is what we expect to see in the Mono Basin creeks." Water and Power's Tom Birmingham shot back, "Sure. A long, skinny fish." It was day forty-six, the last of the water board hearings. By now the transcripts ran to 30,000 pages.

THE WATER BOARD DECISION

As some last repeat witnesses re-turned already well-tilled ground, cameras flashed. Then came the final arguments, followed by a round of mutual compliments and almost regretful farewells.

Closing briefs, reply briefs, rebuttal briefs flew back and forth for another month or two. There was even something called a surrebuttal brief. The experts twiddled with their computer models. And, well out of the public view, the final analysis began. Insiders say that the lake level choice was never deeply in doubt, but other elements of the decision—streamflows and restoration requirements, in particular—were hotly contested among the water board members and staff.

On September 16, 1994, the State Water Resources Control Board published the final version of its Environmental Impact Report. The new plan actually went somewhat beyond the old 6,390-foot alternative. In order to eliminate the dust pollution problem, it would keep another foot or two of water in the lake most of the time. It also set streamflows—somewhat lower, especially in Rush Creek, than the Department of Fish and Game had recommended. It instructed Water and Power to prepare and execute, under board supervision, a plan for continued stream restoration. It added a new restoration mandate: Water and Power must prepare a parallel plan to restore duck habitat, to whatever degree the selected lake level would permit. The plan also placed an upper limit on discharge from the Mono Craters tunnel into the upper Owens River, to stem erosion damage downstream, and it called for a Grant Lake reservoir operations plan to protect recreation values there in light of changing water operations.

In order to get the lake up to the target level, Water and Power could make no diversions until the lake reached 6,377 feet; could take only 4,500 acre-feet a year of diversions until the level was 6,390 feet; and could then divert 16,000 feet a year until the lake reached 6,391 feet. At higher levels, all water in excess of the fish flows (always required) could be diverted. This would yield an average of 30,800 acre-feet a year. Should

Bruce Dodge

Bruce Dodge, lead counsel in the Audubon/Mono Lake Committee suits against Los Angeles Water and Power. (Photo by Gerda S. Mathan)

"You're a wonderful attorney, Mr. Dodge." It was the final minute of the State Water Resources Control Board hearings of 1994, and Hearing Officer Marc Del Piero had compliments for all the assembled counsel, but his words to Dodge were conspicuously fulsome.

What made F. Bruce Dodge, long-standing lead attorney in Audubon's Mono Lake effort, so effective? He is not especially quotable, like Barrett McInerney, CalTrout counsel in the early days; not especially gracious in manner, like Water and Power's Adolph Moskovitz. In court he is the opposite of a grandstander. He executes no dazzling maneuvers. He doesn't glitter when he talks. But with his lanky posture, gravelly Jimmy Stewart voice, and air of controlled irritation, he seems always to be speaking on behalf of offended common sense.

Dodge's briefs are short, straightforward, and based on the narrowest and least alarming interpretations of law that will serve his purpose. What better messenger to entrust with legal dynamite like the expansion of the public trust doctrine into the field of water rights? "His respectable, conservative legal message," says colleague Patrick Flinn, "has carried us for fifteen years."

In court Dodge is engaging and often funny. (One recalls him asking Del Piero, "Can I object to Mr. Flinn's question?") Out of court he is rather unapproachable. "He thinks of himself as a curmudgeon," says Flinn, "but it's not personal, it's directed at everyone." At Morrison & Foerster in the early 1980s, young Flinn attached himself to Dodge—resolving to ignore the famous gruffness—and got "good and subtle teaching." Other partners might simply correct a novice's brief and send it to the typist. "Bruce would hand it back with comments and let me make my own repairs." Flinn feels he owes his MoFo partnership to this mentor.

And what did Marc Del Piero himself have in mind when he singled Dodge out for praise? "Dodge exemplifies something that is becoming somewhat quaint," says Del Piero. "Real honesty and fairness in the practice of the law."

drought drive the lake down (as from time to time it will), permitted diversions would shrink; at 6,388 feet they would cease altogether. The effect of these rules, hydrological models predicted, would be to maintain an average level of 6,392.6 feet and to hold the lake above 6,390 feet about 90 percent of the time.

Why 6,390 feet, after all, rather than 6,405 feet? According to project manager Jim Canaday, two considerations above all went into this solution: ducks and tufa. The water board staff thought that a portion of the duck habitat might be regained even at 6,390 feet, given active restoration work to bring back wetlands. But it questioned whether the enormous pre-diversion flocks could be restored at any lake level, even 6,405 feet, given habitat losses elsewhere along the Pacific Flyway.

It was the tufa issue, however, that was decisive. The board staff agreed with David Carle, ranger at the Mono Lake Tufa State Reserve, that there must be a "major visitor site" for tufa and that only South Tufa would serve. It is here that most people get their first close look at the lake today. The tufa grove is extensive, and the dryland portions are neither swampy nor brushy; you can move around. At a lake level of 6,390 feet, the upland area would shrink but would still accommodate a large number of visitors; at higher levels the usable area would vanish. At 6,390 feet, many of the towers would protrude from the water, their most spectacular setting; at higher levels the towers would be entirely submerged. As for tufa groves elsewhere around the lake, recommended by Audubon as alternate attractions, the board staff felt they just wouldn't do: they are smaller, their upland portions are swampy, and they are altogether harder to use.

Back in the early 1980s, the Mono Lake Committee had launched a campaign to put Mono Lake on the recreation map. The water board decision of 1994 was partly a consequence of that choice. The presence of parks around the lake had been an argument for high lake levels, up to a point; now that point had been reached, and the park managers signaled, "No more."

During the thirteen days between release of the final EIR on September 16, 1994, and the climactic water board hearing on September 28, the question was no longer what the decision would be. The question was whether any of the parties would appeal it to Judge Finney.

On the environmental side, there was some genuine disappointment that the board had not gone all the way to 6,405 feet; the Department of Fish and Game was also unhappy with the board's trimming of fish flows in Rush Creek. But there was ready agreement that the decision, so much more generous than anything on the horizon before 1993, would do. The state agencies and the environmental parties planned a press conference to announce their unified support.

In Los Angeles, most of the people in charge—the mayor, the Water and Power commissioners, even new Water and Power General Manager Bill McCarley—were anxious above all to see the matter settled. A year before, swayed by upbeat predictions from counsel, they had declined to force the issue. But now the time had plainly come. There was still internal resistance in two places, however: among the department's second-level staff, the people who had been fighting this battle for a decade; and among the department's attorneys. The sticking point was not so much the lake level, which had been expected, as it was the strong mandate for restoration work on the streams and now on lake-fringing wetlands as well.

Overpowered though they seemed to be, the old guard did not concede. The legal

Jim Wickser, head of water operations, at the Los Angeles headquarters of the Department of Water and Power. (Photo by Gerda S. Mathan)

appeal was written and ready to go. And when the final Environmental Impact Report came out, water chief Jim Wickser sought to give the story an alarming spin. In an interview with the *Los Angeles Times*, he spoke of a "further threat to the city's water supply." He made no mention of the AB 444 agreement, which had already removed part of the water from contention. The wire services picked up the item in Wickser's terms.

Martha Davis hurried to counter the effects of the publicity, especially at City Hall. And on September 24, the *Times* weighed in with a stern editorial. "The train known as the Mono Lake issue has been roaring down the tracks toward Los Angeles for 16 years," it said. "Yet the Department of Water and Power just stood there. Now, predictably, it has been run over. . . . What is needed at the DWP is not just more water, but more vision, leadership, and courage."

On Monday, September 26, Davis, McCarley, Wickser, and Dennis Tito of the Board of Water and Power Commissioners sat down together. Davis promised that the committee would help secure outside funding for the restoration work. At the close of the meeting, Tito and McCarley announced they would not appeal. The following day, the Water and Power commissioners made it official.

So the news conference in the capitol on Wednesday, September 28—originally planned as a rally for one side—became instead a peace proclamation by both. With the notable exception of Water and Power staff, most of the characters involved in the story were present, either in the audience or at the microphone. "We are here to accept the state's decision," said Dennis Tito. Asked to comment on Jim Wickser's statement of the week before, Ruth Galanter responded, "He was outgunned." "The battle of Mono Lake ends September 29, 1994," said State Senator Tim Leslie. "No other area of the state," Davis emphasized, "will be injured by this decision." Dan Beard, head of the U.S. Bureau of Reclamation, promised continued funding for water reclamation projects. Jim Edmondson of CalTrout announced that he was headed over the hill to the Mono Basin—going fishing.

Then the group trooped upstairs to a special meeting of the State Water Resources Control Board in the mural-bedecked California Room. The hearing that followed was essentially ceremonial. After the 5–0 vote adopting the Draft Decision, the two hundred spectators stood up and applauded. It was the first time anyone could recall such a demonstration at the water board.

Looking back over the years since the launching of the public trust lawsuit in 1979, since the beginning of diversion in 1940, or even since William Mulholland's first visit to the Mono Basin in 1904, it is easy to gain a false impression. It appears as though the abstract beast "society" had created a problem at Mono Lake and then evolved an organ, so to speak, that could correct it. There seems a kind of inevitability to it all, as if events could not have taken any other form.

This is an illusion. The solution at Mono Lake depended on incredible individual tenacity; on efforts that often seemed hopeless; on more than a little dumb luck. Even the early and seemingly futile local resistance to the will of the Department of Water and Power turned out to play a role. Elden Vestal's notes had their hour. Over the decades, one after another, players stepped forward, shouldered the Mono burden for a few months or years, and then passed it on. Many of the people involved never knew each other. Of the ones that did, quite a number didn't like each other. And no two of them seem to have agreed about just who did what. But they formed a collective force that proved irresistible.

Yet perhaps the impression of a society correcting a misstep isn't so wrong after all. If our complex, flawed, and multicentric democracy does not guarantee an outcome like the one at Mono Lake, it does at least permit it if the necessary people will step forward. We are never truly stuck with our mistakes, even the ones we think we have cast in stone. That fact should arouse, in the most disillusioned mind, a secret stirring of hope.

"It's a great decision," Martha Davis said after the water board action, "but there's a lot of implementation ahead." Indeed there was, and the next phase began in some confusion. The restoration planning described in the decision left no place for the existing Restoration Technical Committee; it would take some months to determine how much of the earlier thinking would be carried forward. A few other questions remained for further study.

But for all the fuzziness of a few of the brushstrokes, the picture was distinct. Mono Lake has been saved.

When the lake was sinking toward its nadir, only a few people paid close attention. As it rises, the world will be watching.

THE NEW FUTURE
OF MONO LAKE

Martha Davis

Martha Davis at South Tufa, 1994.
(Photo by Gerda S. Mathan)

"Nobody else could have done it," said Barrett McInerney. "Write that." McInerney, the lawyer who launched and won the early creek cases for CalTrout, was talking about Martha Davis, Mono Lake Committee executive director since 1984 and chief architect of the committee's political victory.

The first adjective people attach to Martha Davis is some variant of stubborn. *"My sense from the time I met Martha was that she was the kind of person who would get hold of an issue and wouldn't let go," says Ed Grosswiler, who first invited Davis onto the Mono Lake Committee staff. "She's a baby-faced killer," Assemblyman Phil Isenberg has said. "She looks like an endearing and charming cocker spaniel but has the jaw strength of a pit bull." Mike Gage, her erstwhile negotiating partner at Water and Power, described her as "personable, pleasant, tenacious, and rigid." An assistant to Los Angeles Mayor Riordan used the warmer word "persistent" and added, "It's a quality I admire."*

But sheer determination is only part of the Davis approach. The other part is a willingness to accommodate the opposition on everything but the essential. Her strategy might be paraphrased, "If you have to lick 'em, try also to join 'em."

The point, she says, is not just to win. In fact, victory can be dangerous. "Our society tends to reject very one-sided outcomes." Interests that are simply beaten down tend to live to fight another day, in another arena. Davis's goal is what she calls "closure": reaching a solution that will stick because it is accepted by all.

For this reason Davis sat down with the Department of Water and Power and other interests in the long-winded, often frustrating Mono Lake Group. For this reason she promoted the effort to locate replacement water sources for Los Angeles and to subsidize their development. For this reason she kept on trying for a lake-level agreement when others, confident of the trend of the battle, would simply have waited it out.

For this reason she regards the limited agreement of December 1993, by which Water and Power gave up all claim to 41,000 acre-feet or more of Mono water, as a truly important gain. The fiats of the water board are subject to revision; the contract of 1993 is binding.

At the beginning of the Mono Lake battle, Davis recalls, the Mono Lake Committee was very much alone. Whatever government agencies took note of its efforts were opposed or studiously neutral; the rest of the environmental movement (Friends of the Earth and Audubon excepted) tended to see the campaign as a noble waste of time. "We were marginal," Davis says, "even within our own community."

The history of the last ten years can be seen as a long process of moving the Mono Lake Committee into the mainstream—and subtly shifting the Department of Water and Power out of it. The committee defined itself as moderate and, as court victory followed court victory, began in fact to seem so. Until 1993, it resisted the temptation to increase its demands as its fortunes improved. Water and Power, on the other hand, clung to old positions far longer than reality allowed, and as a result it came to seem merely intransigent. At the end, the Mono Lake Committee stood in a common front not only with other environmentalists but also with the state and most of the Los Angeles city government; the Department of Water and Power stood alone, unsupported even by its colleagues in the water industry. If Martha Davis did not create the currents that carried the committee to this goal, she rode them masterfully.

The achievement of Martha Davis is largely invisible, because it took place in an endless series of confidential conversations. One thinks of David Gaines standing by Mono Lake or before an audience. If they ever cast a statue of Martha Davis, it will have to be cradling a telephone.

At the Old Marina, the site for years of the annual Bucket Walk and "rehydration ceremony," the true rehydration will proceed. The muddy edge will disappear; the path to the lake will shorten. In the end, the water will cover most of the present parking lot. Boat ramps, built in the 1960s and useless for thirty years, will once again slant suggestively into the waves. Where U.S. 395 borders the lake, the water will come markedly closer to the road.

At the tufa groves, the rising tide will spread among the towers. Tufa masses now at the shoreline will become islands; towers now standing in the bushes, barely glanced at by people striding on toward the lake, will rise again beside their reflections in the water. At South Tufa, some towers will fall.

Negit Island will regain its isolation. First a strait will sever the land bridge near the island end, and another waterway will open near the mainland. As the lake continues to rise, the flat, pale islet between the straits will shrink until, in the target elevation, it skims just above the waves or forms a shoal below them. Negit itself will stand well off shore. Though coyotes are known to swim, the widening waters should eventually discourage them, and the gull colony should return.

On the great arc of the lake's eastern rim, the alkali band will shrink until, in most places, lakewater meets either vegetation or dark-colored sand. From a distance the lake will appear "full." Dust will blow here and there, but the great regional storms should be no more.

Along the shore, wetlands will more commonly be found near open water, providing good habitat for ducks. The lake will reoccupy abandoned coves. In these wind-sheltered bights, fresh water from runoff will tend to remain separate, floating above the salt. Brackish surface waters, too, are good for ducks. Waterfowl numbers should increase.

On the west shore, the lake will invade the eroded channels made by the streams in the years of decline. The result will be fiordlike inlets called *rias*, that favorite word of crossword-puzzle writers. Where fresh water meets salt, well up the rias, new marshes should form.

Upstream along the creeks, the natural recovery of woods and habitats will continue. So will some degree of deliberate restoration. At the Lee Vining Creek diversion dam, the Department of Water and Power is to install a low-level bypass through which sediment can feed into the lower reach of the creek; this should hasten the rebuilding of the soil. A dry subsidiary channel that runs alongside Highway 120 is slated to receive water, giving trans-Sierra drivers a glimpse of restoration at work.

On Rush Creek, the rewatering of abandoned channels, proposed by the earlier planners and endorsed by the water board, seems certain to go forward. Unclear is the fate of a more ambitious plan to restore the springs near the narrows, once the heart of the Rush Creek habitat, by recharging an aquifer on the Cain Ranch above. (The key, according to Scott Stine, is to divide the flows of Parker and Walker creeks among their old distributary channels.)

For many decades, the Mono Basin will continue to be a landscape on the way back, rebounding, repairing itself by human permission and with some degree of human connivance. At the same time, it will continue to yield, if in lessened quantity, a utilitarian resource. We have no ready word to describe such a landscape. Despite the presence of a National Forest Scenic Area, it is not precisely a park. Designation as a park ordinarily rules out resource extraction, on the one hand, and on the other it implies a mere defense, the retention of a status quo that can't undergo deliberate improvements. The situation in the Mono Basin is more complex and perhaps even more to be celebrated. If we lack a word for this kind of place, we have a perfectly good and traditional one for what is going to be going on there. We call it, simply, conservation.

Wallace Stegner once wrote of the "geography of hope." He situated parks and wilderness areas in that geography. But maybe the phrase applies even better to what the Mono Basin is becoming: an illustration that we can take something from nature without taking all, a reminder that we can change our minds, sometimes, and give a little back.

11

THE MEANINGS OF MONO

For us who were there, we caused at the frontiers
exceptional accidents, and pushing ourselves in
our actions to the end of our strength, our joy
amongst you was a very great joy.

Saint-John Perse, *Anabasis*

TABLEAU: REPRESENTATIVES OF THE DEPARTMENT of Water and Power, conservation groups, and various powers of government, grouped around a microphone, swearing cooperation and peace, proclaiming that Mono Lake is saved.

With the Mono Lake story at a tentative conclusion, it is possible at last to step back from the action and ask, What happened here? What else is happening as a result? What does the story mean? The thing itself—the preservation, against long odds, of one of the West's remarkable landscapes—might seem enough meaning, enough reward. But the events at Mono Lake will radiate. They have already changed the realities of water in California. And both the solution and the means by which it was reached have more general lessons to teach.

At Mono Lake in 1994, for the first time ever in California, water was removed from the grasp of an anointed appropriative user and assigned, not to some rival diverter, but to an environmental purpose: the restoration of the lake and its feeder streams. And the agency losing water consented, at the end, to this reassignment. The two facts are almost equally astonishing.

Back in 1946, a California governor proclaimed, "In my opinion we should not relax until California has adopted and put into operation a statewide program that will put every drop of water to work." Water in streams, the context made clear, was not "work-

THE PUBLIC TRUST
AND AFTER

ing." By the time the Mono Lake campaign began in 1978, attitudes had softened somewhat. Certain rivers had been classified as "wild," off limits to dam-builders. The use of water for fish and wildlife was recognized as "beneficial." The State Water Resources Control Board asserted the power to limit the scope of new water diversions. But none of those measures touched the very common case where dams already existed and diversions were already underway.

Then came Mono Lake.

Because Los Angeles had acquired its rights here in the old days, the region lay in a sort of time warp, untouched by the general rise in environmental concern. To accomplish anything in this setting, Tim Such, Palmer Madden, Bruce Dodge, and Barrett McInerney had to look unusually deep. "Hard cases," a lawyers' maxim runs, "make bad law." Certainly the Mono Basin cases were hard ones. But here, at least, the law from hard cases was good.

In its public trust ruling of 1983, the California Supreme Court held that the state had an inescapable duty to protect the values of state-owned Mono Lake "as far as feasible," and that even existing water rights must yield to that duty.

The effect of this precedent was first felt in *United States v. State Water Resources Control Board*, a 1986 decision concerning the Sacramento/San Joaquin Delta. The Third District Court of Appeal declared that the water board had both the power and the duty to protect public trust values in the delta more firmly than it had done before. The board has been struggling with that assignment ever since.

The public trust also shifted the balance in a long-standing controversy concerning the lower American River. Threading the Sacramento metropolis, that stream provides a precious greenway, but water diversion upstream threatens to reduce its value. The Mono Lake public trust decision gave environmentalists and the county of Sacramento a powerful new tool for their battle against this degradation.

In the original decision, the trust came into play only because Mono Lake, as a navigable water, triggered special state responsibilities. Later decisions, however, affirmed that fish and other aquatic life in the Mono Basin creeks, also public property, were covered by the public trust duty. In California, therefore, the doctrine no longer depends on the presence of deep water. Any stream in the state that contains life—which means any stream—is, arguably, covered.

In the Mono Basin stream cases, a second and more specific legal lever came to hand. *Dahlgren v. Los Angeles* relied on Fish and Game Code Section 5937, the provision requiring that dams release water for fish downstream. Then came the *California Trout* cases, argued and won on the basis of code section 5946, which mandated enforcement of 5937 in the eastern Sierra only. That raised a curious question: was the original 5937 somehow *not* enforceable elsewhere? Since then, however, 5937 has been cited in cases involving streams west of the Sierra; it appears that the fish requirements, like the public trust doctrine itself, apply statewide. In fact the courts have combined the two imperatives: the Fish and Game Code provisions are seen as a specific expression of the general underlying trust.

Other legal tools, not forged in the Mono Basin, are now also being used to protect water in its native habitat. Water pollution laws have been invoked, since the quality of water in streams obviously depends in part on water *quantity* there. The federal Endangered Species Act is another powerful, if controversial, tool. And the courts may be inching toward a reinterpretation of the California constitutional provision that water diversion must be "reasonable" and "beneficial": is it not "unreasonable" to take water in such a way that streams are ruined?

But if the public trust is not alone in the field, it still remains the most profound statement we have of a common interest—a common *property* interest—in certain vital things. As a specific doctrine, it seems to have almost constitutional status; it is doubtful that the courts would allow the legislature to abolish it. As a broad idea, it can be said to underlie a world of policies and laws.

To the disappointment of some public trust watchers, the California interpretation of the doctrine has not caught on elsewhere. But all the western states are working in their own ways on the problem of protecting adequate flows in streams. In several states, for instance, government agencies or conservation groups are allowed to acquire water for the express purpose of letting it flow undisturbed. In this broader movement, California's version of the public trust is, if not a model, at least an encouraging landmark.

The Mono Lake outcome, the first of the explicit water reallocations in California, will not be the last or the largest; indeed, the water at stake at Mono was trivial in comparison to that required to preserve the ecosystem of the Sacramento/San Joaquin Delta or—another emerging cause—to put water back into the San Joaquin River below the Friant dam.

Understandably, these pending or possible reallocations are troubling to the interests that stand to lose water. Agriculture, which uses four-fifths of California's developed supply, is particularly worried. Its leaders have complained of what they call a "regulatory drought." Do we really have water to spare for fish, for the health of the delta estuarine system, for Mono Lake, for all manner of environmental treasures? Can we actually live on what U.C. Davis law professor Harrison C. Dunning has called "environmentally safe yield"?

The answer is not a plain yes or no but, rather, "Yes—if we choose to." Our society's need for water is not merely biological, like the needs of the fish whose streams we tap. We use water for shifting purposes; we can use it more or less efficiently for any given

DO WE HAVE
ENOUGH WATER?

purpose; how much we use depends largely on how much it costs us. Everything about our water use is, so to speak, fluid.

In the country, farmers are already facing lessened water deliveries and modestly rising water prices. In response, they are changing irrigation techniques to use water more sparingly, and in some cases they have switched from crops that use a lot of water to crops that use less (but may require more labor and time to establish, maintain, and harvest). The irrigated acreage in the state, which used to expand each time another dam went up, is now expected to shrink somewhat. The difficulty of making such adjustments should not be belittled. Nevertheless, they indicate that to speak of shortage in any absolute sense is unjustified.

In urban areas parallel shifts are under way. Conservation and water reclamation are on the agenda everywhere. Such local measures have the advantage of making cities a bit less dependent on their aqueducts and a bit less vulnerable to drought. "The water supply of tomorrow," says Los Angeles City Councilwoman Ruth Galanter, "is the water that's already here."

Plainly, we have enough water in California for great (and growing) cities and for a vast system of agriculture. We have enough for industry. We have enough for all necessities and for a great many luxuries. But we do not have enough water to think of it in the old way. We used to regard water almost like air: a sustaining substance that was simply *there*. It is now becoming more like money: a sustaining substance that nobody seems to have quite enough of.

"Scarcity," economist Kenneth E. Frederick has written, "is characteristic of most resources and something society must constantly deal with." For some decades we persuaded ourselves that water was the exception. Even without our attack of conscience over the environmental effects of our water demands, the illusion of abundance was due to fade. Because of issues like Mono Lake, though, it is fading a little faster.

WAGING THE PEACE An adjustment to the limits of our water supply—or of any other resource we depend on—can be relatively hard or relatively easy. The fifteen-year Mono Lake battle shows how hard the process can be. It also shows how advocates of change can work to smooth the way.

At Mono Lake, a group of rebels set out to disturb long-standing habits and expectations. It brooked no compromise on its basic position. But at the same time it set out to understand the status quo it was challenging—to get inside it, so to speak—and to address the problems, real or alleged, that victory would raise. This turned out to be, politically, quite brilliant; it was also simply the honest way to go.

This project goes back as far as the Mono Lake Committee itself. Committee hydrologist Peter Vorster made himself an expert on Los Angeles's water supply, *from the city's point of view*. In the late 1980s, the committee developed an identity as a Los An-

At one of the water board hearings, fly researcher David Herbst was put on the spot about his relations with the Mono Lake Committee. Water and Power counsel Moskovitz asked the scientist if he would describe the link as one of "close and continuing support." Herbst did not hedge or quibble, but answered simply, "Yes." Later on the same day, however, he offered evidence tending to support a lake level of 6,390 feet, lower than the Mono advocates were by then seeking. Although he had a hunch, says Herbst, that higher lake levels would be as good or better for alkali flies than 6,390 feet, he had not proved it to his own satisfaction.

The story says something about the role of scientists in the Mono Lake story.

From the beginning they are major figures: Israel Russell; David Mason; Kenneth Lajoie; the Davids Winkler, Herbst, and Shuford (to say nothing of Gaines); Peter Vorster; Scott Stine. Scientists launched the Sierra Club Mono Lake Task Force and the Mono Lake Committee. In varying degrees, in varying ways, they kept on aiding the cause of preservation. On the other side of the legal fence, of course, were scientists funded by the Los Angeles Department of Water and Power. The Mono Lake Committee, too, underwrote a little research.

These facts naturally raise some questions and some eyebrows. Did the science suffer either from personal enthusiasms or from loyalty to funders? To be objective, shouldn't one hold to a strict, and unsubsidized, neutrality?

The record, all in all, seems reassuring. If researchers on both sides have stuck their necks out from time to time, they have quickly drawn them back. Their words and observations have been misused and overinterpreted fairly often by friends and clients, but only rarely by scientists themselves. We have seen science in action: not "pure" so much as self-purifying, with built-in rules that work to sort things out sooner or later.

In the Mono case the water board hearings speeded up that sorting. Divergent accounts had to be accepted, rejected, reconciled, or (in some cases) simply allowed to stand as alternatives pending further data. Project manager Jim Canaday and his colleagues performed this synthesis well, and, still more significantly, the board took an action that reflected it.

As the environmental problems of the world become more severe, more interrelated, and more subtle, we will have to rely increasingly on scientists to speak—and on the powers that be to pause and listen.

Getting the Good Out of Science

geles citizens' group, helping the city to address problems of water management that went well beyond the replacement of Mono Lake water. Eventually, of course, the Mono Lake Committee was instrumental in securing state and federal funding to help the city and the wider region forge ahead with water reclamation. The belated reward of all this work was policy change in Los Angeles, and even within the Department of Water and Power.

Six weeks after the Mono Lake water board decision, the November election brought a great shift in political power in Washington, D.C., and to some extent in Sacramento. Many of the ins were out; many of the outs were in. But the solution that had been built at Mono was not in peril, for it did not depend on any one party or viewpoint. There is every reason to believe that it will stick, because it was, after all, accepted, and not merely imposed.

In December of 1994, three months after the Mono verdict, another and no less significant water breakthrough occurred. Representatives of urban, agricultural, and environmental powers reached a compromise concerning flows in the Sacramento/San Joaquin Delta. The resulting state-federal agreement provides more water for fish and a predictable, though somewhat diminished, supply for cities and farms. The timing of this treaty, so soon after the Mono settlement, was coincidental. Yet the Mono example cannot have hurt the process.

CONSIDERING
THE SOURCE

David Gaines used to remark that saving Mono Lake was not his unalterable goal. His real aim was to make people throughout California realize what would be lost if the lake continued to sink. If Californians, and particularly Angelenos, weighed those values, understood them deeply, and decided to sacrifice them for a convenient and inexpensive water supply, Gaines would (so he said) accept that choice. But it had to be a *knowing* choice.

Surely this idea of knowing choice can be applied to more than Mono Lake; indeed, to more than water. Suppose, in consuming *any* resource, we were told exactly where it came from and at what cost to that place? Suppose, like those aboriginal hunters who offer a courteous apology to the creatures they kill, we took with full knowledge of what it is we were taking? Would this not make us more careful, less casual, in our consumption and in our demands?

Of course, in the case of Mono Lake the linkages are unusually, dazzlingly clear. Source, aqueduct, city: it is almost a cartoon of resource use, as the Mono Lake ecosystem itself is almost a cartoon of the more typical multifariousness. But again a principle is apparent. As the Mono Lake Committee has incessantly pointed out, every tap leads back to a Mono Lake—somewhere. So does every board or sheet of paper lead back to a forest; every burning light bulb to an oil well, perhaps, or a hydroelectric dam; every aluminum can to a landscape marked by a mine. It is impossible, in many cases, to particularize the source. But the source is always there.

We cannot live on the land without changing it; not even indigenous peoples do that.

Opposite: *Lakeshore, 1989. (Photo by Lauren Davis, courtesy Mono Lake Committee)*

We probably cannot live on the land without in some ways damaging it. What we can do is what we did at Mono Lake. We can learn about the things at stake, the kinds of damage to be anticipated, the thresholds at which small degradations become large. Then it is up to us, if we have the courage, to adjust our human claims.

At Mono Lake, we got the information and found the courage. Our society reached a decision to reduce its demands on this place, and by more than just a little. After all the talk, it proved not terribly hard to do.

Many such decisions, some of them far more difficult than the one at Mono, lie ahead. Yet, as we go into the hazardous century to come, the rising waters of Mono Lake can serve as a reminder of one test passed, as one confirmation that we are able to assert not only some control over nature but also some control over ourselves.

Selected Bibliography

Note on repositories (all in California). Perhaps the single most useful collection of Mono Lake materials is the Mono Lake Research Library, maintained at Lee Vining by the Mono Lake Committee. The most nearly complete set of relevant legal documents is at the Eldorado County Superior Court in South Lake Tahoe; some case records are in county courthouses in Markleeville (Alpine County), Bridgeport (Mono County), Sacramento (Sacramento County), and Sonora (Tuolumne County), as well as at the Ninth Circuit U.S. Court of Appeals in San Francisco. The State Water Resources Control Board in Sacramento has sketchy records from early Mono Basin actions and voluminous ones after 1989. Many significant nonlegal documents are reproduced in court and water board records as exhibits. Correspondence in the California Trout Mono Basin litigation can be found at the organization's San Francisco headquarters and at the law offices of Barrett W. McInerney in Van Nuys (Los Angeles). Important materials can also be found at the Great Basin Unified Air Pollution Control District (Bishop), the Mono Basin National Forest Scenic Area (Lee Vining), the Mono Lake Tufa State Reserve (Lee Vining), and the California Resources Agency Library, managed by the California Department of Fish and Game (Sacramento).

At the University of California at Berkeley, the Bancroft Library and the Water Resources Center Archives have some historical documents not available elsewhere. (The Mono Lake Committee's inactive files are being transferred piecemeal to the Bancroft.) The library and the photo archive at the Los Angeles Department of Water and Power offer unique materials. The J. B. Clover Collection, including many historic photographs, is housed at the Huntington Library in San Marino, California. The Mono Basin Historical Society in Lee Vining and the Eastern California Museum in Independence also deserve mention.

The Album: Times and Tales of Inyo-Mono. Bishop: Chalfant Press. Local history periodical, quarterly 1987–92, annual since 1993.

Austin, Mary. *The Land of Little Rain*. 1901. Reprint New York: Penguin, 1988. The classic about California east of the Sierra (and an early example of unsentimental nature writing).

Babb, Dave. "The Mono Lake Wars." *Album* (March 1988): 19–21. Oil and radium rushes at Mono Lake around 1900, as reported by the *Inyo Register* and the *Bodie Miner*.

Bailey, Roy A. *Geologic Map of Long Valley Caldera, Mono-Inyo Craters Volcanic Chain, and Vicinity, Eastern California*. Miscellaneous Investigations Series Map 1–1933. Washington, D.C.: U.S. Government Printing Office, 1989. Two sheets and accompanying text. Engrossing account of local vulcanism.

Baiocchi, Joel. "Use It or Lose It: California Fish and Game Code Section 5937 and Instream Fishery Resources." *U.C. Davis Law Review* 14 (Winter 1980): 431–460. A prescient call for enforcement of the law requiring water releases through, or around, dams.

Bean, Betty. *Horseshoe Canyon: A Brief History of the June Lake Loop*. Bishop: Chalfant Press, 1977. The founding of the Mono Basin's largest community.

Botkin, Daniel, Wallace S. Broecker, Lorne G. Everett, Joseph Shapiro, and John A. Wiens. *The Future of Mono Lake: Report of the Community and Organization Research Institute "Blue Ribbon Panel."* Water Resources Center Report No. 68. Riverside: University of California, 1988. The second major government-sanctioned study of Mono Lake turned the debate away from very low lake levels. Five final reports of the subcontractors are separate volumes.

Brechin, Gray. "Elegy for a Dying Lake." *California Living* (*San Francisco Examiner*), 1 October 1978. Much-quoted early lament and call to action.

———. "A Matter of Trust." *San Francisco Focus* (September 1985): 115–118. The role of Tim Such.

Brewer, William H. *Up and Down California in 1860–1864: The Journal of William H. Brewer*. 1930. Reprint Berkeley: University of California Press, 1966. Fascinating throughout; just a few pages on Mono Basin.

Browne, J. Ross. *A Trip to Bodie Bluff and the Dead Sea of the West (Mono Lake) in 1863*. 1865. Reprint Golden, Colorado: Outbooks, 1981. Last section treats Mono islands, volcanoes, tufa towers, alkali flies, and panoramas.

Cain, Ella M. *The Story of Early Mono County*. San Francisco: Fearon Publishers, 1961. A disjointed but valuable series of historical sketches by a descendant of local pioneers.

Calhoun, Margaret. *Pioneers of the Mono Basin*. Lee Vining: Artemisia Press, 1992. Similar to Cain's work.

California Attorney General. Letters from Ralph W. Scott, deputy attorney general, to Seth Gordon, director, California Department of Fish and Game. 26 August 1953: The Hot Creek Agreement excusing the Department of Water and Power from releasing flows through its Mono County dams is valid. 11 July 1955: The new Fish and Game Code Section 5946 does not apply to cases where preliminary permits were issued before the effective date. 26 June 1956: The dewatering of the Owens Gorge is legal and irrevocable.

California Department of Fish and Game. *Rush Creek: Stream Evaluation Report 91–2*. Sacramento: California Department of Fish and Game, 1991. Recommended flow regimes and habitat restoration work for the benefit of brown trout. Similar two-volume reports for Walker Creek (92–1), Parker Creek (92–2), South Parker Creek (92–3), the upper Owens River (93–1), and Lee Vining Creek (93–2).

California Department of Parks and Recreation. *Bodie State Historic Park*. Sacramento: California Department of Parks and Recreation, 1988.

California Senate Committee on Local Governmental Agencies. *Report Concerning Application of City of Los Angeles for Purchase of Federal Lands in Mono County, October 19, 1945*. In 1944, Water and Power sought to acquire 23,851 acres of public land in Mono County, but opposition, exemplified by this report, killed the plan.

California State Water Resources Control Board. *Draft Environmental Impact Report for the Review of the Mono Basin Water Rights of the City of Los Angeles.* Sacramento: California State Water Resources Control Board, 1993. Three volumes, 28 auxiliary reports: the most massive compilation of data concerning Mono Lake.

———. *Final Environmental Impact Report for the Review of the Mono Basin Water Rights of the City of Los Angeles.* Sacramento: California State Water Resources Control Board, 1994. Reassesses the effects of various lake levels, incorporating new findings especially on tufa, sand tufa, and alkali flies.

California Trout. *Streamkeeper's Log.* San Francisco. Organizational newsletter since 1971; regular coverage of Mono events after 1984.

Cameron, Robert, and Harold Gilliam. *Above Yosemite: A New Collection of Aerial Photographs of Yosemite National Park, California.* San Francisco: Cameron & Co., 1983. Includes Mono Basin; text by Gilliam.

Chalfant, Willie A. *The Story of Inyo.* 1933. Reprint Bishop: Chalfant Press, 1975. The Inyo side of the Inyo–Los Angeles story.

Chasan, Daniel Jack. "Mono Lake vs. Los Angeles: A Tug-of-War for Precious Water." *Smithsonian* (February 1981): 42–50. Among the most thorough of the early national articles.

City of Los Angeles, Mayor's Blue Ribbon Committee on Department of Water and Power Rate Structure. *Water Rate Structure Report.* Los Angeles: City of Los Angeles, 1977. Prior to 1977, Los Angeles had rewarded heavy users with lower rates; this report led to adoption of a uniform price per gallon.

City of Los Angeles, Mayor's Blue Ribbon Committee on Water Rates. *Proposed Water Rates.* Los Angeles: City of Los Angeles, 1992. Acting on the advice of this second Blue Ribbon Committee, the city shifted water costs to the heaviest users, encouraging conservation.

Cloud, Preston, and Kenneth R. Lajoie. "Calcite-Impregnated Defluidization Structures in Littoral Sands of Mono Lake, California." *Science* 210 (November 28, 1980): 1009–1012. Sand tufa, with cover photo of lithic tufa.

Constantine, Helen. *Plant Communities of the Mono Basin.* Lee Vining: Mono Lake Committee, 1993. Thirty characteristic plants in ecological context.

Dana, Gayle L., Robert Jellison, John M. Melack, and Gwen L. Starrett. "Relationships Between *Artemia monica* Life History Characteristics and Salinity." *Hydrobiologia* 263 (July 16, 1993): 129–143. A summation growing out of work for the State Water Resources Control Board; incorporates results of experiments conducted by the Department of Water and Power.

Dana, Gayle L., and Petra H. Lenz. "Effects of Increasing Salinity on an *Artemia* Population from Mono Lake, California." *Oecologia* 68 (February 1986): 428–436. Based on laboratory experiments, finds that shrimp cysts fail to hatch when salinity reaches 133 grams/liter, or a lake level of about 6,357 feet.

Davis, Emma Lou. *An Ethnography of the Kuzedika Paiute of Mono Lake, Mono County, California.* University of Utah Department of Anthropology Anthropological Papers 75. Salt Lake City: University of Utah Press, 1965. A basic work on the Kuzedika.

Davis, M. L. *Rivers in the Desert: William Mulholland and the Inventing of Los Angeles.* New York: HarperCollins, 1993. Admiring biography marred by some glaring inaccuracies.

Dunning, Harrison C. "Dam Fights and Water Policy in California: 1969–1989." *Journal of the West* 29 (July 1990): 14–27. The Mono controversy as one of several turning points in reform.

———. "The End of the Mono Lake Basin Water War: Ecosystem Management, Fish, and Fairness to a Water Supplier." *California Water Law and Policy Reporter* 5 (November 1994): 27–31. A satisfied look back.

———. "Instream Flows and the Public Trust." In Lawrence J. MacDonnell and Teresa A. Rice, eds., *Instream Flow Protection in the West.* 2d ed. Boulder: Natural Resources Law Center,

University of Colorado School of Law, 1993. Background and implications of the 1983 public trust decision.

Dunning, Harrison C., ed. *The Public Trust Doctrine in Natural Resources Law and Management: Conference Proceedings.* Davis: University of California, 1981. The September 1980 conference. Includes reports by the opposing lawyers on *Audubon v. Los Angeles.*

———. "The Public Trust Doctrine in Natural Resources Law and Management: A Symposium." *U.C. Davis Law Review* 14 (Winter 1980): 181–460. The principal papers from the conference, with new allied material. Cited several times by the California Supreme Court in its 1983 public trust decision.

Farquhar, Francis P. *History of the Sierra Nevada.* Berkeley: University of California Press, 1965. The standard work. Glancing reference to the Mono Basin.

Feller, Joseph M. Letter to Cathy Catterson, Clerk, United States Court of Appeals for the Ninth Circuit. November 4, 1988. On file at Great Basin Unified Air Pollution Control District, Bishop. Feller's warning caused the court to rewrite an opinion in *Audubon v. Los Angeles* that might have undermined the Clean Air Act.

Fiero, Bill. *Geology of the Great Basin.* Reno: University of Nevada Press, 1986. Describes a dramatic and intricate landscape evolution.

Fletcher, Thomas C. *Paiute, Prospector, Pioneer: A History of the Bodie-Mono Lake Area in the Nineteenth Century.* Lee Vining: Artemisia Press, 1987. The one scholarly history of the Mono Basin. Based on the author's Master's thesis, University of California at Berkeley, 1982.

Frederick, Kenneth D., ed. *Scarce Water and Institutional Change.* Washington, D.C.: Resources for the Future, 1986. Case for water marketing in arid regions.

Gaines, David. *Birds of Yosemite and the East Slope.* Lee Vining: Artemisia Press, 1988. Completed a month before the author's death.

———. Revised by Lauren Davis. *Mono Lake Guidebook.* Lee Vining: Mono Lake Committee, 1989. Fourth edition since 1981. A tremendous amount of basic information, largely reliable.

Geologic Society of the Oregon Country. *Roadside Geology of the Eastern Sierra Region: Bodie, Mono Lake, Yosemite, June Lake, Devils Postpile, Convict Lake, White Mountains.* G.S.O.C. Publication 19. 1962. Reprint Lee Vining: Mono Lake Committee, 1982. A handy though dated guidebook.

Gilbert, Bil. "Is This a Holy Place?" *Sports Illustrated*, May 30, 1983, 76–90. A breakthrough piece in a popular publication.

Gilbert, C. M., M. N. Christensen, Y. Al-Rawi, and Kenneth R. Lajoie. "Volcanism and Structural History of Mono Basin." Pp. 275–330 in *Studies in Volcanism: A Memoir in Honor of Howel [sic] Williams.* Ed. Robert R. Coats, Richard L. Hay, and Charles A. Anderson. Geological Society of America Memoir 116. Boulder: Geological Society of America, 1968. Still the most thorough discussion of the subject. Considers alternate theories and concludes that the Mono Basin is a fault-block structure, not a caldera.

Gilliam, Harold. "The Destruction of Mono Lake Is on Schedule." *This World (San Francisco Chronicle)*, 11 February 1979. Early call to action.

Governor's Commission to Review California Water Rights Law. *Final Report.* Sacramento: State of California, 1978. This commission (staff headed by Harrison C. Dunning) saw the lack of mechanisms for protecting natural streamflows as one of four key defects in the law, and they listed the public trust doctrine among possible correctives. See also Schneider, below.

Grinnell, Joseph, and Tracy I. Storer. *Animal Life in the Yosemite.* Berkeley: University of California Press, 1924. Grinnell's famous trans-Sierra transect study ended on Mono Lake at the mouth of Lee Vining Creek.

Hall, Clarence A., Victoria Doyle-Jones, and Barbara Widawski, eds. *The History of Water: Eastern Sierra, Owens Valley, White-Inyo Mountains.* Proceedings, White Mountain Research Station

Fourth Biennial Symposium, Bishop, September 1991. Los Angeles: University of California White Mountain Research Station, 1992. Significant contributions by Jellison, Dana, and Melack on the lake ecosystem, Herbst on fly habitat, Cahill and Gill on Owens Lake dust pollution, Vorster on historic Owens Valley agriculture.

Hanna, Jim. *Lundy—Gem of the Eastern Sierra: A Day Hiker's and Backpacker's Guide to the Geology, History and Points of Interest.* Virginia City: Gold Hill Publishing Co., 1990. The nineteenth-century mining district on Mill Creek.

Harding, S. T. "Report on Development of Water Resources in Mono Basin Based on Investigations Made for the Division of Engineering and Irrigation, State Department of Public Works." Report, 1922. Water Resources Center Archives, University of California at Berkeley. Early competition for water in the Mono Basin.

Harris, Stephen L. *Fire Mountains of the West: The Cascade and Mono Lake Volcanoes.* Missoula: Mountain Press, 1988. Chapter on past and probable future volcanic activity in the Mono Lake–Long Valley region.

Hart, Terry, and David Gaines. "Field Checklist of the Birds of Mono Basin." Lee Vining: Mono Lake Committee, 1983. Two hundred and fifty-nine species.

Herbst, David B. "Comparative Population Ecology of *Ephydra Hians Say* (Diptera: Ephydridae) at Mono Lake (California) and Abert Lake (Oregon)." *Hydrobiologia* 158 (January 30, 1988): 145–166. The alkali fly prospers in waters of intermediate chemical load: too salty and alkaline for predators and competitors, not too much so for the fly itself.

Herbst, David B., and Timothy J. Bradley. "A Malpighian Tubule Lime Gland in an Insect Inhabiting Alkaline Salt Lakes." *Journal of Experimental Biology* 145 (September 1989): 63–78. How the alkali fly gets rid of excess carbonate and bicarbonate from lakewater. Not stated here is the author's suggestion that excreted lime accretes to tufa structures.

———. "A Population Model for the Alkali Fly at Mono Lake: Depth Distribution and Changing Habitat Availability." *Hydrobiologia* 267 (September 10, 1993): 191–201. The importance of tufa and other hard underwater surfaces for larvae and pupae.

Herbst, David B., and Richard W. Castenholz. "Growth of the Filamentous Algae *Ctenocladus circinnatus* (*Chaetophorales, Chlorophyceae*) in Relation to Environmental Salinity." *Journal of Phycology* 30 (August 1994): 588–593. This alga, a food source for the alkali fly, is suppressed by current high salinity.

Hoffman, Abraham. *Vision or Villainy—Origins of the Owens Valley–Los Angeles Water Controversy.* College Station: Texas A&M University Press, 1981. One of the major accounts, generally favorable to the city's point of view.

Huber, N. King. *Amount and Timing of Late Cenozoic Uplift and Tilt of the Central Sierra Nevada, California—Evidence from the Upper San Joaquin River Basin.* U.S. Geological Survey Professional Paper 1197. Washington, D.C.: U.S. Government Printing Office, 1981. Pinpoints the tectonic events that created the Mono Basin.

Hundley, Norris L. *The Great Thirst: Californians and Water, 1770s–1990s.* Berkeley: University of California Press, 1992. The first overall history. Notes contrast between Spanish-Mexican and Anglo-American water rights doctrines.

Interagency Task Force on Mono Lake. Minutes. During working meetings in the spring of 1979, two sets of minutes were taken, one for public consumption, one for members only. Both sets, as well as the minutes of public hearings in June, are found at the Mono Lake Research Library in Lee Vining or at the Bancroft.

———. *Report.* Sacramento: California Department of Water Resources, 1979. An early official call for a high lake level. In some respects the proposed solution anticipates the water board decision of 1994.

Irwin, Sue. *California's Eastern Sierra: A Visitor's Guide.* Los Olivos: Cachuma Press/Eastern Sierra

Interpretive Association, 1991. From Lone Pine to Bridgeport, with copious color photographs and maps.

Jehl, Joseph R., Jr. "Beauty, Goose and Anna Herman: Mono Lake's Islands and How They Got Their Names." *Album* (January 1992): 13–19. Among other points, takes aim at David Gaines's suggestion that *negit* might mean "gull."

———. *Biology of the Eared Grebe and Wilson's Phalarope in the Nonbreeding Season: A Study of Adaptations to Saline Lakes.* Studies in Avian Biology no. 12. Los Angeles: Cooper Ornithological Society, 1985. A basic work on two of the less controversial Mono species.

———. *The Biology of Waterbirds at Mono Lake, California: A Synthesis.* San Diego: Hubbs–Sea World Institute, 1987.

———. "Mono Lake: A Vital Way Station for the Wilson's Phalarope." *National Geographic* 160 (October 1981): 520–525. New findings.

Jehl, Joseph R., Jr., David E. Babb, and Dennis M. Power. "History of the California Gull Colony at Mono Lake, California." *Colonial Waterbirds* 7 (June 1984): 94–104. Suggests that declining lake levels were actually favorable to the gulls.

———. "On the Interpretation of Historical Data, with Reference to the California Gull Colony at Mono Lake, California." *Colonial Waterbirds* 11 (June 1988): 322–327. Another shot in the gull duel; compare Winkler, below.

Jellison, Robert, Gayle L. Dana, and John M. Melack. "Ecosystem Responses to Changes in Freshwater Inflow to Mono Lake, California." In Hall, Doyle-Jones, and Widawski, *History of Water,* above. Concludes that salinity alone affects the shrimp population less dramatically than lab results suggest; emphasizes available nitrogen as controlling factor.

Johnson, Stephen, ed. *At Mono Lake: A Photographic Exhibition.* San Francisco: Friends of the Earth Foundation, 1983. Catalogue with contributions by Johnson, Page Stegner, historian Thomas Fletcher, and others.

Jones, Holway R. *John Muir and the Sierra Club: The Battle for Yosemite.* San Francisco: Sierra Club, 1965. Yosemite National Park origin and boundary controversies.

Kahrl, William L. *Water and Power: The Conflict over Los Angeles' Water Supply in the Owens Valley.* Berkeley: University of California Press, 1982. The magisterial history of Los Angeles's relations with the Owens Valley, with a thorough discussion of the Mono Extension. Strong emphasis on the L.A. theater of the story. Gives short shrift to Mono events after 1975.

———, ed. *The California Water Atlas.* Sacramento: State of California, 1979. An opulent book, still of great value, on sundry aspects of the water supply scene. Mono Lake gets a bare mention.

Kelsey, Louise. "The Lost Benchmark." *Album* (October 1989): 23–26. Locating Israel Russell's benchmark on Negit Island.

Kirshenbaum, Jerry. "Will the Flow from Rush Creek Swamp the Dreaded DWP?" *Sports Illustrated,* 4 February 1984, 7. A report on the Dahlgren case.

Kramer, E. W. "Report on the Use for Irrigation of Rush and Leevining [*sic*] Creeks by the Cain Irrigation Company." Report for U.S. Forest Service, San Francisco, 1928. Over-irrigation of Cain Ranch fields in anticipation of buyout by Los Angeles. Los Angeles Department of Water and Power Exhibit 7, State Water Resources Control Board hearings, 1993.

Kusko, Bruce H., and Thomas A. Cahill. *Study of Particle Episodes at Mono Lake: Final Report to the California Air Resources Board on Contract No. A1–144–32.* Davis: Air Quality Group, Crocker Nuclear Laboratory, University of California, 1984. An important study reflecting the low-lake and high-dust period around 1980.

Lajoie, Kenneth R. "Quaternary Stratigraphy and Geologic History of Mono Basin, Eastern California." Ph.D. diss., University of California, Berkeley, 1968. Still basic; identifies the Bishop Tuff in logs of old Paoha Island oil drilling.

Lawton, Harry W., Philip J. Wilke, Mary DeDecker, and William M. Mason. "Agriculture Among the Paiute of Owens Valley." *Journal of California Anthropology* 3 (Summer 1976): 13–50. Argues that the Owens Valley Paiutes practiced true irrigation and not merely "water spreading."

Leopold, Aldo. *A Sand County Almanac, and Sketches Here and There.* 1949. Reprint New York: Oxford University Press, 1989. For the remark about "quality in nature" cited in the introduction to the color plates, see the essay "Marshland Elegy."

Los Angeles Department of Water and Power. *Facts and Figures.* Los Angeles: Los Angeles Department of Water and Power, 1995. Includes a valuable chronology (key dates from 1769) and current system data.

———. *Intake.* Inhouse publication. Significant Mono articles appear in August 1978, June 1979, May 1980, June 1980, September 1980, September–October 1982, March–April 1983, July–August 1991, November–December 1991, November–December 1994.

———. *Los Angeles Aqueduct System.* Los Angeles: Los Angeles Department of Water and Power, 1989. A useful orientation.

———. *The Mono Lake Management Plan.* Los Angeles: Los Angeles Department of Water and Power, 1993. A statement for the public of the proposals made by the Department of Water and Power to the State Water Resources Control Board.

———. *Mono Lake Report.* Los Angeles: Los Angeles Department of Water and Power, [1989]. Report on the situation as the water board's review of the city's water diversion licenses was getting under way.

———. *Sharing the Vision: The Story of the Los Angeles Aqueduct.* Los Angeles: Los Angeles Department of Water and Power, undated. Celebratory history.

———. *Statistical Report for the Fiscal Years 1983–1994.* Los Angeles: Los Angeles Department of Water and Power, 1995. A ten-year record, revised annually.

———. *Urban Water Management Plan, City of Los Angeles.* Los Angeles: Los Angeles Department of Water and Power, 1987. Assessment of supply, demand, conservation, and reclamation.

———. *Urban Water Management Plan, City of Los Angeles.* Los Angeles: Los Angeles Department of Water and Power, 1991. An update reflecting both policy evolution and the challenge of drought.

———. *A Water Recycling Plan for the Los Angeles Department of Power: Water Recycling 1991–2000.* Los Angeles: Los Angeles Department of Water and Power, 1994. Plans for generating and distributing reclaimed water, with a target of 80,000 acre-feet a year in 2010.

———. "Water Rights and Operations in the Mono Basin." Unpublished report, 1974. Growing protest led water chief Paul H. Lane and his colleagues to review the situation and consider means of stemming the lake's decline without reducing exports. Letter to Toiyabe Chapter, Sierra Club, appended.

Los Angeles Times. Editorials track shifting attitudes. See February 11, 1980; February 20, 1983; May 29, 1983; July 25, 1983; November 10, 1983; December 11, 1984; April 30, 1985; August 26, 1986; August 7, 1987; September 26, 1988; June 17, 1989; August 23, 1989; September 7, 1992; December 19, 1993; September 24, 1994.

McPherson, Wallis. Interview by David Gaines and Ilene Mandelbaum, June 28, 1985. Transcript and tape recording, Mono Lake Research Library, Lee Vining.

———. Interview by Mono Lake Committee, undated. Transcript and tape recording, Mono Lake Research Library, Lee Vining.

Mason, David T. "Limnology of Mono Lake, California." Ph.D. diss., University of California, Davis, 1966. Also University of California Publications in Zoology 83. First modern limnological study.

Means, Thomas H. "Report on the Value of Property Sold by the Southern Sierra Power Company and Associated Companies to the City of Los Angeles in 1934 and 1935 Under Contract Dated

Oct. 20, 1933." 1938. Thomas Means Papers, Water Resources Center Archives, University of California at Berkeley.

Melack, John M. "Large, Deep Salt Lakes: A Comparative Limnological Analysis." *Hydrobiologia* 105 (September 1, 1983): 223–230. Compares Mono with other saline lakes over fifteen meters deep on three continents. Mono is the saltiest of the group and the only one without fish.

Mono Basin Ecosystem Study Committee of the National Research Council, National Academy of Sciences. *The Mono Basin Ecosystem: Effects of Changing Lake Level.* Washington, D.C.: National Academy Press, 1987. Historically important, though in large part superseded.

Mono Lake Committee. *Mono Lake: Endangered Oasis. Position Paper of the Mono Lake Committee.* Lee Vining: Mono Lake Committee, 1989. (See also 1982 edition.) Contains much of the material included in David Gaines's *Mono Lake Guidebook.*

———. *Mono Lake Newsletter.* Quarterly from 1978; early issues titled *Mono Lake Committee Newsletter.*

Moore, Barbara. "Mono Inn: A Grand Old Lady." *Album* (January 1990): 36–39. Part of the history of the McPhersons.

———. "Paoha: Island of Shattered Dreams." *Album* (July 1991): 40–49. More on the McPherson family.

Muir, John. *John of the Mountains: The Unpublished Journals of John Muir.* Edited by Linnie Marsh Wolfe. 1938. Reprint Temecula: Reprint Services, 1991. This and the next three of Muir's books contain different but overlapping accounts of the Mono Basin, based on the journals of two visits.

———. *The Mountains of California.* 1894. Reprint San Francisco: Sierra Club, 1989. See the chapter "The Passes of the High Sierra."

———. *My First Summer in the Sierra.* 1911. Reprint New York: Penguin, 1987. Mono Basin is discussed on pp. 306ff.

Muir, John, ed. *Picturesque California: The Rocky Mountains and the Pacific Slope.* San Francisco: J. Dewing, 1894. Another version of "Passes of the High Sierra."

Nadeau, Remi A. *The Water Seekers.* Salt Lake City: Peregrine Smith, 1974. This lively account should be read in conjunction with Karhl's *Water and Power.*

National Academy of Sciences. See Mono Basin Ecosystem Study Committee.

Public Policy Program, UCLA Extension. *Mono Lake: Beyond the Public Trust Doctrine. Conference Proceedings.* Los Angeles: Public Policy Program, UCLA Extension, 1984. Lively give-and-take marks the beginning of attempts to find common ground.

Puetz, James R., ed. "Symposium on the Public Trust and the Waters of the American West: Yesterday, Today and Tomorrow." *Environmental Law* 19 (Spring 1989): 425–735. Includes contributions by Harrison C. Dunning, Ralph E. Johnson, Joseph L. Sax, Jan S. Stevens, and others; reports on the limited echoes of the California public trust cases in Idaho, Montana, Oregon, and Washington.

Putnam, William C. "Quaternary Geology of the June Lake District, California." *Bulletin of the Geological Society of America* 60 (August 1949): 1281–1302. Discusses drilling of the Mono Craters Tunnel.

Reisner, Marc. *Cadillac Desert: The American West and Its Disappearing Water.* 2d ed. New York: Penguin, 1993. History and denunciation of the federal reclamation (dam-building) program; new afterword sees us "undoing the wrongs caused by earlier generations doing what they thought was right."

Reisner, Marc, and Sarah Bates. *Overtapped Oasis: Reform or Revolution for Western Water.* Washington, D.C.: Island Press, 1990. Calls for removing barriers to water marketing, raising the prices of subsidized federal water, protecting the public trust and instream flows, and other environmental protection and efficiency measures.

Rinehart, C. Dean, and Ward C. Smith. *Earthquakes and Young Volcanoes Along the Eastern Sierra Nevada.* Mammoth Lakes: Genny Smith Books, 1982. In 1980 and 1981, earthquakes in Long Valley raised fears of an eruption and prompted this accurate review.

Rowell, Galen. "Mono Lake: Silent, Sailless, Shrinking Sea." *Audubon* (March 1978): 102–106. One of the first discussions of the Mono issue in a national periodical.

Russell, Israel C. *Quaternary History of the Mono Valley, California.* 1889. Reprint Lee Vining: Artemisia Press, 1984. The granddaddy of all Mono Lake studies, from the Eighth Annual Report of the U.S. Geological Survey.

Sax, Joseph L. "The Public Trust Doctrine in Natural Resource Law: Effective Judicial Intervention." *Michigan Law Review* 68 (January 1970): 471–566. In the article that inspired Tim Such, Sax sees the doctrine as a powerful general tool but does not mention an application to water rights.

Schneider, Anne J. *Legal Aspects of Instream Water Uses in California: Background and Issues.* Sacramento: Governor's Commission to Review California Water Rights Law, 1978. "While consumptive water rights themselves have not yet been impaired by the assertion of the public trust doctrine, there is nothing in theory to prevent it" (27).

Schultheis, Robert. "Exploring California's Inland Sea: If There Were a Lake on the Moon, It Would Look like Mono." *Outside* (March 1978): 29–35. Another in the first swarm of articles.

Scoonover, Mary. "Mono: The Lake, the Legacy." *Environs* 18, no. 1 (1994): 26–34. Scoonover, who represented the State Lands Commission and the Department of Parks and Recreation before the water board, reviews the history of the controversy.

Smith, Felix E. "The Public Trust Doctrine as a Resource Management Philosophy." Sacramento: U.S. Fish and Wildlife Service, 1980. Aggressive early call for application of the public trust doctrine to any stream with fish, and for the federal government to play a role.

Smith, Genny, ed. *Deepest Valley: A Guide to Owens Valley, Its Roadsides and Mountain Trails.* 2d ed. Mammoth Lakes: Genny Smith Books, 1978. Guidebook, history, and natural history, with an update on the groundwater pumping dispute after 1970. Third edition in press.

———. *Mammoth Lakes Sierra: A Handbook for Roadside and Trail.* Mammoth Lakes: Genny Smith Books, 1991. Includes the Mono Basin.

———. *Sierra East: Edge of the Great Basin.* Berkeley: University of California Press, forthcoming. A natural history of the eastern slope of the Sierra Nevada mountain block and the adjacent valleys, including the Mono Basin.

Stanley, Barbara, and David A. Wright. "West Portal: The Memory, the Fact, the Ghost." *Album* (1993): 170–177. Exploring the site of the Mono Craters construction camp, with accounts from *Intake.*

Steinhart, Peter. "The City and the Inland Sea." *Audubon* (September 1980): 98–125. Comprehensive discussion.

Stine, Scott. "Extreme and Persistent Drought in California and Patagonia During Mediaeval Time." *Nature* 369 (June 16, 1994): 546–549. Evidence from sites including Mono Lake suggests past droughts far exceeding those in recorded history.

———. "Geomorphic, Geographic, and Hydrographic Basis for Resolving the Mono Lake Controversy." *Environmental Geology and Water Science* 17 (October 1991): 67–83. Identifies thresholds to be considered in choosing a lake level. The highest alternative discussed is 6,380 feet plus a drought buffer.

———. "Late Holocene Fluctuations of Mono Lake, Eastern California." *Palaeogeography, Palaeoclimatology, Palaeoecology* 78 (June 1990): 333–381. Fascinating narrative of a rising and falling lake and the evidence that records its behavior.

———. "Mono Lake: The Past 4000 Years." Ph.D. diss., University of California, Berkeley, 1987. A more leisurely tour of relatively recent events.

————. *A Reinterpretation of the 1857 Surface Elevation of Mono Lake*. Water Resources Center, University of California, Report no. 52. Davis: Water Resources Center, 1981. Debunks the traditional view that Mono Lake had been low in the nineteenth century.

————. *Restoration Conceptual Plan: Concepts and Principles Guiding the Restoration of Rush and Lee Vining Creeks, Mono County, California*. Report to the Mono Basin Restoration Technical Committee for the El Dorado County Superior Court. 1994.

Stine, Scott, Peter Vorster, and David Gaines. "Destruction of Riparian Habitat due to Water Diversions in the Mono Basin, California." In R. E. Warner and K. M. Hendrix, eds., *California Riparian Systems: Ecology, Conservation, and Productive Management*. Berkeley: University of California Press, 1984. A pioneering assessment.

Trexler, Keith A. *The Tioga Road: A History, 1883–1961*. Washington, D.C.: Yosemite Natural History Association, 1975. How the Great Sierra Wagon Road became the modern highway.

Trihey and Associates. Numerous reports to the Mono Basin Restoration Technical Committee for the El Dorado County Superior Court, concerning Rush and Lee Vining creek restoration work, 1991–1994.

Twain, Mark. *Roughing It*. 1872. Reprint Berkeley: University of California Press, 1972. For Mono Lake, see chapters 38 and 39.

U.S. Congress. House. Committee on Environment and Commerce. *Clean Air Act Amendments of 1990: Report on HR 3030, together with Additional, Supplemental, and Dissenting Views*. 101st Cong., 2d sess., 1990. Report 101–490, Part 1. Specifies that dust from exposed alkali flats at Mono and Owens lakes is "anthropogenic" and subject to pollution law.

U.S. Congress. House. Committee on Interior and Insular Affairs. Subcommittee on Public Lands and National Parks. *Hearings on Public Land Management Policy*. 97th Cong., 2d sess., 1982. Vol 5. Hearings in Washington, D.C., on May 18, 1982, concerning the Mono Lake National Monument and related bills.

U.S. Congress. House. Committee on Interior and Insular Affairs. Subcommittee on Public Lands and National Parks. *Hearings on Public Land Management Policy*. 98th Cong., 1st sess., 1983. Vol. 3. Includes hearings in Lee Vining on March 29, 1983, and in Washington, D.C., on June 2, 1983, concerning the Mono Lake National Monument and land transfer bills.

U.S. Congress. Senate. Committee on Energy and Public Works. *Report on the Clean Air Act Amendments of 1989, Together with Additional and Minority Views; to accompany S. 1630*. 101st Cong., 1st sess., 1989. Report 101–278. Parallel to House report above.

U.S. Department of Agriculture. Forest Service, Pacific Southwest Region, Inyo National Forest. *Comprehensive Management Plan, Mono Basin National Forest Scenic Area*. Bishop: U.S. Department of Agriculture, Forest Service, Inyo National Forest, 1990. Compares five management alternatives varying in intensity of visitor-serving development and permitted uses. Discusses effects of differing lake levels.

————. *Final Environmental Impact Statement for the Comprehensive Management Plan, Mono Basin National Forest Scenic Area*. Bishop: U.S. Department of Agriculture, Forest Service, Inyo National Forest, 1990. Adopts a strategy of very modest development; advocates that lake surface be kept between 6,377 and 6,390 feet.

Vestal, Elden H. "Creel Returns from Rush Creek Test Stream, Mono County, California, 1947–1951." *California Fish and Game* 40, no. 2 (1954): 89–104. Results of a fish-planting experiment on Rush Creek as diversions increased.

Vorster, Peter. "The Development and Decline of Agriculture in the Owens Valley." In Hall, Doyle-Jones, and Widawski, *History of Water*, above. A scrupulous assessment of what Owens Valley agriculture "before Los Angeles" was—and was not.

————. "A Water Balance Forecast Model for Mono Lake, California." Master's thesis, California State University at Hayward, 1985. Remains the basic reference on the hydrogeography of the

Mono Basin. Distributed by U.S.D.A. Forest Service, California Region, San Francisco, as *Earth Resource Monograph 10.*

Walston, Roderick E. "The Public Trust Doctrine in the Water Rights Context: The Wrong Environmental Remedy." *Santa Clara Law Review* 22 (Winter 1982): 63–93. The author, who represented the State of California in *Audubon v. Los Angeles*, argues that the public trust doctrine reinforces the state's right to change its mind about water allocations but does not require special consideration for environmental values.

Walton, John. *Western Times and Water Wars: State, Culture and Rebellion in California.* Berkeley: University of California Press, 1992. A sociological history of the Owens Valley, with an emphasis on continued resistance to Los Angeles's water-gathering policies.

Wedertz, Frank S. *Mono Diggings: Historical Sketches of Old Bridgeport, Big Meadows and Vicinity.* Bishop: Chalfant Press, 1978. Another local history, rich but to be used with caution.

Winkler, David W., and W. D. Shuford. "Changes in the Numbers and Locations of California Gulls Nesting at Mono Lake, California, in the period 1863–1986." *Colonial Waterbirds* 11 (June 1988): 263–274. Rival interpretation to Jehl, Babb, and Power, "History of the California Gull Colony," above.

Winkler, David W., ed. *An Ecological Study of Mono Lake, California.* University of California Institute of Ecology Publication 12. Davis, 1977. The study that launched the modern controversy. The Mono Lake Committee edition (Lee Vining, 1979) includes Stine's findings on historic lake levels.

Wright, David A. "The Wooden Legacy of the Bodie and Benton." *Album* (1993): 145–163. Unfulfilled plans to tie Mono Basin rail lines in with the outside world.

Young, Gordon. "The Troubled Waters of Mono Lake." *National Geographic* 160 (October 1981): 504–519. The Mono Lake Committee files contain a prepublication draft with proposed amendments by the Los Angeles Department of Water and Power.

STATUTES AND LEGAL DOCUMENTS (IN CHRONOLOGICAL ORDER)

City of Los Angeles v. Aitken. Superior Court of Tuolumne County No. 5092, 1935. The condemnation suit to acquire riparian and littoral water rights in the Mono Basin. The massive record is informative about the values of the lake, contemporary attitudes, and project history. Copy in Mono Lake Research Library, Lee Vining.

City of Los Angeles v. Aitken. 10 Cal. App. (2d) 460 (1935). Los Angeles sought to reduce the Tuolumne jury's awards to lakeshore property owners. The Third District Court of Appeal in Sacramento upheld the awards, declaring, "Irrigation and household uses of water are not the only reasonable or beneficial purposes for which [water] may be employed" (474).

California Fish and Game Code Section 5937. Enacted in 1937, this law provides that "The owner of any dam shall allow sufficient water at all times to pass through a fishway, or in the absence of a fishway, allow sufficient water to pass over, around or through the dam, to keep in good condition any fish that may be planted or exist below the dam."

California Department of Public Works. "Before the Division of Water Resources, April 11, 1940. Opinion and Order." This document gave Los Angeles the go-ahead for Mono Basin diversions.

California Fish and Game Commission. "Order of the Fish and Game Commission in Respect to Hot Creek Fish Hatchery Site in Mono County, California, August 19, 1940." Allowed Los Angeles to build the Hot Creek Hatchery instead of providing fishways at Grant Lake and the Long Valley reservoir (Lake Crowley).

California Fish and Game Commission. "Agreement by and Between the City of Los Angeles and the State of California re Hot Creek Hatchery Site, November 25, 1940." Going beyond the concession made in the preceding document, this contract purported to exempt the Department of Water and Power from the requirement to pass water for fish through its Mono County dams.

Opinion No. 50–89. *Opinions of the Attorney General of California* 18 (1951): 31–40. Attorney General Edmund G. Brown declared that Fish and Game Code Section 5937 did not apply where all waters had been appropriated.

California Fish and Game Code Section 5946. Enacted in 1953, this law provides that "no permit or license to appropriate water in District 4 1/2 shall be issued . . . after September 9, 1953, unless conditioned upon full compliance with section 5937."

Opinion No. 73–44. *Opinions of the Attorney General of California* 57 (1974): 577. Attorney General Evelle J. Younger partially reversed Brown's interpretation: the water board may enforce 5937 but has no duty to do so.

California State Water Resources Control Board. "License for Diversion and Use of Water 10191, January 25, 1974" and "License for Diversion and Use of Water 10192, January 25, 1974." The documents that supposedly made Los Angeles's rights in the Mono Basin permanent.

National Audubon Society v. Los Angeles. Superior Court of Alpine County No. 6429. The original public trust suit, filed in 1979. See *In the Matter of Mono Lake Water Right Cases* (pending).

National Audubon Society v. Superior Court. 33 Cal. 3d 419 (1983). *Audubon v. Los Angeles* carried this title when it reached the California Supreme Court. The court declared that existing water rights must be modified to protect the public trust.

California Health and Safety Code Section 42316. This language, added by SB 270 in 1983, requires Los Angeles to pay for measures to mitigate dust pollution caused by its water-gathering activities in the eastern Sierra but otherwise renounces state authority on the issue.

Dahlgren v. City of Los Angeles. Mono County Superior Court No. 8092. Filed November 1984. In his Order of August 1985, Judge Otis directed that a flow be retained in Rush Creek pending fish studies. See *In the Matter of Mono Lake Water Right Cases* (pending).

Mono Lake Committee v. City of Los Angeles. Mono County Superior Court No. 8608. The Lee Vining Creek case, filed in August of 1986, temporarily broke the alliance between the Mono Lake Committee and CalTrout. See *In the Matter of Mono Lake Water Right Cases* (pending).

In re Water of Hallett Creek Stream System. 44 Cal. 3d 448 (1988). The State Supreme Court ruled that the federal government can assert water rights as a riparian owner under certain circumstances, thus strengthening the hand of the U.S. Forest Service as a backup protector of Mono Lake.

California Trout, Inc., v. State Water Resources Control Board. 207 Cal. App. 3d 584 (1989). This decision, which came to be known as CalTrout I, required that Los Angeles's diversion licenses to divert from the Mono Basin be amended to comply with Fish and Game Code sections 5937 and 5946.

California Trout, Inc., v. Superior Court. 218 Cal. App. 3d 187–212 (1990). "CalTrout II" required that streamflow requirements be added to Los Angeles's licenses immediately, not after study, and it laid the groundwork for stream restoration.

California State Water Resources Control Board. *Draft Decision and Order Amending Water Right Licenses to Establish Fishery Protection Flows in Streams Tributary to Mono Lake and to Protect Public Trust Resources at Mono Lake and in the Mono Lake Basin.* Sacramento: State Water Resources Control Board, 1994. The draft was adopted unchanged on September 20, becoming Decision 1631.

In the Matter of Mono Lake Water Right Cases. El Dorado County Superior Court Coordinated Proceeding Nos. 2284 and 2288. The combined cases before Judge Terrence Finney. At this writing, despite the water board's decision, the matter remains open.

INTERVIEWS AND PERSONAL COMMUNICATIONS

Andrews, Jerry, and Terry Andrews. Mono Basin residents. Interview by author, Mono Basin, May 29, 1992.

Bailey, Roy A. Geologist. Telephone conversation with author, February 17, 1994.

———. Letter to author, October 18, 1994.

Banta, Don. Mono Basin resident. Interview by author. Tape recording. Lee Vining, June 26, 1992.

Becker, Carlisle. Landscape architect. Conversation with author, Mono Basin, June 11, 1993.

Brechin, Gray. Writer and activist. Telephone conversation with author, May 26, 1994.

Brower, David. Conservationist. Telephone conversations with author, February 21 and 25, 1994.

Brown, Russ. Water Resources Team Leader, Mono Basin EIR, Jones & Stokes. Letter to author, March 21, 1994.

Cahill, Thomas A. Researcher, air pollution. Telephone conversations with author, January 25 and 26, 1994.

Cahill, Virginia A. Counsel to California Department of Fish and Game. Telephone conversation with author, August 5, 1994.

Cain, John. Science Associate, Mono Lake Committee. Interview by author, Mono Basin, July 5, 1992.

———. Telephone conversations with author, 1992–93.

Canaday, Jim. Staff, State Water Resources Control Board. Telephone conversations with author, 1994–95.

Carle, David. Ranger, Mono Lake Tufa State Reserve. Telephone conversation with author, September 9, 1994.

Casaday, Ken. Project Manager, Mono Basin EIR, Jones & Stokes. Conversation with author, Sacramento, October 28, 1993.

Cassidy, Tom. Former Mono Lake Committee lobbyist. Conversation with author, San Francisco, November 20, 1994.

———. Telephone conversation with author, May 25, 1995.

Dahlgren, Richard O. Fly fisherman. Telephone conversation with author, March 12, 1994.

———. Letter to author, April 19, 1994.

Dana, Gayle L. Biologist. Interview by author. Tape recording. Crowley Lake, April 29, 1992.

———. Telephone conversations with author, 1992–95.

Davis, Martha. Executive Director, Mono Lake Committee. Interview by author. Tape recording. Burbank, April 25 and 27, 1992.

———. Interview by author. Tape recording. Nicasio, May 9, 1993.

———. Interview by author, Mill Valley, December 31, 1993.

———. Letter to author, October 31, 1994.

———. Interview by author, San Francisco, November 4, 1994.

———. Telephone conversations with author, 1991–95.

de Laet, Grace. Former Mono Lake Committee board member. Interview by author, Sausalito, February 1, 1994.

Del Piero, Marc. Member, State Water Resources Control Board. Telephone conversations with author, 1994.

Dodge, F. Bruce. Counsel to National Audubon Society. Interview by author, Larkspur, April 12, 1994.

———. Telephone conversation with author, April 12, 1994.

Dondero, John, and Dorothy Andrews. Mono Basin residents. Interview by Ilene Mandelbaum. Lee Vining, May 27, 1992.

Downey, Kenneth W. Assistant City Attorney, Los Angeles. Telephone conversation with author, January 26, 1995.

Dunning, Harrison C. Professor, University of California, Davis, School of Law. Interview by author. Tape recording. Davis, March 9, 1993.

———. Telephone conversation with author, March 3, 1995.

Edmondson, Jim. Vice President, California Trout. Conversation with author, Mono Basin, June 11, 1993.

———. Interview by author. Tape recording. Los Angeles, August 17, 1993.

———. Telephone conversations with author, 1993–94.

Eller, Stan. Former Assistant District Attorney, Mono County. Interview by author. Tape recording. Mammoth Lakes, April 29, 1992.

English, Scott. Restoration consultant. Conversation with author, Lee Vining, July 10, 1992.

Estolano, Cecelia. Aide to Mayor Tom Bradley. Interview by author, Los Angeles, August 28, 1992.

Finney, Terrence. Superior Court Judge, Eldorado County. Conversation with author, Mono Basin, July 20, 1992.

Flinn, Patrick. Counsel to National Audubon Society. Interview by author. Tape recording. Palo Alto, May 14, 1994.

———. Interview by author, San Francisco, November 4, 1994.

———. Telephone conversations with author, 1994.

Fontaine, Joe. Sierra Club activist. Telephone conversation with author, January 26, 1994.

Forstenzer, Edward. Former counsel to Dahlgren et al. Telephone conversation with author, March 27, 1994.

Gage, Mike. President, Los Angeles Board of Water and Power Commissioners. Interview by author. Tape recording. Los Angeles, August 28, 1992.

Gaines, Sally. Co-chair, Mono Lake Committee. Interview by author. Tape recording. Lee Vining, October 13, 1991.

———. Telephone conversations with author, 1991–95.

Galanter, Ruth. Councilwoman, City of Los Angeles. Telephone conversation with author, January 17, 1995.

Georgeson, Duane L. Former Assistant General Manager for Water, Los Angeles Department of Water and Power. Interview by author. Tape recording. Los Angeles, August 27 and 28, 1992.

Gewe, Gerald A. Engineer, Los Angeles Department of Water and Power. Telephone conversation with author, January 5, 1995.

Graff, Thomas J. Attorney, Environmental Defense Fund. Telephone conversation with author, September 23, 1994.

Graymer, LeRoy. Director, Public Policy Program, University of California, Los Angeles. Interview with author, Berkeley, October 12, 1994.

———. Telephone conversations with author, 1994.

Grosswiler, Ed. Co-chair, Mono Lake Committee. Telephone conversation with author, June 15, 1994.

Hansen, Jeff. Mono Basin resident; co-founder, Friends of Mono Lake. Telephone conversation with author, September 12, 1994.

Hardebeck, Ellen. Control Officer, Great Basin Unified Air Pollution Control District. Interview by author. Tape recording. Bishop, April 30, 1992.

——. Telephone conversations with author, 1994.

Heim, Jon S. Former extern to California Supreme Court Justice Alan Broussard. Telephone conversation with author, January 3, 1995.

Herbst, David B. Biologist. Interview by author. Tape recording. Crowley Lake, May 12, 1992.

——. Telephone conversations with author, 1992–95.

Hess, August. Interview by author. Tape recording. Lee Vining, May 12, 1992.

Huber, N. King. Geologist. Telephone conversations with author, August 23 and 27, 1993.

Isenberg, Phillip. Assemblyman. Interview by author, Sacramento, October 5, 1993.

Jehl, Joseph R., Jr. Telephone conversations with author, July 30, 1993, May 31, 1994.

Jimenez, Mike. Aide to Councilman Zev Yaroslavsky. Interview by author, Los Angeles, August 28, 1992.

Johnson, Huey. Former Secretary of Resources, State of California. Telephone conversations with author, September 23, 1992, February 14, 1994.

Johnson, Stephen. Photographer. Telephone conversation with author, March 24, 1992.

——. Interview by author, Pacifica, April 24, 1992.

Jones, Robert A. Reporter, *Los Angeles Times*. Interview by author, Pasadena, April 25, 1992.

Kahrl, William L. Journalist/historian. Interview by author, Sacramento, May 8, 1993.

Katz, Richard D. Assemblyman. Interview by author. Tape recording. Sacramento, August 27, 1993.

Kodama, Mitchell. Senior Waterworks Engineer, Mono Basin Litigation and Operations. Interview by author, Los Angeles, August 26, 1992.

——. Telephone conversations with author, 1992–95.

Lajoie, Kenneth R. Interview by author. Tape recording. Menlo Park, December 8, 1993.

——. Interview by author. Tape recording. Menlo Park, March 29, 1994.

——. Telephone conversations with author, 1994–95.

Larsen, Eric. Stream restoration consultant. Conversation with author, Mono Basin, July 22, 1992.

Lawrence, Andrea. Mono County Supervisor. Interview by author. Tape recording. Mammoth Lakes, April 28, 1992.

——. Telephone conversations with author, 1992–95.

Lehman, Richard. Congressman. Telephone conversation with author, July 23, 1994.

Levine, Barbara. Mono Lake Committee board member. Conversation with author, San Francisco, March 1, 1992.

McCarley, William. General Manager and Chief Engineer, Los Angeles Department of Water and Power. Telephone conversation with author, June 22, 1995.

McInerney, Barrett W. Attorney. Interview by author, Los Angeles, August 16, 1993.

——. Interview by author. Tape recording. Los Angeles, August 31, 1992.

——. Telephone conversations with author, March 30, 1994, October 14, 1994.

McPherson, Wallis R. Mono Basin resident. Interview by David Gaines and Ilene Mandelbaum. Tape recording. Bridgeport, June 28, 1985.

——. Interview by Ilene Mandelbaum. Tape recording. Bridgeport, March 7, 1989.

——. Interview by author. Tape recording. Bridgeport, May 11, 1992.

——. Interview by Emilie Strauss. Tape recording. Lee Vining, undated.

Madden, Palmer Brown. Former counsel to National Audubon Society. Interview by author. Tape recording. Walnut Creek, November 23, 1993.

Mandelbaum, Ilene. Associate Director, Mono Lake Committee. Interview by author. Tape recording. Sacramento, January 30, 1992.

——. Telephone conversations with author, 1992–95.

Martin, Dennis. Supervisor, Inyo National Forest. Telephone conversation with author, September 16, 1994.

Mason, David T. Limnologist. Telephone conversation with author, January 31, 1994.

May, Richard. President, California Trout. Telephone conversation with author, January 26, 1994.

Melack, John M. Limnologist. Telephone conversation with author, March 12, 1995.

Messick, Tim. Biologist, Jones & Stokes. Telephone conversation with author, June 4, 1994.

Nichols, Mary. Member, Los Angeles Board of Water and Power Commissioners. Interview by author, Los Angeles, August 28, 1992.

Pestor, Randy. Inyo County representative, Interagency Task Force on Mono Lake, 1979. Telephone conversation with author, February 2, 1994.

Peyton, George. National Audubon Society's liaison with Morrison & Foerster. Telephone conversations with author, March 12, 1994, March 25, 1994, January 3, 1995.

Phillips, David. Mono Lake Committee board member. Telephone conversation with author, February 22, 1994.

Pickard, Alan. Biologist, California Department of Fish and Game. Telephone conversation with author, August 8, 1994.

Pister, Phil. Biologist, formerly with California Department of Fish and Game. Tape recording. Lee Vining, June 27, 1992.

———. Telephone conversation with author, September 23, 1992.

Reifsnider, Betsy. Associate Director, Mono Lake Committee. Telephone conversations with author, February 5, 1993, August 18, 1993.

Reveal, Arlene. Mono County Librarian. Telephone conversation with author, January 12, 1995.

Robie, Ronald. Director of Water Resources under Jerry Brown. Telephone conversation with author, August 28, 1994.

Roos-Collins, Richard. Counsel to California Trout. Telephone conversation with author, March 4, 1994.

Ross, Mark. Lifelong friend of David Gaines. Telephone conversation with author, February 19, 1994.

Rossmann, Antonio. Attorney. Interview by author. Tape recording. San Francisco, November 12, 1993.

———. Telephone conversations with author, May 4 and 6, 1994.

———. Letter to author, May 6, 1994.

Sax, Joseph L. Professor of Law, University of California at Berkeley. Telephone conversation with author, April 11, 1994.

Scoonover, Mary J. Deputy Attorney General. Telephone conversation with author, July 28, 1994.

Shuford, W. David. Ornithologist. Letter to author, October 4, 1994.

———. Telephone conversations with author, 1992–95.

Silver, Laurens. Attorney. Telephone conversations with author, July 7, 1994, September 29, 1994.

Simis, Charlie. Mono Basin resident. Interview by author. Tape recording. Mono Basin, May 29, 1992.

Smith, Felix. Biologist, U.S. Fish and Wildlife Service. Interview by author. Tape recording. Sacramento, May 7, 1993.

Smith, Gary E. Biologist, California Department of Fish and Game. Telephone conversations with author, June 3, 1994, August 5, 1994, February 18, 1995.

Smith, Genny. Publisher, Mono Lake Committee Board Member. Interview by author. Tape recording. Cupertino, January 29, 1992.

———. Telephone conversations with author, 1992–95.

Stevens, Jan S. Deputy Attorney General, State of California. Telephone conversation with author, September 30, 1994.

Stine, Scott. Geomorphologist. Conversations with author, Mono Basin, July 19–22, 1992.

———. Interview by author. Tape recording. March 16, 1993.

———. Conversation with author, Berkeley, July 24–25, 1994.

———. Telephone conversations with author, 1992–95.

Stodder, John. Former aide to Mayor Tom Bradley. Telephone conversation with author, August 26, 1994.

Such, Tim. Interview by author, San Francisco, March 22, 1994.

———. Interview by author. Tape recording. Menlo Park, March 29, 1994.

———. Telephone conversations with author, 1994–95.

Taylor, Dan. Western Regional Representative, National Audubon Society. Interview by author, Sacramento, January 28, 1994.

Taylor, Dean. Biologist. Telephone conversation with author, January 12, 1995.

Thomas, Harold M. Attorney, California Department of Fish and Game. Conversation with author, Sacramento, September 28, 1994.

Trihey, E. Woody. Trihey & Associates, Aquatic Resource Specialists. Stream restoration consultant. Telephone conversations with author, September 23, 1993, October 21, 1994.

———. Interview by author. Tape recording. Walnut Creek, January 14, 1994.

Vestal, Elden H. Biologist, California Department of Fish and Game (retired). Interview by author. Tape recording. Napa, October 1, 1991.

———. Interview by author. Tape recording. Napa, March 26, 1992.

———. Telephone conversation with author, January 15, 1995.

Vorster, Peter. Hydrologist. Interview by author. Tape recording. Oakland, April 11, 1992.

———. Telephone conversations with author, 1992–95.

Wagtendonk, Jan van. Research scientist, Yosemite National Park. Telephone conversation with author, September 27, 1993.

Wickser, James F. Assistant General Manager and Chief Engineer for Water, Los Angeles Department of Water and Power. Interview by author. Tape recording. Los Angeles, August 27, 1992.

———. Interview by author, Los Angeles, August 16, 1993.

Williams, Dennis C. Engineer, Aqueduct Division, Los Angeles Department of Water and Power. Interview by author. Tape recording. Los Angeles, August 27, 1992.

Winkler, David W. Ornithologist. Telephone conversations with author, 1993–95.

Wood, Wallace. Lakeshore visitor, 1940s. "Draft Interview with Mr. Wallace Wood." Telephone interview by Emilie Strauss, April 8, 1992.

Yaroslavsky, Zev. Los Angeles City Councilman. Interview by author. Tape recording. Los Angeles, August 28, 1992.

———. Interview by author, Los Angeles, August 16, 1993.

Index

in *Inyo v. Los Angeles*, 59, 62–63, 98; in *Los Angeles v. Aitken*, 40; in *U.S. v. State Water Resources Control Board*, 180

Tidelands, covered by public trust, 64

Tioga Pass, 28

Tito, Dennis, 170, 174

Toiyabe Chapter, Sierra Club, 59, 76

Tourism, in Owens Valley, 58

Trihey, E. Woody, 141, 143, 150–52, 154

Trout, 15, 25, 118–19, 133, 137, 153; in Rush Creek, 39–40, 47–49, 109–12, 116–17, 140

Tufa, 17, 20–21, 30, 66, 80, 101; affected by lake-level changes, 50–51, 122, 125, 138, 160–62, 176; considered by Water Board, 158, 165–66, 172–73; sand tufa, 50, 158, 160

Tuolumne County Superior Court, 39

Twain, Mark, 2, 27

Twain islet, 67, 72, 121–22, 135, 162, 163; affected by lake-level changes, 95, 100, 125

U.S. Bureau of Reclamation, 113, 147, 174. *See also* U.S. Reclamation Service

U.S. Congress, 103–4, 106, 126, 147, 154–56, 159

U.S. Court of Appeals for the Ninth Circuit, 119, 129, 155

U.S. Department of the Interior, 126

U.S. District Court for the Eastern District of California. *See* Karlton, Lawrence

U.S. Fish and Wildlife Service, 85, 163

U.S. Forest Service, 85, 92, 127, 131, 135, 138, 144–45; as manager of Mono Basin National Forest Scenic Area, 40–41, 80, 103, 106, 125–28, 157

U.S. Geological Survey, 86, 96

U.S. Reclamation Service (later U.S. Bureau of Reclamation), 32, 37

U.S. Supreme Court, 102

United States v. State Water Resources Control Board, 180

University of California at Davis, Institute of Ecology, 71

University of California at Los Angeles, Public Policy Program, 105. *See also* Mono Lake Group

University of California at Santa Barbara, Community and Organization Research Institute. *See* CORI report

Up and Down California (William Brewer), 15, 22, 27

Upper Gorge Power Plant, 153

Urban Water Conservation Council, 149

Van Norman, H. A., 43, 47

Van Vleck, Gordon, 102

Venita (vessel), 29, 44

Vestal, Elden H., 47–49, 54, 140, 175

Vining, Leroy, 24, 28

Virginia Creek, 24

von Schmidt, Alexis Waldemar, 26–27, 86

Vorster, Peter, 84, 87, 96, 114, 138, 141, 167, 182–83

Walker, Joseph Reddeford, 24

Walker Creek, 23, 42, 108, 128; restoration of, 139–40, 143, 163, 178

Walker River, 85, 153

Water balance models, 68–69, 87–88

Water conservation, 76–77, 85, 88, 147, 149, 158, 165–66, 169, 182

Water marketing, 131, 147–48

Water pollution laws, 181

Water quality, 181

Water rates, 136, 149, 182

Water reclamation, 77, 88, 147–48, 158, 165, 170, 174, 182, 183

Water rights law, California, 31, 36, 39, 56, 126, 132, 179–81; and Fish and Game Code, 112–13, 117, 180–81; and public trust doctrine, 65, 91, 98, 102, 180–81

Water supply, California, 148, 181–82, 184

Waterfowl. *See* Ducks

Waters, Daniel, 169, 170

Waters, Norman S., 84, 88, 90, 106

Watt, James, 92

Watterson family, 36

Weigen, Christine, 66

West Basin Municipal Water District, 147–48

West Portal, 42–43

Western Hemisphere Shorebird Reserve Network, 20

Weston, Brett, 80

Wet Year/Dry Year Plan, 114–15, 146

Wetlands, 49–50, 64, 138, 161; in Owens Valley, 59; possible restoration at Mono, 172–73, 175, 177–78

White Mountains, 32

Wickser, James F., 170, 174

Wild rivers, 180

Wildlife, 115, 126

Wilson, Pete, 106, 132, 144, 164, 165, 169, 170

Wilson Creek beds, 62

Wilson's phalarope, 18–19, 67–68

Winkler, David W., 66–68, 71–72, 77, 183; after leaving Mono Lake Committee, 80, 93, 95, 124, 166, 168

Withdrawal, 38, 126

Wodraska, John ("Woody"), 164

Yaroslavsky, Zev, 120, 170

Yokuts Indians, 22

Yosemite National Park, 28, 59

Yosemite Valley, 23, 24

Younger, Evelle, 113

Zelman, Walter, 132

Designer:	Barbara Jellow
Compositor:	G & S Typesetters, Inc.
Text:	10/16 Minion
Display:	Minion
Printer:	Malloy Lithographing, Inc.
Binder:	John H. Dekker & Sons
Insert:	New England Book Components